D0443900

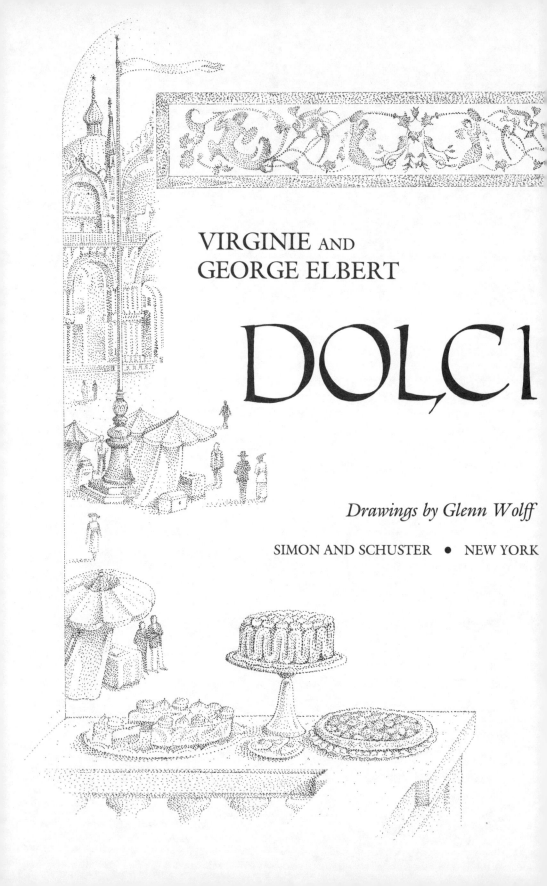

VIRGINIE AND
GEORGE ELBERT

DOLCI

Drawings by Glenn Wolff

SIMON AND SCHUSTER • NEW YORK

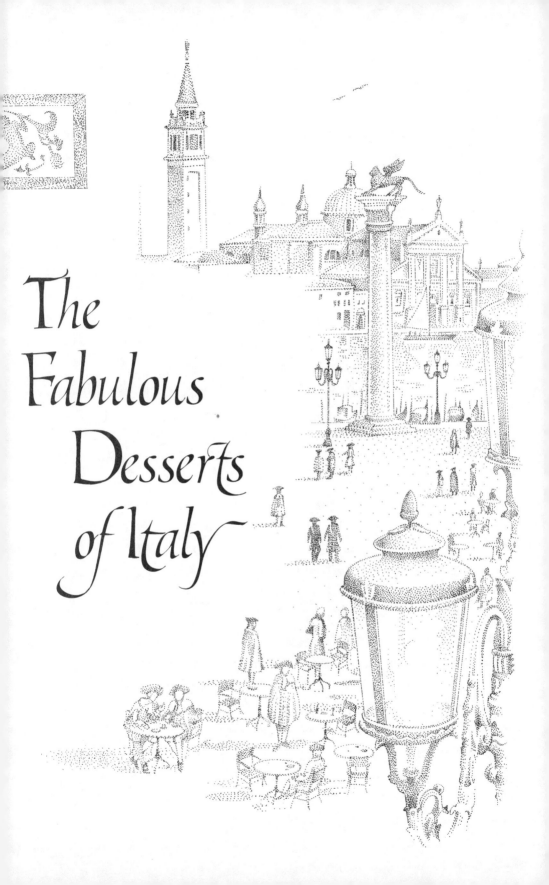

The Fabulous Desserts of Italy

Copyright © 1987 by George Elbert and Virginie Elbert
All rights reserved
including the right of reproduction
in whole or in part in any form
Published by Simon and Schuster
A Division of Simon & Schuster, Inc.
Simon & Schuster Building
Rockefeller Center
1230 Avenue of the Americas
New York, New York 10020
SIMON AND SCHUSTER and colophon
are registered trademarks of Simon & Schuster, Inc.
Designed by Edith Fowler
Manufactured in the United States of America

10 9 8 7 6 5 4 3 2 1

Library of Congress Cataloging-in-Publication Data

Fowler, Virginie, date.
    The fabulous desserts of Italy.

    Includes index.
    1. Desserts. 2. Cookery, Italian. I. Elbert, George,
date. II. Title.
TX773.F72 1987 641.8'6'0945 87-4577
ISBN: 0-671-54374-1

Acknowledgment

Many thanks to *Gourmet* magazine for their kind permission to reprint two recipes, Italian Chestnut Jam Cake and Whipped Cream Cake Eolia, from our article, "Caterina Cornaro's Asolo," December 1980.

To Suzanne

Contents

How This Book
Came About

We return

to Italy over and over again. There is always something new to see: the golden light against amber and rust-toned buildings; towns perched on hillsides with their buildings and windows facing the valleys below; geometrically cultivated fields; espaliered orchards; garlanded grape vines; fantasy-shaped haystacks; solid barns, farmhouses, and villas. These are the basic components, but the specific designs change from province to province. The views are magical yet familiar, reminiscent of early primitive and Renaissance paintings; homes, fields, and villages are of human proportions, all part of centuries of unchanged living.

In that long, narrow peninsula, food dishes change depending on the available local ingredients, the seasons, and the absorbed cooking styles of the many invaders: Greeks, Turks, North Africans, Middle Easterners, then Normans, Austrians, French, and Spanish. Later, the expatriate English inspired zuppa inglese.

In the south, flaky pastries are filled with honey and ground almonds or walnuts, clearly the influence of Greeks and Turks who brought in the original trees. Small pastries are fried in olive oil for lack of butter and are sometimes filled with ricotta cheese made from ewe's milk. Orange and lemon rinds add flavoring, or the pastries are filled with chocolate and nuts and oven-baked. For centuries pistachio nuts came across the Mediterranean from Persia to be made into pastries and ice cream, which originally was frozen with the snow from the high mountains that rise up behind the Gulf of Taranto. Batters are baked between patterned hot irons into thin waffles called *pizzelle,* a distant cousin of the *warka* of North Africa.

These specialties of the south give way to the fruit tarts of the north where miles of orchards sprawl out from Ferrara: pear, apple, peach, apricot, and cherry, all espaliered to increase their production. In the flat, sandy plains near the east coast, strawberries flourish in the springtime. Further inland, in the richer soil of the Lombard plains, are the rice paddies and cornfields. These plains are also rich in grass, gathered to feed the herds of cows that produce the rich milk, butter, and heavy cream lavishly used for the northern sweets. Here, too, is where the basic cakes originated— Pan di Spagna (Spanish sponge cake) and Genoise (from Genoa) —and classic spices from the East were introduced by Venetian merchants.

Our first trip to Italy in early spring solved a mystery that had long puzzled us. We knew from historical readings that the art of pastry making had spread from Italy to Europe many centuries ago and that the Italians were the first to serve a separate course of sweet dishes at the end of a meal. Yet most current food and travel writers report with complete aplomb that Italians "eat only fruit or cheese for dessert," until this phrase has become a self-perpetuating cliché.

But as we traveled we found that most restaurants, large and small, had a dessert table at the entrance with cakes, tarts, and puddings elegantly displayed. The pasticcerias, their windows filled with pastries, were crowded with customers during the day; and in the evening people stopped by for a leisurely espresso and pastry, or settled at a gelato-bar table for ice cream or sherbet. Yes, cheese and fruit *are* eaten at the end of a meal after the entree, but as a clearing-the-palate course preceding dessert or after a sweet dessert. We concluded that American travelers as well as many food and travel writers arrive in Italy during the summer when the local residents very sensibly favor the ripe fruits of the season and the new production of cheeses. Even at this time of year, though, the pastry shops are full of cakes and tarts. The tourists may not notice them because they are often off the beaten track of tourist attractions, or perhaps they have gorged on the main part of the meal and can face only an espresso at the end, ignoring that fabulous dessert table near the entrance.

Loving desserts as well as all other foods and loving to cook, each day during our many trips to Italy we made copious notes on the ingredients of our purchases at the pasticcerias. We splurged on small tarts, tiny cakes, and cookies, purchased for picnics along our routes when we were driving from place to place. When we were living in Italy, we crowded into the pastry shops along with our neighbors to buy the evening dessert, discovering that we could buy half a large cake, cake by the slice, or sometimes a whole small cake or tart. Our restaurant meals always ended in dessert (we each chose a different one) from that unforgettable display on the table in front.

While staying in Italy we found many products in the markets that were new to us, and so we comfortably settled into an Italian way of life, buying in a normal way some supplies and products that can be found only in gourmet shops in the United States. Vanilla flavoring, or vanillina, is sold in measured, individual packets of powder with directions specifying one or two packets to be used; vanilla extract as we know it is not available. Baking powder, too, is sold in individual packets rather than in cans; each packet is sixteen grams, which means a lot of "filler" because each packet is to be used with two and one-half cups of flour. The grocery shelves contain several grades of flour: pastry, bread, and all-purpose. Sugar is fine or granulated, both white and unbleached. There are cake mixes, too, but they have a European orientation, such as exotic (for us) St. Honore. On the other hand, there are the familiar Royal gelatins and custard pudding mixes packaged in Europe.

From these forays into groceries and supermarkets, and from our detailed diary notes about desserts, we gradually developed this book as we traveled the length and breadth of Italy. We have enjoyed the memories recalled during the writing and retesting of these recipes—memories not only of the pastries but of the places where they were bought and eaten.

General Directions

While we are baking,

especially when reproducing a remembered cake, tart, pudding, or other dessert, we constantly make notes and change proportions, reworking and adjusting recipes made from our on-the-spot notes while traveling.

Many decisions take place based on experience, but these are not repeated in each recipe unless they are needed for a particular process. We decided to pass these basics along as hands-on tips that form a background for the recipes.

Recipe Servings

Since there are only two people in our family, we find that making a dessert for four is a very comfortable amount because the servings can be used for either another couple or for ourselves on a second day. Many of the recipes in this book, therefore, are based on this practical approach for couples or small families. Perhaps this is in rebellion against all the time we've spent reducing the standard recipes meant for eight to ten servings!

If we are having several guests, we can double these recipes for eight servings or increase them by half to serve six. Normally there is no change in the balance of a recipe formula when increasing or decreasing ingredients. To halve a whole egg, beat it and measure with a tablespoon; for a separated egg, measure each part after separating.

Recipe Style

The ingredients are listed in their order of use, which means that ingredients for ahead-of-time preparation are given first and all others are listed as they are needed. We have always been disturbed by cake recipes that stress beating the dough well for lightness and *then* direct you to beat the egg whites while the dough sits there deflating! We beat the egg whites before mixing the dough and then, when ready to be added, the whites need only two or three turns of the beater to freshen. The same holds true for other ahead-of-time preparations. The step-by-step directions include all the necessary preparatory additions so that the final assembly is a continuous operation.

Equipment

Utensils listed in the recipes are standard kitchen equipment, and we have tried to simplify the number needed. We have adapted some of the recipes to fit American pans; conversely, when we lived and kept house in Italy, we had to adapt some of our baking routines to fit the available kitchen equipment there.

You will need straight-sided *cake and tart pans* with either fluted or plain sides. It is preferable to have removable bottoms for tarts because they are meant to be served out of the pan, not in it, as are most American pies. Frequently we have specified a quiche pan because they are shallow and fluted, and have removable bottoms. Small tarts and cakes are made in individual fluted pans (some have slightly slanting sides), but lacking these, use muffin pans. The only time we use the standard American slant-sided pie plate is for some cakes that have a traditional slanted side when turned upside down.

Usually Italian cakes are made in *springform pans*. The cake is split into layers rather than baked as separate layers in separate pans.

But a layer cake pan, as we know it, is often used for baking a plain cake that will not be split into layers but will be either frosted on top or dusted with vanilla-flavored confectioners' sugar.

Springform pans come in a bewildering variety of sizes, both imported and domestic, with half-inch variations from five to twelve inches in diameter. You will find that in some recipes we have listed two measurements because we know the quantity of cake batter can be used in either size pan, depending on the one you have in your cupboard. For instance, some of the basic cakes, such as Chocolate Torta (page 74), when baked in a large layer cake pan are served as a shallow, single layer but when baked in a smaller, deep springform pan, can be split into layers.

Though ovens come equipped with their own thermostatically controlled temperature settings, they are often unreliable, so we recommend an *oven thermometer* for a more reliable reading. An oven thermometer can also help you determine how much preheating your oven needs to reach the desired temperature. In most cases, however, we have given instructions to preheat at the beginning of each recipe. If you know your oven heats up very quickly, use your own judgment.

For draining, we like the fine-mesh plastic or stainless steel *sieves* rather than those made of aluminum, which reacts with acidic ingredients such as lemons and oranges and changes their flavor.

The modern, smooth-geared *hand beaters, wire whisks,* and *wooden spoons* with angled bottoms are the mixing tools that seem to work best in putting together these Italian desserts. We have tried using electric mixers for dough-making but the final result is too homogeneous, so we have returned to the classic utensils that we enjoy using to achieve a superior texture. Perhaps the only exception is in making Génoise, where the lukewarm eggs and sugar have to be beaten to maximum lightness to triple in bulk; but even here with effort the hand beater can do its job.

A *kitchen scale* is an invaluable piece of equipment when it comes to determining the quantity of nuts, chocolate, and other small, bulky items needed in a recipe, rather than depending on spoons and cups. In Europe, every ingredient is weighed, which overcomes that question of how large an egg, how small an apple, or how many almonds in a tablespoon.

Flavorings

We have always been puzzled by the small measures of flavorings specified in many American recipes, a tradition harking back to long-ago measurements. In fact, the strength of flavorings—such as vanilla, lemon, almond, and orange—has been weakened by the manufacturers through the years; to compensate, one has to increase the amounts, a practice we have always followed in baking. So do not be surprised at the amounts listed in our recipes—they work! This is especially true for ice cream and some other cold desserts where cooling and freezing reduce the strength of the flavor.

Italian cooks freely use *dark rum* in baking; it takes away the "floury" taste in cakes while adding an underlying richness of flavor. Rum also masks the "boiled milk" flavor in custard puddings and in ice creams that have a cooked milk or cream base.

Grated lemon zest is a favorite Italian flavoring. Lemons in Italy not only have thick, moist skins that are perfect for grating, but they are also extremely aromatic; and the juice is sweeter than that of American lemons, not sharp and sour. Often, the only lemons we can buy in the States are the thin-skinned variety that grate into a powdery dust with little flavor; for this reason we look for thick-skinned lemons and often supplement the grated zest with lemon extract or substitute lemon extract entirely.

When making cakes, tart pastry, and cookies that include grated *almonds* as an ingredient, we often find it a good idea to add almond extract because almonds do not always have a really pronounced "almond" flavor, and unless toasted, they have barely any flavor at all. In Italy and other parts of Europe, bitter almonds are legally used in addition to regular or sweet almonds for their more assertive "almond" flavor, although bitter almonds are, in fact, apricot pits. Because of their prussic acid content, bitter almonds are not sold in the United States.

Italian cocoa is less flavorful than ours or at least less flavorful than the richer Dutch dark cocoa we have always used. When we were told in Italy that cocoa was used in a recipe, we substituted the dark and strongly flavored Italian chocolate.

For coffee flavor we use *instant espresso coffee powder* because it has the right intensity for Italian sweets.

Ingredients

We freeze *unused egg whites* by dropping them first into a ramekin and freezing them uncovered, then turning them out, transferring them to a plastic storage bag labeled with the date and number of whites, and returning them to the freezer. Defrost in a ramekin or cup when ready to use; frozen egg whites will not be appreciably different from fresh egg whites. *Egg yolks* can be frozen in the same way. This method solves the nagging problem of what to do with the leftover part of an egg.

In cakes, puddings, and ice creams we've specified *half-and-half* because it most nearly resembles "real" whole milk in the classic sense; our milk is a poor, thinned-out product by comparison.

As for *heavy cream,* we avoid ultrapasteurized, not only for its evaporated milk flavor but also for its poor whipping quality.

Sweet or unsalted butter is used throughout. If you arc on a butterless diet, margarine can be substituted.

When *apples* are called for, green Granny Smiths are our choice. Their flesh is firm, juicy, and full of flavor, and they do not become mushy when cooked.

Basic Recipes

In the following pages

are basic cake formulas to make and serve as they are or to use as part of the various, more elaborate "assembled" cakes that follow. Be sure to note that one pan size may be specified in the basic recipe while another may be given for the "assembled" version.

Also found here are instructions for the preparation of frequently used ingredients: lemon and orange peel, the nuts that so often are part of a cake or meringue batter, and some of the more popular icings and glazes for cakes.

The basic Italian cake formulas that follow are in themselves so flavorful that they, too, can be served as plain cakes. You will be referred back to these recipes many times because they are the basis for most of the frosted and decorated layer cakes.

On their own, plain cakes are cut into slices or wedges and eaten with sweet dessert wines or coffee. Sometimes they are served with a sweet fruit sauce or a dollop of whipped cream.

Génoise

This Genoa cake acquired the internationally known French name of Génoise when it traveled centuries ago to France in the sixteenth century with the pastry chefs of both Caterina de' Medici, who became the queen of Henry II, and Maria de' Medici, queen of Henry IV.

It is a buttery but light cake that is, along with Sponge Cake (Pan di Spagna), a classic base for layer cakes. Dusted with vanilla-flavored confectioners' sugar, it often accompanies a sweet dessert wine between meals or at the end of a meal.

6½- to 7-inch springform pan for a cake ½-inch deep or more, or as specified in another recipe

> 3 tablespoons unsalted butter
> ⅓ cup flour
> Pinch of salt
> 2 large eggs
> ⅓ cup sugar
> 1 teaspoon vanilla extract
> ¼ teaspoon lemon extract

1. Preheat the oven to 350°.

2. Butter the bottom and sides of the springform pan. Fit a circle of wax paper into the bottom; butter it and dust the bottom and sides with flour.

3. Melt the butter and set it aside to cool.

4. Put the flour and salt into a flour sifter placed on a plate. Set aside.

5. Using a small wire whisk, beat the eggs and sugar together in the top of a double boiler (preferably round-bottomed) until just combined.

6. Bring the water in the bottom of the double boiler to *almost boiling*. Place the top pan over the water, but do not allow the water to touch the top pan. Lightly stir the mixture with the wire whisk 2 or 3 times to prevent the eggs from thickening too quickly. They should be lukewarm in about 1½ or 2 minutes. Check the temperature with a fingertip. When the eggs are lukewarm and syrupy, remove the top of the double boiler to the work surface.

7. Beat the mixture with a hand beater or an electric mixer on high for 10 minutes. Scrape down the sides of the pan every so often with a plastic or rubber spatula. When the mixture is foamy,

has tripled in quantity, and is cool, beat in the vanilla and lemon extracts.

8. Sift the flour, a little at a time, over the whipped eggs, folding it in with a plastic spatula after each addition so it does not lump. After each addition of flour mix in a tablespoon of the cooled melted butter. Alternate until the flour and butter are used up. Add the next addition of flour and butter when the previous amount is not quite mixed in. Do not overmix or the eggs will deflate.

9. Spoon the mixture into the springform pan. With a spatula or the spoon, push the batter slightly away from the center toward the sides. Bake for 25 to 30 minutes or as specified in another recipe, until the top is light brown and a thin skewer inserted into the center of the cake comes out clean. The cake will separate from the edge of the pan; it will be high but will fall once it is out of the oven. Run a knife around the edge to be sure the separation is complete. Remove the cake from the pan by loosening the side of the springform; turn it upside down, remove the metal bottom, and then carefully remove the wax paper. Cool on a cake rack top side up so the moist top will not stick to the cake rack. (The bottom will become the top of the final iced cake.)

10. Preheat the broiler.

11. When the cake is cool and ready to be iced, the top may still be moist and sticky, so place the cake briefly under a preheated 300° broiler to crisp the top and dry it out. Watch the cake carefully because it can quickly burn. If the cake is too high for your broiler, split it in half horizontally (as you would do anyway for a layer cake) and slip the top layer under the broiler. Cool on a cake rack before turning over.

VARIATIONS

Depending on filling or decorations, other flavors can be substituted for the lemon extract—orange, almond, or rum—but vanilla extract is always used as well.

Double the recipe for a 10-inch springform pan. The single recipe can also be baked in a 7-x-7-inch square pan.

Sponge Cake
Pan di Spagna

Pan di Spagna is one of the two basic layer cakes in Italy, the other being Génoise. Why it is the "bread of Spain" is lost in the mists of ancient history, and any explanation is pure speculation.

This recipe can be cut in half or doubled. We tend to follow the full recipe and use up any leftover batter for filled or plain cupcakes, an extra cake layer, or for ladyfingers (see *Variations*). All of these extras freeze nicely, though they rarely stay in our freezer for any length of time.

When baking sponge cakes, the pans are left unbuttered *on the sides* to facilitate rising, but the bottoms are covered with buttered wax paper.

10-inch springform pan for full recipe, or two 6-inch springform pans, as specified in another recipe

> 3 eggs, separated
> 1 egg white
> ¼ teaspoon cream of tartar
> 7 tablespoons plus 1 teaspoon sugar
> ⅛ teaspoon salt
> ¾ teaspoon lemon extract
> ½ cup plus 1 tablespoon cake flour

1. Preheat the oven to 325°.

2. Fit a circle of wax paper into the bottom of the springform pan and butter it, or butter muffin tins or ladyfinger molds.

3. Beat the egg whites with the cream of tartar; when soft peaks form, add 2 tablespoons of the sugar and beat until the whites are stiff. Set aside.

4. Put the egg yolks in a large bowl and beat with a wire whisk or electric beater. Slowly add the remaining 5 tablespoons plus 1 teaspoon of sugar, beating constantly. Add the salt and

lemon extract, and beat the mixture until it is a pale lemon color.

5. Freshen the egg whites by beating them once or twice, then lightly fold ¼ of the whites into the yolk-sugar mixture. Heap the rest of the whites on top and sift the cake flour over the whites. Fold the flour, beaten egg whites, and yolk mixture together until just mixed. Do not overmix.

6. Spoon the batter into the prepared pan and bake for a recipe's specified time. Bake in a 10-inch springform pan for 45 to 50 minutes, in a 6-inch pan for 35 minutes, or until a thin skewer inserted into the center comes out clean.

7. Loosen the edge of the cake from the pan with a thin knife and allow to cool for 10 to 15 minutes. Unhinge the springform sides and turn out the cake onto a cake rack. Remove the bottom of the form and the wax paper, and turn the cake upright to finish cooling. When cold, if the top is too moist and sticky, place it briefly under a preheated 300° broiler to crisp the top and dry it out. Watch the cake carefully because it can burn quickly. If the cake is too high for your broiler, split it in half horizontally (as you would do anyway for a layer cake) and slip the top layer under the broiler.

VARIATIONS

When using this recipe to make cupcakes or ladyfingers, the muffin pans and ladyfinger molds are buttered on the sides and bottoms. Cupcakes are baked for 15 to 20 minutes and ladyfingers for 10 to 12 minutes. Allow to cool for 10 minutes, then remove from the pan to a cake rack. (See also Ladyfingers, page 119.)

Almond Cake

This nut-flour cake can be baked in layers or as small cakes; it can be combined with a meringue layer or spooned into an un-baked crust of puff pastry or pasta frolla (a rich tart pastry).

6-x-1¾-inch round cake pan for plain cake, or as specified in another recipe

Serves 6

> 3½ ounces Almonds, Blanched and Toasted, page 48
> ½ cup flour
> 1½ teaspoons baking powder
> Pinch of salt
> 2 eggs, separated
> ¼ teaspoon cream of tartar
> 4 tablespoons unsalted butter, slightly softened
> ½ cup sugar
> 1 teaspoon almond extract

1. Preheat the oven to 375°.
2. Butter the cake pan and dust it lightly with flour.
3. Prepare the almonds. Grind them, but not too fine. There should be some nut texture to the cake.
4. Sift the flour, baking powder, and salt into a bowl. Stir in the ground almonds until well mixed. Set aside.
5. Beat the egg yolks in a small bowl, then set aside 1 or 2 teaspoons of the beaten yolks for brushing the top of the cake.
6. Beat the egg whites with the cream of tartar until stiff.
7. Cream the butter, add the sugar, and blend. Gradually add the beaten egg yolks and almond extract, beating until a pale lemon color.
8. Stir in the flour-nut mixture a little at a time, blending after each addition. After all the dry ingredients have been incorporated, add ¼ of the beaten egg whites, stirring until the batter is moistened, then lightly fold in the remaining beaten egg whites.
9. Spoon the batter into the prepared cake pan and bake for about 40 minutes or as specified in another recipe.

VARIATION

The flavor can be varied by using toasted hazelnuts instead of toasted almonds.

Basic Baked Meringues

Meringues are a favorite dessert or snack all over Italy. Their sweet lightness can be enjoyed out-of-hand, at a sidewalk cafe with coffee, as a finale to a dinner, or as one component of a dessert.

This basic recipe is based on one egg white; if more meringues are needed, all amounts can be increased proportionately depending on the number needed.

11-x-17-inch baking pan
Makes 8 meringues, 2½ inches in diameter, or 1 layer 8 inches in diameter

> *⅛ teaspoon cream of tartar*
> *1 egg white*
> *5 tablespoons sugar*
> *1¼ teaspoons cornstarch*
> *Pinch of salt*
> *½ teaspoon vanilla extract or ¼ teaspoon almond extract*

1. Preheat the oven to 225°.
2. Lightly oil the baking pan. Smooth on a sheet of wax paper but do not oil it.
3. Sprinkle cream of tartar over the egg white and beat until the egg white holds soft peaks. Beat in 2 tablespoons of the sugar.
4. Mix the remaining 3 tablespoons of sugar with the cornstarch and salt. Sprinkle over the egg white and beat in. Add vanilla or almond extract and beat well until the meringue is stiff.
5. For a meringue layer, mark an 8-inch circle on the wax paper by drawing around the edge of an 8-inch plate, cake pan, or pot lid. Spoon the mixture into a pastry bag fitted with a plain ½-inch tube. Starting at the outer edge, cover the circle with a ½-inch-deep spiraled layer of meringue; smooth the surface with a plastic or rubber spatula or leave it spiraled, depending on the

recipe you are following. Or spoon the meringue directly onto the circle, smoothing it with a spatula.

6. Bake the meringue layer in the preheated oven for 45 minutes. Turn off the oven heat and allow the layer to cool and dry in the oven for 20 to 30 minutes. Remove the pan from the oven and carefully slip the wax paper out of the pan and onto a cake rack. Delicately remove the meringue layer from the wax paper and cool on the rack.

7. For separate meringues, form 8 round mounds with a tablespoon on the wax paper–covered baking pan, or form the mounds with a pastry bag and a number 8 star tube. Bake in the preheated oven for 45 to 50 minutes, then turn off the heat and leave the meringues in the oven for 20 to 30 minutes to dry out. The tops will be light tan and crisp. Carefully remove the meringues from the paper and allow to cool on a baking rack.

Nut-Meringue Layers for Cakes
Giapponese

This is a more substantial meringue than the simple basic recipe (page 35). In many of the meringue layer recipes a nut-meringue can be substituted for a plain meringue. Use either toasted almonds or hazelnuts ground into a powder, and flavor the mixture with either vanilla or almond extract. In the Nut-Meringue Whipped Cream Cake (page 91), both instant coffee powder and unsweetened cocoa powder are added to this basic recipe.

1 plate, 8 inches in diameter
Two 11-x-17-inch baking pans
Makes three 8-inch round meringues

3 ounces Almonds, Blanched and Toasted, page 48, or
Toasted Hazelnuts, page 49

1 cup less 1 tablespoon sugar
Pinch of salt
4 teaspoons cornstarch, sieved
3 egg whites
¼ teaspoon cream of tartar
1½ teaspoons vanilla extract or ¾ teaspoon almond extract,
    or to taste

1. Lightly oil the baking pans. Smooth on sheets of wax paper or aluminum foil, but do not oil the wax paper or foil. Mark 3 8-inch circles on the paper or foil with a pencil or blunt instrument, using the plate as a pattern.

2. Toast and grind the almonds or hazelnuts into a powder.

3. Mix ½ of the sugar with the salt and sieved cornstarch. Set aside.

4. Preheat the oven to 225°.

5. Put the egg whites in a large bowl and sprinkle with the cream of tartar. Beat until the whites hold soft peaks, then beat in the plain sugar. Slowly add the sugar-cornstarch mixture, beating the meringue after each addition. Add the vanilla or almond extract, and beat until the meringue is stiff.

6. Fold in the ground almonds or hazelnuts.

7. Spoon the meringue into a pastry bag with a ½-inch star or plain tip and fill in the three 8-inch circles on the prepared baking pans.

8. Bake the meringues in the preheated oven for 45 to 50 minutes, then turn off the heat and leave the meringues to cool and dry out in the oven for 20 to 30 minutes. Remove the pan from the oven and carefully separate the meringue layers from the paper or foil; cool on a cake rack.

Notes: For smaller amounts, the recipe can be cut to ½ or ⅓.

Three 8-inch rounds are the approximate sizes because the amount of egg whites varies depending on the size of the eggs used. Pipe each meringue starting at the center and complete only half of the intended size of each finished meringue; gradually enlarge each in turn so that all 3 are the same size. The meringue will spread slightly in baking.

VARIATION

This recipe can also be used to make cookies. It makes 24 cookies. Follow the directions for forming shapes and sizes in meringue-based cookies, page 148.

Thin Cake Layer

This is a crisp, thin cake layer one-fourth to three-eighths inch thick, similar to a single layer in a seven-layer cake.

9-inch round or springform pan, or as specified in another recipe

> *Confectioners' sugar*
> *1 egg, separated*
> *⅛ teaspoon cream of tartar*
> *1 teaspoon plus 2 tablespoons sugar*
> *½ teaspoon vanilla extract*
> *Pinch of salt*
> *3 tablespoons flour*

1. Preheat the oven to 475°.
2. Butter the outside bottom of the round or springform pan. Cover with wax paper and butter it. Place a sheet of wax paper on a cake rack and dust lightly with confectioners' sugar.
3. Beat the egg white with the cream of tartar until it holds soft peaks. Add 1 teaspoon of the sugar and continue beating until stiff and shiny. Set aside.
4. In a separate bowl, beat the egg yolk, add the 2 tablespoons of sugar, and beat until thick. Add the vanilla extract and salt, and mix well. Fold in the flour. Freshen the egg white and fold into the mixture.

5. Spread the batter into an even ¼-inch-thick layer over the wax paper–covered bottom of the cake pan. Put the pan on the lowest shelf of the oven and bake for 5 to 7 minutes, until light brown.

6. Remove the pan from the oven. Turn the cake layer out on the sugared wax paper, and when slightly cool, remove the bottom circle of wax paper from the cake. Turn the cake over on the rack and remove the sugared wax paper. Allow the layer to cool completely, sugar side up.

Cake/Tart Crust

In northern Italy one constantly encounters a crustlike cake or cakelike crust—whichever way one wishes to describe it. This is filled with fruit or a second type of cake, all baked together. You will find several recipes in this book for these fillings.

Since these crusts are never used alone, specific pan sizes and oven temperatures will be found in the finished recipes.

> *8 tablespoons (1 stick) unsalted butter*
> *½ cup plus 2 tablespoons sugar*
> *¹⁄₁₆ teaspoon salt*
> *2 eggs, separated*
> *1 teaspoon lemon extract or grated zest of ½ lemon*
> *¼ teaspoon almond extract*
> *2 teaspoons dark rum*
> *⅛ teaspoon cream of tartar*
> *1 cup flour, sifted*

1. Preheat the oven.
2. Butter and flour the cake pan.
3. Cut the butter into slices and soften in a mixing bowl.
4. Cream the butter, ½ cup of sugar, and salt together with a wooden spoon. Add the egg yolks and beat the mixture. Beat in

the lemon extract and grated lemon zest, almond extract, and rum.

5. Beat the egg whites with the cream of tartar. When soft peaks form, add the remaining 2 tablespoons of sugar and continue beating until the egg whites are stiff.

6. To the butter-egg mixture, alternately fold in ⅓ of the egg whites and ⅓ of the sifted flour, starting with the egg whites. Consistency will be that of a cake batter, yet it will be stiff enough to support itself as a side wall around the edge of a tart pan.

7. Spoon the batter into the pan and bake according to the directions given for the size pan used.

Vanilla-Flavored Confectioners' Sugar

A dusting of vanilla-flavored confectioner's sugar is a must for the tops of plain cakes, small cakes, and fruit tarts. It is a staple on our pastry supply shelf where the sugar shaker is kept in a plastic storage bag to keep in the flavor. To make vanilla-flavored confectioners' sugar, fill a metal sugar shaker halfway with confectioners' sugar. Add two 2-inch lengths of vanilla bean and cover them with 3 or 4 additional tablespoons of confectioners' sugar (the sugar should not come up to the top of the container). Let stand for about a week before using, but from then on the shaker can be continually replenished with sugar and, from time to time, new vanilla beans. When we use a piece of vanilla bean to flavor a custard or ice cream, we fish it out of the hot liquid, wash it off, dry it well, and then drop it into the shaker to give up its remaining fragrance to the sugar.

Simple Icing

A quick but professional thin white icing for the tops of cookies, sweet ravioli, and plain cakes such as Plum Cake (page 102),

Panforte di Siena (page 98), and for Round Cake or Roll Cake (page 78) in place of the confettilike nonpareils.

Makes ½ cup icing

> 1 cup plus 2 tablespoons confectioners' sugar, sifted
> 2 tablespoons cold water
> ¼ teaspoon vanilla, lemon, or almond extract, or to taste

1. Preheat the oven to 300°.

2. In the top of a double boiler, mix the sugar with the water to make a dense cream, adding more sugar or water to make the proper consistency. Add the flavoring.

3. Put the pan over simmering hot water until the mixture is tepid. Remove from the hot water and spread the icing on with a narrow spatula, smoothing the surface.

4. Place the iced sweet in the oven for just 3 minutes to form a shiny surface. Remove from the oven and cool before serving.

Almond Icing

This is an ideal icing for Plum Cake (page 102) and any other loaf cake or ring-mold cake, as well as small cupcakes and cookies. The quantities listed are for a top icing on a loaf cake four and one-half by twelve inches. Use your own judgment on the amount to make for other baked goods.

> ¾ cup plus 2 tablespoons confectioners' sugar, sifted
> 3 teaspoons white wine
> 1½ teaspoons Amaretto liqueur
> ¼ teaspoon almond extract
> Pinch of salt

1. Sift half of the sugar into a small bowl. Add the white wine,

Amaretto liqueur, almond extract, and salt. Stir and smooth the mixture until all the sugar has been mixed in.

2. Gradually sift the remaining sugar into the bowl, mixing until the consistency is stiff but still soft.

3. Smooth the icing evenly over the top of the cake with a narrow metal spatula.

Lemon Icing

This is a sweet-and-sour icing with a strong lemon flavor. It goes well with plain cupcakes, thin cakes served with coffee, cream puffs, and layer cakes.

Makes ¾ cup icing, approximately

> *1½ cups confectioners' sugar, sifted*
> *Juice of ½ lemon*
> *½ teaspoon lemon extract*

1. Sift half of the sugar into a bowl. Add half of the lemon juice and all the lemon extract. Mix the liquid into the sugar, smoothing out any lumps. Add more sifted sugar and the rest of the lemon juice, and mix again. Add the remaining sugar, thinning the mixture with a little water until it is the right consistency. It should spread on the cake top without running over the edge and form a smooth, shiny icing surface.

Orange Icing

This semi-thin icing for a plain cake is used as a decorative "drizzle," allowing the cake top to show through. On a round cake you can make a snaillike pattern with lines of varying thicknesses and widths; on a loaf cake you can make parallel or crosshatched lines of icing.

Makes ¼ cup icing

> *½ cup plus up to 1½ tablespoons confectioners' sugar*
> *Pinch of salt*
> *1 tablespoon orange juice*
> *1 teaspoon rum*
> *⅛ teaspoon orange extract*
> *Whole almonds, blanched (optional), (page 48)*
> *Butter*

1. Sift ½ cup of confectioners' sugar into a small bowl. Stir in the salt, 1 tablespoon of orange juice, rum, and orange extract. The icing should be thin enough to be dribbled from a teaspoon in a concentric circle on top of the cake but thick enough to hold ridges of icing in place; the continuous line will vary from thick to thin. Add up to 1½ tablespoons of confectioners' sugar if needed to adjust the thickness of the icing.

2. Brown the almonds, if used, in a little butter and drain on paper towels. While the icing is still soft, randomly press the almonds securely in place.

Hard Chocolate Glaze

One of the simplest icings is plain melted chocolate; without any additions, it is poured while still liquid over a cake's surface. A thin layer of apricot glaze can be brushed over the cake surface before pouring on the chocolate glaze. Unsweetened chocolate will melt to a thinner consistency than semisweet or sweet. *Warning:* Both the top of the double boiler used for melting the chocolate and the spoon used for stirring *must be absolutely dry;* even a drop of water will cause the chocolate to lump.

Makes enough to cover the top of a 8- to 10-inch cake

4 ounces unsweetened chocolate

1. Break up the chocolate into small pieces. Put the pieces into the perfectly dry top of a double boiler, over simmering water. As the chocolate melts, stir with a dry tablespoon until fully melted.

2. Remove the pan from the water; allow the liquid chocolate to cool, stirring continuously. When slightly thickened, pour over the cake top. Immediately put the cake into the refrigerator to stiffen. The hardened chocolate will not melt at room temperature.

Note: Semisweet or sweet chocolate may be substituted for unsweetened chocolate. Cookies may be dipped halfway into chocolate that is melted in this manner.

Soft Chocolate Glaze

This is a cooked icing with an intense bittersweet chocolate flavor and a creamy texture.

Makes enough to cover the top and sides of a 6½-inch cake

> *1 ounce unsweetened chocolate*
> *2 ounces semisweet chocolate*
> *⅓ cup half-and-half or heavy cream*
> *2 tablespoons light corn syrup*
> *1 tablespoon unsalted butter, cut into bits*
> *1 teaspoon instant espresso coffee powder*
> *½ teaspoon vanilla extract*

1. Break the chocolate into small chunks and place in the bowl of a food processor fitted with a steel blade. Process until finely ground.

2. Pour the half-and-half or heavy cream into a saucepan. Add the light corn syrup and the butter. Sprinkle the instant coffee powder over the surface. Place over medium heat and bring to a boil. Turn off the heat and stir in the vanilla extract.

3. Sprinkle the ground chocolate over the hot mixture and stir to mix. Cover the saucepan for 5 or 6 minutes. Remove the cover and lightly stir again to blend all the ingredients. If necessary, reheat the mixture to fully melt the chocolate, stirring lightly, but do not boil.

4. Cool the glaze until lukewarm, then place in the refrigerator. Chill until the glaze is stiff enough to spread without running. Return the cake to the refrigerator to set the glaze.

Marzipan Topping

This is a popular topping in Italy for a thin layer cake and makes an elegant and flavorful decoration.

Makes enough to cover the top of a 6½- to 8-inch cake

> *7 ounces (two 3½-ounce packages) marzipan, or almond*
>   *paste (see Note)*
> *4 teaspoons beaten whole egg*
> *1½ teaspoons Amaretto or maraschino liqueur, or dark rum*
> *Almond extract to taste*

1. In a small bowl, mash the marzipan with a fork.

2. Mix in the beaten egg, add the liqueur, and beat well. The mixture should be soft enough to be squeezed through a pastry tube, yet stiff enough to hold its shape.

3. Depending on how much almond flavoring there is in the packaged marzipan, or almond paste, add almond extract, starting with 4 drops and gradually working up to ⅛ teaspoon or more.

4. Put the mixture in a pastry bag and pipe out, following the pattern called for in the cake recipe.

5. Set the marzipan topping by putting the decorated cake in a 450° oven for 5 to 10 minutes, then briefly under the broiler to lightly brown the surface. Be careful, though, because the topping may burn, so watch it every second.

Note: The brand of marzipan, or almond paste, most readily available has separate 3½-ounce rolls, one labeled marzipan and the other almond paste, with very little difference between them.

Stiffened Whipped Cream

Whipped cream, used as a filling between cake layers, as a top decoration, and as icing, needs to be stiffened; otherwise, it collapses, the cake becomes soggy, and the icing becomes soft. By adding melted, unflavored gelatin to the whipped cream the cake and filling can be completed early in the day, placed in the refrigerator, then brought to room temperature before sitting down to dinner or during dinner. This is much more relaxing than having to put the cake together just before serving.

Makes about 3 cups

> 1 rounded teaspoon unflavored gelatin
> 3 tablespoons cold water
> 1½ cups heavy cream (not ultrapasteurized)
> 3 to 6 tablespoons sugar, or to taste
> 1 teaspoon vanilla extract
> Pinch of salt

1. In a small ramekin, soften the gelatin in the water. When soft, bring a small saucepan of water to a boil. With the heat *turned off,* place the ramekin in the water until the gelatin is clear and

liquid. Remove the ramekin from the pan and cool the gelatin at room temperature. Do not allow the gelatin to solidify.

2. Beat the heavy cream just until it begins to thicken. Spoon a little of the cream into the cooled gelatin, then scrape this mixture into the rest of the cream, stirring it in. Add the sugar, vanilla, and salt. Continue beating until the cream is thick.

3. Cover the bowl with clear plastic wrap and place it in the refrigerator to allow the gelatin to stiffen the cream.

Mocha Butter Cream

This is a soft butter cream that readily stiffens in the refrigerator and holds its shape when squeezed through a pastry tube into an edging design. Its softness or hardness can be controlled by the amount of beaten egg white added to the butter mixture. The food processor speeds things up.

Makes enough for the top, sides, and filling of a 2-layer 6½-inch cake

> *11 tablespoons (1 stick plus 3 tablespoons) unsalted butter*
> *1½ teaspoons instant espresso coffee powder*
> *1 tablespoon hot water*
> *2 egg yolks*
> *6 tablespoons sugar*
> *1½ teaspoons unsweetened cocoa powder*
> *1 teaspoon vanilla extract*
> *Pinch of salt*
> *1 egg white*
> *⅛ teaspoon cream of tartar*

1. Cut the butter into thin slices and then into ¼-inch dice. Set aside on a small plate to soften to room temperature.

2. Dissolve the instant coffee powder in the hot water.

3. In a food processor fitted with a steel blade, put the egg yolks and 3 tablespoons of the sugar mixed with the cocoa powder.

Add the dissolved instant coffee, vanilla extract, and salt.

4. Start the processor and, when the ingredients are blended, add the butter gradually until it is all incorporated.

5. Turn off the processor. Scrape the butter cream into a bowl, cover with plastic wrap, and place in the refrigerator for at least 15 minutes, or until slightly stiffened.

6. In a small bowl, beat the egg white with the cream of tartar. When the egg white holds soft peaks, slowly add the remaining 3 tablespoons of sugar (1 tablespoon at a time) and continue beating until the egg white is stiff.

7. Remove the butter cream from the refrigerator and gradually fold in the beaten egg white. Start with 2 rounded tablespoons of egg white well mixed in. The butter cream must be spreadable but not so thin that it oozes out of a center filling, runs off the edge of a cake top, or refuses to stick to the side of a cake. In any case, you will not use all the egg white; what is left over can be used for tiny decorative meringues that can be frozen for later use. Return the butter cream to the refrigerator, covered, until ready to use.

VARIATION: Chocolate Butter Cream

The ingredients and process remain the same, except for the following *additions:*

> *4 tablespoons unsweetened cocoa powder*
> *2 tablespoons hot water (to go with cocoa powder)*

Almonds, Blanched and Toasted

1. Preheat the oven to 300°.

2. Blanch the almonds by half-filling a small pot with water and bringing it to a boil. When boiling, turn off the heat and drop in the shelled almonds. Let them soak for 4 or 5 minutes. Scoop out a few almonds at a time with a slotted spoon. Cut off a sliver of skin at the blunt end of the nut and pop the almond out of its

skin. Repeat with all the almonds, placing them on an ungreased baking pan; the size will depend on how many nuts you use.

3. Place the pan in the preheated oven and turn the nuts over every few minutes so they brown evenly on both sides. When the almonds are well toasted, approximately 10 to 15 minutes, remove the pan from the oven and turn the nuts out on a plate to cool.

4. According to the recipe being followed, the nuts can be left whole, coarsely chopped, or ground into "flour" in a food processor fitted with a steel blade or in a Mouli nut grater.

Note: Throughout the book all measurements of almonds are based on shelled nuts.

Toasted Hazelnuts

Hazelnuts must be toasted to bring out their flavor.

1. Preheat the oven to 300°.
2. Spread the nuts in a single layer on a baking pan. Put the pan into the preheated oven, turning the nuts over every few minutes so they brown evenly. When well toasted but not burned, approximately 10 to 15 minutes, remove the pan from the oven. Turn the nuts out on a plate until cool enough to handle.
3. Taking a few nuts at a time, rub off as much skin as possible between sheets of paper or cloth towels folded over the nuts and held between the palms of your hands. We prefer paper towels to cloth because they can be discarded. Not all the skin will come off, but the remaining bits do not harm the final flavor.
4. According to the recipe being followed, the nuts can now be coarsely chopped or ground into "flour" in a food processor fitted with a steel blade or in a Mouli nut grater.

Note: Throughout the book all measurements of hazelnuts are based on shelled nuts.

Candied Lemon Peel

A number of recipes call for candied lemon rind or mixed candied fruits. Packaged candied lemon peel has very little flavor and often has a metallic taste, but you can make thin strips or dice of candied lemon peel in small quantities, using leftover skins after squeezing a lemon or two for juice. The candied peel will keep indefinitely in a covered jar in the refrigerator.

Rind of 1 lemon
1 cup water
½ cup sugar plus sugar for separating and drying peel

1. Cut lemon rind in quarters. With a teaspoon, scoop out the white membrane on the inside. With a sharp knife cut the rind into ¼-inch dice or thin strips.
2. Put the rind into a small saucepan and cover with the water.

Bring to a boil and boil for 10 minutes. Pour the contents of the saucepan into a small bowl and cool. When cool, cover with plastic wrap and keep in the refrigerator overnight.

3. The next day, pour the rind and liquid back into the small saucepan. Add the ½ cup of sugar and bring to a boil. Boil gently, until the syrup is reduced and slightly colored, but do not let it burn or turn brown.

4. While the rind is cooking, spread a sheet of wax paper over a dinner plate or on a work surface and sprinkle the paper heavily with sugar.

5. Remove the saucepan from the stove and drain the rind in a metal sieve over a small bowl. Quickly turn the rind onto the sugared paper and separate the pieces with 2 forks. Lift up the sides of the paper to flip sugar over the top of the pieces. As soon as the rind is cool enough, separate the pieces with your fingers. When well separated, sprinkle 1 more tablespoon of sugar over the rind, stir, and allow to cool completely.

6. When cool, pour the rind and any extra sugar on the paper into a glass jar and cover with a top. Put the jar in the refrigerator until needed.

Note: Save the syrup if there is enough to pour over ice cream or squares of cake. If only a small amount is left, it can be discarded. To prepare larger quantities, increase the recipe ingredients accordingly.

Candied Orange Peel

All proportions are based on the rind of one orange. Increase the ingredients according to the number of orange peels that you are candying. We prefer soft, thick-skinned oranges because the peel cooks quickly and stays tender. You can candy one orange peel at a time and store it in a jar kept in the refrigerator, adding additional peel from time to time.

Rind of 1 orange
1 cup water
¾ cup sugar plus sugar for separating and drying peel

1. Remove any thin white skin or membrane from the inside of the peel. Cut the peel into ¼-inch dice or long ⅛-inch-wide strips. Put the pieces of peel into a small stainless steel saucepan, add the water, and bring to a boil. Continue to boil for 10 minutes, then turn down the heat to moderate.

2. Add ¾ cup of sugar to the peel and liquid in the saucepan. Gently boil down the liquid until there is approximately 2 tablespoons of syrup left. Remove the saucepan from the heat before the syrup caramelizes.

3. Scrape the candied peel and any syrup into a metal sieve and drain off the syrup. Turn the candied peel out onto a well sugared dinner plate and sprinkle more sugar over the top of the peel. Separate the still-hot pieces with 2 forks, adding more sugar if needed. When the peel can be handled with the fingers, finish separating the pieces.

4. Spread the sugared peel on a sheet of wax paper placed on a baking rack and allow to dry for 1 hour. Store the candied peel in a covered glass jar in the refrigerator.

Almond Brittle
Il Croccante alle Mandorle

This preparation is also known as praline or nougat. All pastry chefs have a jar of crushed almond or hazelnut brittle stored away. It adds a professional—and flavorful—decoration to cake icings, meringues, ice creams, or any other dessert that needs a sprinkling of crisp nut brittle. Toasted Hazelnuts (page 49) may be substituted for almonds, following the directions for making almond brittle.

10-x-15-inch baking pan
Makes 1¼ cups

> ¾ *cup Almonds, Blanched and Toasted, page 48*
> ½ *cup sugar*
> 2 *tablespoons water*

1. Cut the prepared almonds into small pieces.
2. Butter the baking pan and set aside.
3. Put the sugar and water into a small saucepan and let stand until the sugar is nearly dissolved. Place the saucepan over low heat. Let the sugar bubble slowly *without stirring* until caramelized, tipping the saucepan now and then to mix the syrup so that it caramelizes evenly. When golden brown but not burned, add the nuts and mix with a fork. When the nuts are coated with the syrup, remove the saucepan from the heat.
4. Turn the mixture out onto the buttered baking pan, spreading the mixture as thinly as possible with a fork and the back of a tablespoon. Allow to cool.
5. When cold and stiff, break the brittle into pieces with your fingers. Put the pieces into a double plastic bag (one inside the other) and place flat on a pastry board. Break the brittle into small pieces with a small rolling pin or hammer. Place in a covered glass jar and store in the refrigerator. The brittle will keep indefinitely.

Cakes

Italian cakes

are one or two inches high (low by American standards); with few exceptions they are "raised" with eggs rather than baking powder, and this makes them richer and moister. Finely ground nuts are often substituted for white flour or blended with white flour.

Rather than baking a layer cake in two separate layers, the Italians bake one thick layer and then split it in half with either a long knife or a length of button thread. (Circle the thread around the outside of the cake, cross the ends over when they meet, and pull on the two ends; the thread will slowly cut the cake.) In this whole new world of baking, the flat bottom of the cake becomes the top; any center bump on the original top caused by the cake's uneven rising is trimmed off before turning it over. The result is a cake that is easier to ice and decorate.

Most often the layers are filled with jam, butter cream, custard, or whipped cream; sometimes the layers are first sprinkled with a liqueur or rum. The top and sides of a cake are covered with thin icings, sometimes over a brushing of jam that helps keep the icing and cake moist. Decorations include fruits, nuts, meringues, and whipped cream. In all cases these tempting confections are served cut into narrow wedges. They are savored slowly for their blended and contrasting flavors, and are an elegant finish to a meal, not yet another dish to fill up on.

The Italians make many buttery and eggy plain cakes, both loaf-shaped and flat rounds. Some have raisins, nuts, or candied fruit added, and the cakes often are dusted with vanilla-flavored confectioners' sugar. There is something very appetizing about the sight of confectioners' sugar sprinkled on plain cakes just before serving with the browned top showing through the snow white of the sugar.

Almond Coffee Cake (Vigoreto)

Between Mantua and Parma is the small walled town of Sabbioneta, with its exquisite trompe l'oeil church interior and the small Olympic Theater reminiscent of both Palladio's theater in Vicenza and the Farnese theater in Parma. We have visited the town several times, and each time we have eaten lunch at the Parco Cappuccini in nearby Vigoreto. We rarely duplicate each other's choices at restaurants, so over the years we have collected a set of memorable dishes, including desserts; several from the Parco are in this book.

This one is a light cake made with nut-flour and strongly flavored with almonds. The cake batter is baked in a shell of puff pastry. It is the perfect cake to serve with espresso or cappuccino coffee or a slightly sweet wine.

6-x-1¾-inch round cake pan
Serves 6

> *Puff Pastry, page 174, or a frozen commercial sheet*
> *Almond Cake, page 33*

1. Line the bottom and sides of the cake pan with thinly rolled puff pastry, leaving 1 inch of pastry hanging over the edge. If using frozen, commercially made puff pastry, you will need about ¾ of a sheet. Prick the bottom of the pastry all over with the tines of a table fork. Place the pan in the refrigerator while you are making the cake batter.

2. Prepare the almond cake batter.

3. Preheat the oven to 375°.

4. Remove the puff pastry–lined pan from the refrigerator. Spoon the almond cake batter into the pan, heaping it a little in the

center and filling the pan ⅔ full. Lightly fold the 1-inch overhang of puff pastry over the edge of the cake batter. Do not press it against the batter. The puff pastry will overlap itself here and there, and have an irregular edge.

5. Put the pan in the preheated oven and bake for 30 minutes. Brush the top with the reserved teaspoon of egg yolk mixed with ½ teaspoon of water. Bake 10 minutes more or until the top is a rich brown and a metal skewer inserted into the center comes out clean. Remove the cake from the oven and place the pan on a cake rack to cool for 15 minutes. Transfer the cake from the pan to the rack to finish cooling. Serve at room temperature.

Note: There will be enough almond cake batter left over for 6 to 8 tiny cupcakes that can be iced with Almond Icing (page 41). Or make a thin single layer in a 6½-inch quiche pan and combine it with a Basic Baked Meringue layer (page 35), for a variation of Torta Margherita (page 106).

VARIATION

We were served a similar cake at a restaurant on the Brenta Canal near Dolo. It had a pasta frolla crust and whole almonds pressed into the top. It was a shallower cake with a flat top and a crimped edge of pasta frolla showing just above the cake.

A Cake Bombe (Naples)

One day we drove up from Sorrento to Naples along the clifftop road that parallels the Bay of Naples, catching glimpses of Vesuvius and the blue, blue water below us. Then we traveled down into the muddled traffic along the waterfront and out into the blessed openness and greenery of the Municipio/Castel Nuovo park where, in an unheard-of piece of luck, a car pulled out of a parking slot and we slipped in. By that time we felt we needed R & R before tackling the National Museum on the other side of town; at that time the museum was open until 4 P.M. A relaxing lunch at a nearby trattoria ended with a wedge of a cake bombe, a splendid creation somehow expressing the past glories of Naples with its succession of Bourbon and Napoleonic rulers.

As we subsequently found out, a cake bombe can be simple or elaborate, but in any form it is an enchanting dessert. The bombe starts with a sponge cake baked in a round-bottomed stainless steel bowl. After baking, the cake is hollowed out and filled with whipped cream and a mixture of fresh fruit dice, if served in the spring or summer, or with whipped cream and chopped toasted almonds or hazelnuts, if served in the fall; or an egg custard mixed with whipped cream and diced candied fruits or toasted nuts, if in the winter. The outside can be dusted with vanilla-flavored confectioners' sugar, as we had it that day in Naples. In another restaurant we saw a cake bombe decorated with piped lines of whipped cream decorated with red and green candied cherries. At holiday or birthday celebrations, confettilike multicolored nonpareils replace the candied cherries.

7-x-4-inch stainless steel bowl or round-bottomed top of a double boiler
Serves 4 to 6

> *Sponge Cake, page 32*
> *Stiffened Whipped Cream, page 46*
> *Apricot Jam Glaze, page 178; double the recipe*
> *½ to ¾ cup diced fruit (depending on size of bombe hollow):*
> > *fresh peaches, apricots, nectarines, cherries, strawberries,*
> > *or pineapple*
> *Vanilla-Flavored Confectioners' Sugar, page 40 (optional)*

1. Preheat the oven to 325°.
2. Pour the sponge cake batter into the unbuttered stainless steel bowl or the top of the double boiler. Bake for 40 to 50 minutes or until a thin skewer inserted into the center comes out clean. Brown the top of the cake under a broiler to crisp it so it will not become moist as it cools and stick to the cake rack. (If the cake

does not fit under your broiler, see Step 1 of the assembling directions.) Turn out the cake and cool on the cake rack. Wash and dry the pan.

3. While the cake is cooling, make and chill the stiffened whipped cream.

4. Make the apricot jam glaze and let it cool slightly until it starts to thicken.

5. Drain the fruit and pat dry with paper towels; put the fruit into the refrigerator to chill.

To Assemble:

1. Holding the cake carefully, cut away a ¾-inch-thick slice from the flat bottom of the cake and set it aside with the cut side upward. If the browned side is still sticky, slip the slice under a preheated broiler to crisp the surface; remove and allow to cool with the browned side up. Return the rest of the cake to the pan it

was baked in to add support during the scooping and filling of the cake.

2. With a sharp knife and a tablespoon, cut and scoop out the center of the cake, leaving a ¾- to 1-inch-thick wall on the bottom and sides. Try to cut out pieces as large as possible without tearing the cake: these pieces can be frozen and used in other desserts, such as Black-and-White Pudding (page 243). Brush away any loose crumbs from the inside of the hollow.

3. Brush the inside of the cake hollow and the upper edge of the cake wall with a little more than half the apricot glaze, giving the bottom a double coat of glaze. Brush the cut surface of the slice of cake with a thick coating of the apricot glaze. The glaze will keep the filling from soaking into the cake.

4. Remove the stiffened whipped cream and the diced fruits from the refrigerator. Fold the whipped cream and fruit together, making your own judgment of how much filling will be needed, proportioning fruit and whipped cream according to your taste. You may have enough whipped cream left over to pipe on the outside of the cake.

5. Spoon the filling into the cake hollow. Cover the filling with the top slice of cake, apricot glaze side down. Place the cake bombe in the refrigerator, still in the pan, until ready to serve. Just before serving, carefully turn out the cake bombe onto a serving dish and dust the outside with vanilla-flavored confectioners' sugar. Cut the bombe into wedges when serving.

Note: As you can see, this is a spectacular dessert that is simple to put together but has infinite variations, so it can be served many times with different fillings and decorations.

VARIATIONS: Ingredients include:

> *Almonds, Blanched and Toasted, page 48, or Toasted*
> *Hazelnuts, page 49, to taste*
> *Candied whole fruits to taste*
> *Egg Custard, page 237, or Time-Saver Custard, page 240*

Additional ¼ to ½ cup heavy cream
Red and green candied cherries
Multicolored nonpareils

Follow the cooking directions through Step 4, then:

If nuts instead of fruit are being added to the stiffened whipped cream, chop them coarsely and set them aside in a small bowl.

If candied fruits are being added to the stiffened whipped cream, cut the whole fruits into ¼- to ⅜-inch dice and set aside.

If the cake is to be filled with egg custard mixed with freshly whipped cream, make the custard and chill it.

If decorating the cake with red and green cherries, put them into separate small bowls and cover with boiling water. Carefully wash off the sticky syrup and place the cherries on paper towels to drain and dry.

Continue with Step 1 of the assembly directions but note the following:

For the variations, the toasted chopped nuts or diced whole candied fruits can be mixed with the stiffened whipped cream.

For the egg custard filling, fold ¼ to ½ cup (depending on the amount of filling needed) of freshly whipped cream into the chilled custard. Add the toasted chopped nuts or diced candied fruit and follow the directions in assembly Steps 4 and 5.

Instead of dusting confectioners' sugar on the outside of the bombe, decorate it about 1 hour before serving with whipped cream. Pipe on either the reserved stiffened whipped cream or ½ cup or more of freshly whipped heavy cream flavored with sugar and vanilla to taste; use either a ½-inch star tube or a ½-inch toothed ribbon tube in the pastry bag. The fancy strip design down the sides is your choice; leave the whipped cream strips plain or add either candied cherries or multicolored nonpareils to the strips. Return the bombe to the refrigerator until just before serving.

Cake of the House (Villa Cipriani in Asolo)
Torta della Casa

Over a long weekend at the Villa Cipriani in Asolo, we lived splendidly: had breakfast at the edge of the garden overlooking the valley; explored the town; visited not only the remaining wing of Catarina Cornaro's Barca (now a series of barns and farmers' homes) but also Villa Emo and Villa Barbaro; then went up into the still snow-covered mountains to the north. In the evenings we unwound over drinks, were pampered with deft serving in the charming dining room, and talked with other guests over espresso coffee and grappa in the softly lighted lounge.

One evening the special house dessert was a light and airy cake: a well-browned round of flaky puff pastry split in half and thickly filled with unctuous whipped cream, the top thickly dusted with vanilla-flavored confectioners' sugar. A thoroughly sybaritic experience.

10-x-15-inch baking pan, unbuttered
Serves 6 to 8

> *Puff Pastry, page 174, or a 9½-x-10½-inch sheet of commercial puff pastry*
> *1½ cups heavy cream*
> *6 to 8 teaspoons sugar, or to taste*
> *1 teaspoon vanilla extract, or to taste*
> *Vanilla-Flavored Confectioners' Sugar, page 40*

1. Preheat the oven to 375°.
2. Prepare and bake the 9-inch round of puff pastry or cut a 9-inch round from a sheet of frozen puff pastry, baking it according to the manufacturer's instructions, approximately 20 minutes.
3. Remove the baking pan from the oven and transfer the pastry to a cake rack to cool.

4. Thirty minutes to 1 hour before serving, whip the heavy cream, adding the sugar and vanilla extract to taste.

5. Split the puff pastry round into 2 layers. Return the bottom half, cut side up, to a cake rack covered with a sheet of wax paper. Spread the pastry surface with the whipped cream in an even layer. Replace the top layer and heavily dust it with the vanilla-flavored confectioners' sugar.

6. Transfer the cake to a serving plate and keep it chilled in the refrigerator until ready to serve.

Candied Fruit and Marzipan Cake (Mira)

We have driven many times along the length of both sides of the Brenta Canal, from Fusino on the Adriatic to Padua. It is not hard to project oneself back to the period of the sixteenth to eighteenth centuries when the luxurious villas were new, built by wealthy Venetian patricians as refuges from the summer heat of Venice. The canal was the easiest avenue of travel for the water-oriented Venetians' elaborate burchiellos, as well as the working barges that carried supplies and farm produce.

Many side canals cut across the wide, flat fields and drain into the Brenta Canal. In this area, from the Villa Pisani at Stra down to the brooding Villa Malcontenta, many restaurants are tucked away in the countryside. Since we once stayed in Dolo, we explored the neighborhood and dined on fantastic fish preparations and glorious desserts. This cake is from Della Clara, inland from the Brenta at Mira, and we have made it many times since we returned home.

Slightly related to the Pineapple Marzipan Cake we bought in Chioggia (page 100), this is a slant-sided, one-inch-high cake filled with strained apricot jam, topped with a thin brushing of jam, and sprinkled with an even dusting of unsweetened cocoa. Marzipan decorates the sides and top; candied cherries and pieces of candied figs and other fruits are tucked into the spaces left by the marzipan swirls; and the top is quickly browned in the oven.

8-inch slant-sided pie plate, 1 inch deep
10-x-15-inch baking pan
Serves 6 to 8

> *Génoise, page 29; double the recipe*
> *Marzipan Topping, page 45; 1½ times the recipe*
> *Apricot Jam Glaze, page 178; 1½ times the recipe*
> *Unsweetened cocoa powder*
> *A few candied fruits, cherries, figs, citron, pears, and so*
> *forth, for decoration*

1. Preheat the oven to 350°.

2. Butter the pie plate, fit a circle of wax paper in the bottom, butter the paper, and dust the pan with flour.

3. Make the Genoise. Pour the batter into the prepared pan and bake for 30 to 40 minutes following the recipe directions. Remove the cake from the pan and cool, top side up, on a cake rack.

4. Make the marzipan topping and set aside.

5. Make the apricot jam glaze and set it aside to cool until it begins to thicken.

6. Slip the cooled cake under a preheated broiler to crisp and brown the top, about 1 or 2 minutes. Cool the cake on a cake rack.

7. When cool, turn the cake upside down (the bottom now becomes the top of the cake) and cut it in half horizontally, marking the side with a vertical nick so the 2 halves can be matched when putting them together again. Place the 2 halves on the upended bottom of a baking pan because the cake will be returned to the oven to brown the marzipan topping.

8. Spread the apricot glaze on the cut surface of the lower layer, reserving enough glaze for a thin coat on top of the cake. Cover the apricot filling with the top layer, matching the nicked line on the side.

9. Spread a thin coat of apricot glaze over the top and sprinkle it with an even dusting of cocoa.

10. Fit a pastry bag with a ½-inch star tip and spoon the

marzipan topping into the bag. Cover the sides with a continuous looped line. Cover the cake top with irregular swirls of marzipan and tuck pieces of candied fruit into the swirls. Follow the directions for baking and browning the marzipan; you can brush the top surface with the remainder of the egg mixed with a little cold water.

11. Cool the cake, then carefully slip it off the baking pan onto a serving plate.

Chestnut Jam Cake
Torta Castelvecchio

On one of our trips to Verona from our apartment in Desenzano on Lake Garda, we parked the car and walked along the river to the fourteenth-century Castelvecchio, now the Museo d'Arte, with its matchless collection of paintings by Veronese painters. When it closed at lunchtime, we crossed the street to a simple fish restaurant where we had wonderful fish soup and broiled shrimp. Then, as was often our custom, we strolled down the street looking for espresso and a sweet.

We had our espresso at a bar, but the sweet eluded us until we reached Pasticceria Castelvecchio. There we bought a fabulous nut-dough cake with filling and sides of mocha butter cream, its top covered with chestnut jam and decorated with thin grid lines of chocolate and a wavelike edging design of mocha butter cream. It was packed into a box with its own stiff white plastic doily that we kept as a souvenir.

We also sampled from the lavish variety of cookies and small cakes on display in the shop's glass case. We went down the line pointing for two of this and four of that, the cheerful lady behind the counter smiling appreciatively as she filled a box cradled in her arm. We would eat some on the drive home and the remainder on picnics during the next few days. Several of these are part of the Small Cakes and Cookies section, which begins on page 115.

6½- to 7-inch springform pan
Serves 6 to 8

> *1 ounce (about 23) almonds, unskinned*
> *¼ cup plus 1 teaspoon flour*
> *⅛ teaspoon salt*
> *Zest from ½ lemon*
> *Juice from ½ lemon*
> *3 eggs, separated*
> *⅛ teaspoon cream of tartar*
> *½ cup sugar*
> *1 teaspoon vanilla extract*
> *¼ teaspoon almond extract*
> *Mocha Butter Cream, page 47*
> *2 ounces Almonds, Blanched and Toasted, page 48*
> *1 ounce unsweetened chocolate*
> *Chestnut jam topping (⅓ cup Chestnut Creme Preserve*
> *   [Bonne Maman] mixed with 1 tablespoon dark rum)*
> *   (see Note)*

1. Preheat the oven to 350°.
2. Butter only the bottom of the springform pan. Fit a circle of wax paper in the bottom, butter the paper, and dust it with flour.
3. In a food processor fitted with a steel blade, grind the 1 ounce of almonds along with 1 teaspoon of flour. When very fine, pour the almonds into a small bowl and mix with ¼ cup of flour and ⅛ teaspoon of salt. Set aside.
4. Grate the lemon zest, and squeeze the lemon juice from the ½ lemon and set aside.
5. Beat the egg whites in a mixing bowl with the cream of tartar. When soft peaks form, gradually add the sugar, 1 tablespoon at a time, until the whites are stiff.
6. Beat the egg yolks with the wire whisk. Beat in the lemon juice and vanilla and almond extracts; and add the grated lemon zest.

7. Spoon the egg yolk mixture over the top of the egg whites. Dust with the almond flour and fold in until just mixed.

8. Spoon the batter into the springform pan, heaping it a little in the center because the cake will sink a bit after it is baked. Bake for 25 to 30 minutes, until a thin skewer inserted in the center comes out clean. Take the cake out of the oven and place the pan on a cake rack.

9. While the cake is baking, make the mocha butter cream and put it in the refrigerator.

10. Chop the 2 ounces of blanched, skinned and toasted almonds into small pieces. Set aside.

11. Cool the cake slightly in the pan. Loosen the edge with a sharp knife and turn the pan upside down on a cake rack until the cake is almost cold. Turn the pan right side up and open and remove the springform and the bottom wax paper. Let the cake cool completely on the rack, upside down, so that the bottom of the cake is the top.

12. Melt the chocolate in the top of a double boiler over hot water.

To Assemble:

1. The bottom of the cake becomes the top. If there is a hump in the middle of the original top of the cake, cut it off so that the cake will lie flat on the plate. Split the cake in half horizontally, cutting a vertical mark on the edge as a guide for putting the layers back together again. Place the now lower half on a cake rack covered with a sheet of wax paper.

2. Spread approximately ⅓ of the butter cream on the lower layer and top with the other layer, matching the knife cut on the side. Cover the sides with the butter cream. Scrape the remainder of the butter cream into a pastry bag fitted with a ½-inch star tip or a decorating tip toothed on one side and plain on the other. Put the bag into the refrigerator until needed.

3. Cover the top with a smooth layer of chestnut jam mixture, leaving a ½-inch border around the edge.

4. Shape a piece of wax paper into a small cone and cut a ⅛-

inch opening at the tip. Fill with melted chocolate and form a diamond-shaped grid of thin chocolate lines over the chestnut jam.

5. Cover the butter cream on the sides of the cake with the chopped toasted almonds.

6. Take the pastry bag out of the refrigerator and fill in the ½-inch border on the top of the cake with the butter cream, making a wavelike design around the edge.

7. Carefully transfer the cake to a serving dish and place it in the refrigerator to stiffen the butter cream. Remove from the refrigerator **30** minutes before serving.

Note: If the Bonne Maman Chestnut Creme Preserve is unavailable, use canned chestnut puree, adding 1 tablespoon of rum and enough light corn syrup to sweeten and thin the puree to a spreading consistency.

Chocolate African Cake (Verona)
Torta Africano

As we started up Via Mazzini, the traffic-free shopping street in Verona, on our way to the Piazza delle Erbe, we passed an elegant pasticceria. In the window there was a beautifully decorated chocolate cake labeled *Africano.* After wandering around Verona for the day, we bought the cake on our way back to the car, adding it to the thick Bolsano white asparagus, red radicchio, and farm-fresh eggs bought at the open-air market in the Piazza delle Erbe.

This has a sponge cake "sandwich" between a thin hard chocolate base and a thin hard chocolate topping. Between the two sponge layers is a light chocolate butter cream, which is also spread around the sides and then covered with chocolate sprills. The same butter cream is formed into cups around the edge of the chocolate topping, and each holds a candied cherry, one for each serving. A chocolate cake for chocoholics!

Serves 6 to 8

> *Sponge Cake, page 32, using a 6- to 8-inch springform pan
> (see* Note)
> *Hard Chocolate Glaze, page 43*
> *Mocha Butter Cream, page 47, plus 1 tablespoon cocoa pow-
> der*
> *Chocolate sprills, narrow ¼-inch-long chocolate cylinders
> variously called Choc-o-Trims and Dark Vermicelli*
> *6 to 8 candied cherries*

1. Prepare the sponge cake following the recipe directions but using the springform pan size above.

2. Make the hard chocolate glaze and allow to cool a bit so it will be thick enough to stay in place.

3. Cut the sponge cake into two equal layers with a broad sharp knife, not with a sawing motion but with single strokes pulled toward you to prevent the cake from crumbling. The original top of the cake will eventually become the bottom. If there is a hump in the middle, cut this off so you will have a flat surface.

4. Cover the original top of the cake with a thin layer of chocolate glaze. Put this cake layer on a plate, chocolate side up, and place in the freezer to harden the chocolate coating. Also place the metal disk of the springform pan in the freezer to chill.

5. Prepare the butter cream and spread ½ on the *cut* surface of the other cake layer. Place in the refrigerator.

6. When the chocolate coating is hard, remove the first cake layer from the freezer and place on the chilled metal disk, chocolate side against the metal; this is now the bottom layer.

7. Put the butter-creamed layer in place over the bottom layer, butter cream between the cake layers.

8. Cover the sides of the cake with approximately ¾ of the remaining butter cream, bringing it up to form a small rim around the top edge in order to contain the chocolate glaze when it is added. Cover the butter cream with chocolate sprills.

9. Spread a very thin coat of chocolate glaze over the top of the cake; if it is too thick, it will be hard to cut through when serving. Put the cake into the refrigerator to stiffen the chocolate topping.

10. Wash off the candied cherries in hot water to remove the sticky surface, and dry with paper towels.

11. When the top glaze is stiff, add 6 to 8 circles of butter cream around the edge of the top, 1 for each serving, and press a candied cherry into the center of each circle. Put the cake into the refrigerator until about 1 hour before serving, then transfer to a serving plate. Keep the metal disk from the springform pan under the cake on the serving plate.

Note: The sponge cake can be made the day before and stored overnight in a plastic bag, unrefrigerated. If the top has softened or becomes sticky overnight, place the cake under a preheated broiler for a few minutes to dry out the top. The mocha butter cream, too, can be made the day before and stored in the refrigerator in a covered container.

Chocolate-Almond Loaf Cake (Rimini)
Dolce del Passatore

This rich, moist loaf cake, baked in a half-round pan, is a specialty of Emilia-Romagna on the northern Adriatic Sea. It was in Rimini that we sampled the cake. It is the same shape as the half-round loaf of Latte Imperiale (page 248) that we bought in Ravenna. Literally translated, it means passenger's or traveler's cake, and one can speculate that this plain cake was carried on journeys or that its rounded top was reminiscent of the old rounded-top trunks. Who knows?

A rounded-bottom loaf pan is hard to come by, so we have made this cake in a long, narrow loaf pan.

4¼-x-12-x-3½-inch loaf pan
Makes approximately 24 slices

> 1 ounce unsweetened chocolate
> 2 ounces semisweet chocolate
> 4 ounces almonds, unskinned
> 4 eggs, separated
> ¼ teaspoon cream of tartar
> ¾ cup sugar
> 10 tablespoons (1 stick plus 2 tablespoons) unsalted butter
> ½ teaspoon almond extract
> 1 tablespoon dark rum
> 4 tablespoons flour
> Pinch of salt, or to taste
> Vanilla-Flavored Confectioners' Sugar, page 40

1. Preheat the oven to 375°.
2. Lightly butter and flour the pan.
3. Break up the chocolate and melt it in the top of a double boiler over hot water. When the chocolate has melted, remove the pan from the hot water and allow the chocolate to cool.
4. Grind the unskinned almonds as finely as possible in either a nut grinder or a food processor fitted with a steel blade. If using the processor, add 1 teaspoon of flour to the almonds before grinding to keep the almond particles separate.
5. Beat the egg whites with the cream of tartar. After the egg whites are stiff, beat in 2 tablespoons of sugar. Set aside.
6. Cream the butter and the remaining sugar. Add the egg yolks, beating with a wire whisk or wooden spoon. Add the almond extract and the rum, and beat in the melted chocolate.
7. Mix the flour, ground nuts, and salt together.
8. Freshen the egg whites and add 3 or 4 tablespoons to the chocolate mixture to soften it. Alternately fold in the flour-nut mixture and the egg whites. Do not quite fold in each one before adding the other.

9. Pour the batter into the prepared loaf pan. Bake for 50 to 60 minutes; it is done when a thin skewer inserted into the center comes out clean. The cake shrinks away slightly from the edge of the pan. Remove from the pan and cool on a cake rack. To serve, dust the top heavily with vanilla-flavored confectioners' sugar.

Chocolate Torta (Ostia)

We had driven into Ostia, the Lido di Roma, from the south, deciding to stay two or three days at this seaside resort before taking the plane home from nearby Leonardo da Vinci Airport at Fiumicino. It was a chance to unwind and relax after a strenuous but exciting trip through Sicily and the southern area.

The Lido is a place of small hotels and substantial summer villas, many lined up facing the beach and sea across the shore road, and there is a busy shopping street a few blocks in from the water.

We sunned ourselves on the beach, people-watched, and ate lunch at the open-air beach restaurant. A highlight at one day's lunch was a plain but subtly flavored chocolate cake whose "flour" was finely ground almonds.

9-inch layer cake pan
Serves 8 to 10

> *3½ ounces semisweet chocolate*
> *1 ounce unsweetened chocolate*
> *10 tablespoons (1 stick plus 2 tablespoons) unsalted butter*
> *4½ ounces shelled almonds*
> *2 teaspoons cocoa powder*
> *2 teaspoons flour*
> *½ teaspoon baking powder*
> *Pinch of salt*
> *3 eggs, separated*
> *¼ teaspoon cream of tartar*

⅔ cup plus 2 teaspoons sugar
2 tablespoons orange juice
1 teaspoon dark rum
1 teaspoon Bianco Cinzano (sweet)
Grated zest of approximately ½ large thick-skinned orange
½ teaspoon vanilla extract
¼ teaspoon almond extract
Vanilla-Flavored Confectioners' Sugar, page 40

1. Preheat the oven to 325°.

2. Butter the cake pan; fit a circle of wax paper in the bottom, butter the paper, then dust the pan with flour.

3. Melt the chocolate in the top of a double boiler over gently boiling water. Remove from the heat and cool.

4. Cut the butter in pieces into a large bowl and allow to soften.

5. Place the unskinned almonds in a food processor fitted with a steel blade and partially break them up. Add the cocoa, flour, baking powder, and salt, and whirl until the almonds are as powdered as they can get without becoming a paste. There will be some small pieces, but that is all to the good. Set aside.

6. In a large bowl, beat the egg whites with the cream of tartar. When soft peaks form, add 2 teaspoons of sugar and beat until stiff. Set aside.

7. Cream the softened butter with a wooden spoon. Gradually add the remaining ⅔ cup of sugar and beat well. Add the egg yolks and beat until the mixture is lemon-colored. Add the orange juice, rum, and Bianco Cinzano, and continue to beat with the wooden spoon. Mix in the grated orange zest and add the vanilla and almond extracts.

8. Add the cooled melted chocolate and mix thoroughly. Add the almond-flour mixture and mix thoroughly.

9. Freshen the egg whites with the beater, add ⅓ to the cake batter, and mix. Fold in the rest of the egg whites.

10. Scrape the batter into the prepared layer cake pan. Because the cake has a tendency to sink in the middle, heap slightly in

the center. Bake for 45 minutes to 1 hour. The cake is done when a thin skewer inserted into the center comes out clean. Remove the cake from the oven and cool on a cake rack for 10 minutes. Turn out of the pan and remove the wax paper. Allow the cake to finish cooling, top side up. When cold, dust with vanilla-flavored confectioners' sugar.

Chocolate with Chocolate Cake (Venice)

Once one leaves the St. Mark's Square area of tourist shops and restaurants, one enters the Venice of winding streets linked by the narrow bridges that span the canals. Here are the local food shops, pasticcerias, dress and jewelry shops, hardware and home supplies stores, as well as coffee bars and small trattorias, all catering to the Venetians who live in the old buildings lining the streets and canals. In one of the pasticcerias we saw an elegant chocolate cake, and without a moment's hesitation we went in and bought two slices to go; they were eaten later on the steps of a small bridge as we waited in the sun for the Dalmation Scuola di San Giorgio degli Schiavoni to open so we could see its collection of Carpaccio paintings. (We had some plastic forks tucked away in one of our photographic bags, just in case.)

A round chocolate cake, one and one-half inches high, is split into two layers and filled with dark brown mocha butter cream one-fourth inch thick. The top and sides are covered with the same butter cream. Fancy rosettes of the butter cream are piped around the top edge of the cake, alternating with meringues of the same size, plus a larger meringue in the center. Each wedge-shaped serving gets one each of the butter cream and meringue rosettes.

6½-inch springform pan
Serves 6 to 8

Chocolate Torta, page 74
Mocha Butter Cream, page 47; 1½ times the recipe plus
    additional 2 tablespoons cocoa powder and 1 teaspoon
    instant espresso coffee powder
Basic Baked Meringues, page 35

1. Preheat the oven to 325°.
2. Make the chocolate batter and bake it. Remove the cake from the oven and cool it on a cake rack. Turn down the oven temperature to 225° for the small meringues.
3. While the cake is baking, prepare the mocha butter cream, adding the additional 2 tablespoons of cocoa powder and 1 teaspoon of instant espresso coffee to the recipe. When finished, spoon the butter cream into a covered container and place in the refrigerator to stiffen.
4. Prepare the meringue mixture and transfer it to a pastry bag fitted with a ½-inch star tube. Pipe out 6 to 8 meringues approximately ¾ inch in diameter and 1 meringue 1½ inches in diameter for the center. Bake and cool according to directions in the recipe.

To Assemble:
1. If there is a hump in the center of the cake's top, level it with a sharp knife. Turn the cake over so the flat bottom is the top and split the cake in half with a sharp knife. Place the lower layer on a cake rack and spread the butter cream ¼ inch deep on the cut side of the lower layer. Cover with the upper layer and smoothly cover the top and sides of the cake with the butter cream, reserving enough for six to eight ¾-inch rosette decorations.
2. If the butter cream has started to soften, put the cake and the reserved butter cream back into the refrigerator to stiffen. After stiffening, remove the cake and butter cream from the refrigerator and slide the cake onto a serving plate.
3. Spoon the butter cream into a pastry bag fitted with a star tip and form rosettes around the outside edge of the cake top,

spacing them so that a meringue rosette can be put between each one. There will be 6 to 8 each of the meringues and the butter cream rosettes, a pair for each wedge-shaped serving of cake. Set the small meringues in place around the edge and put the larger one in the middle of the cake.

4. Return the cake to the refrigerator to stiffen the butter cream. Remove the cake about 30 minutes before serving.

Note: With any remaining meringue mixture, make an even number of swirled peak forms 2½ inches in diameter; these can be used for Meringues with Chocolate Glaze (page 129).

Round Cake or Roll Cake (Emilia-Romagna)
Ciambella

Ciambella is a thin, dry cake with or without raisins, formed either into a ring or, as sometimes seen in the Emilia-Romagna area, into a square-ended elliptical roll only one and one-half inches high. It is the best sort of cake to eat with a glass of wine or cappuccino coffee because it is not too sweet. Freshly baked, it is often sold in some of the small "family" supermarkets by the slice.

11-x-17-inch baking pan
Makes 26 to 28 slices

> 2½ *cups flour*
> 3 *teaspoons baking powder*
> ½ *teaspoon salt*
> 6 *tablespoons sugar*
> 3 *ounces dark or golden raisins*
> 1½ *tablespoons dark rum or Marsala*
> 6 *tablespoons unsalted butter*
> 2 *eggs*
> 5 *tablespoons half-and-half*

1 teaspoon vanilla extract
1 teaspoon lemon extract or grated zest of 1 lemon
Sugar for dusting
Multicolored nonpareils

1. Preheat the oven to 350°.
2. Cover the baking pan with a length of aluminum foil. With a dull-pointed instrument or pencil, draw a square-ended ellipse in the middle of the foil, 14 inches long, 5½ inches wide at the center, and 3 inches wide at each end. Pull the outer part of the foil up into a 1½-inch-high edge around the ellipse, pinching the foil together to form a stiff upright double wall to contain the batter.
3. Mix the dry ingredients together and sift into a mound in a large mixing bowl, then make a well in the center.
4. In a small bowl, soak the raisins in the rum or Marsala.
5. Place the butter in the top of a double boiler over simmering water to melt slowly. While the butter is melting, beat the 2 eggs in a small bowl with a wire whisk. Reserve 1½ tablespoons of the beaten eggs in a ramekin, then add the half-and-half to the remaining eggs. When the butter has just melted, add the egg mixture in a thin stream, beating all the while. Remove from the heat and hot water and continue beating until slightly thickened and foamy.

6. Add the vanilla extract and lemon extract or lemon zest, and beat well. Slowly pour the liquid into the flour well, mixing it in with a fork and gradually incorporating all the liquid with the flour. The batter will be soft but not so soft that it will not hold its shape. Mix in the raisins and their liquid. If the batter seems crumbly, add a little more half-and-half.

7. Form the batter into an ellipse to fit the foil. Place it on the aluminum foil between the foil walls, pressing the batter into shape between the walls. Cover as many raisins as possible with the batter so they will not burn, then smooth the top. Mix the reserved beaten egg with 1 teaspoon of cold water and brush the top with half of the mixture. Sprinkle the top with sugar and with the multicolored nonpareils. Bake the cake in the preheated oven for 30 to 35 minutes. About 10 minutes before the cake is done, brush the top again with the remaining egg mixture. When the cake is done, place it under the broiler to brown the top.

8. Remove the cake from the broiler and let it stand for 10 minutes, then transfer it to a rack to cool. Serve it cut in ½-inch-wide slices. The slices can also be brushed with melted butter and toasted under the broiler.

Flaked Caramel and Mocha Butter Cream Cake (Desenzano)

Along one side of the narrow shopping square at Desenzano we stopped in front of an elegant pastry shop. After looking at the cakes in the window, we entered and walked slowly past the high glass-fronted counter, looking at all the cakes and tarts, trying to decide which to try first. Our choice was one with crisp brown crumbles all over and stripes of confectioners' sugar decorating the top, but it was a large twelve-inch cake, too much for two people. We were delighted to find we could buy a quarter of a cake, and this opened up a whole new world of cake and tart tastings. We haunted the lavish displays of this pasticceria, knowing now that nothing in that glass case was beyond our tasting!

6½- to 7-inch cake pan (for a thick cake)
Serves 4 to 6

> *Sponge Cake, page 32*
> *Mocha Butter Cream, page 47*
> *¼ cup sugar*
> *2 teaspoons light corn syrup*
> *2 teaspoons water*
> *½ teaspoon baking soda, sifted*
> *Vanilla-Flavored Confectioners' Sugar, page 40*

1. Preheat the oven to 325°.
2. Prepare and bake the sponge cake.
3. While the cake is baking, make the mocha butter cream and put it in the refrigerator to chill.
4. To make caramel flakes, put the sugar, corn syrup, and water in a saucepan large enough to allow the syrup to foam up when the baking soda is added. Stir until sugar is moist.
5. Place the saucepan over medium heat and boil to a hard-crack test or until 310° on a candy thermometer is reached. Do not allow it to get too brown or to burn, which is so easy to do.
6. Remove from the heat and add the baking soda. Stir quickly, bringing syrup up from the bottom of the pan with a spoon. When *just* mixed and thick, scrape out onto an unoiled metal cake pan, without spreading.
7. When cool, turn the caramel out onto a sheet of wax paper and cover with a second sheet, or place inside a plastic bag. With a rolling pin break up into large and small pieces; there will be many small pieces. Place in a bowl and set aside.
8. To make the pattern for the confectioners' sugar design, draw on a sheet of typewriter paper using a compass or baking pan 2 circles, one 8½-inch and an inside one 6½ to 7 inches, depending on the size of your cake. Within the smaller circle measure and

draw lines ⅝ inch apart. Cut out the first ⅝-inch-wide strip, then alternate, leaving solid and open strips.

9. After the cake has cooled, trim off the hump in the center of the top so the cake is level. Make a small wedge cut up the side in order to match the layers after filling. Split the cake in half horizontally and turn over so the bottom becomes the top. Separate the layers and place the bottom layer on a cake rack covered with a sheet of wax paper and the top layer on a plate, cut side up.

To Assemble:

1. Spread the butter cream on the cut surface of the bottom layer. Put the top layer over the filling, matching the side cut. Cover the sides and top with butter cream, smoothing it to a flat top surface.

2. Place the cake in the refrigerator, still on the cake rack, until about 1 hour before serving.

3. When you remove the cake from the refrigerator, sprinkle the top and sides heavily with the caramel flakes, using the larger pieces. The small pieces can be kept in a glass jar to use in meringues, on ice cream, or to flavor whipped cream.

4. Quickly place the strip pattern over the top of the flakes and sieve confectioners' sugar through the openings. Lift the paper up carefully so as not to allow sugar to spill out over the caramel flakes. If any does fall onto the cake in the unsugared areas, add flakes to cover the sugar.

5. Carefully transfer the cake to a serving plate. It can be returned to the refrigerator briefly until just before serving. However, the flaked caramel tends to soften the butter cream, and the butter cream in turn softens the flaked caramel, and the crisp look and texture can be lost. So complete the cake as close to serving time as possible.

Marsala Custard and Whipped Cream Cake (Mira)

At the Ristorante Castagnara just south of the Brenta Canal near Mira, we each had narrow wedges of the specialty, a cake of several seductive levels of flavor. It was rich but not cloying.

A sponge layer was cut horizontally into two and filled with a cooked egg custard strongly flavored with Marsala and Amaretto liqueur. The custard was heavily sprinkled with mini-chips of chocolate before the top layer was put in place. The top was thinly spread with custard that soaked into the cake and then decorated with three circular rows of tiny—one inch in diameter—unfilled cream puffs, alternating with rows of equal-size whipped cream rosettes. The side of the cake was covered with vertically swirled whipped cream.

Serves 4 to 6

> *Sponge Cake, page 32, using a 6½- to 7-inch round, straight-sided cake pan*
> *Cream Puff Dough, page 118*

> *Egg Custard, page 237; half the recipe; or Time-Saver Custard, page 240. Add 1 tablespoon Marsala and 2 teaspoons Amaretto liqueur, or to taste, to the recipe.*
> 3 *tablespoons chocolate mini-chips*
> *Stiffened Whipped Cream, page 46*

1. Make and bake the sponge cake. Place on a cake rack to cool.

2. Prepare the cream puff dough and bake 18 small puffs, ¾ inch in diameter (they will expand in baking). Set aside to cool on a cake rack.

3. Prepare the egg custard and spoon it into a bowl. Set aside to cool with a circle of wax paper over the top to prevent a skin from forming.

To Assemble:

1. Level the top of the cake by cutting away any center hump that has formed. If the top is moist, place the cake under a preheated broiler to crisp the surface. Turn the cake over (the smooth, flat bottom becomes the top of the finished cake) and cut the cake in half horizontally.

2. Place the now bottom layer on a serving dish, cut side up. Spread more than half of the egg custard on the bottom layer, reserving just enough for a thin layer to be spread over the top of the cake. Sprinkle the chocolate mini-chips on the custard. Cover with the other cake layer and spread a thin layer of custard on the top.

3. Put the filled cake in the refrigerator. The custard will soak into the cake and the chocolate mini-chips will soften.

4. Make the stiffened whipped cream and place the bowl in the refrigerator.

5. About 2 hours before serving, crisp the puffs in the oven and then cool to room temperature. Remove the cake and the stiffened whipped cream from the refrigerator. Spoon the whipped cream into a pastry bag fitted with a ½-inch star tip. Cover the side of the cake with continuous vertical lines curved at the top and

bottom. Arrange the puffs in 2 or 3 circular rows on top of the cake and add whipped cream rosettes in circular rows between the rows of puffs.

6. Transfer the cake to a serving platter and return it to the refrigerator until 30 minutes before serving.

Note: Both the cake and the puffs can be made the day before and stored in the refrigerator in plastic bags.

Marzipan Cake/Tart (Desenzano)

This sensuous cake/tart with its five layers of flavors is another triumph of the pasticceria in Desenzano on Lake Garda. After dinner on an early summer evening, we sat on our terrace with a view of the lake and a still snow-capped mountain, making careful notes on the cake so we could reproduce this confection once we were back in our home kitchen.

The cake/tart starts with a crisp-baked pasta frolla shell, spread with apricot glaze and covered with a thin cake layer. A second brushing of apricot glaze is topped with piped-on marzipan and then browned under the broiler. Both the baked pasta frolla shell and the thin cake layer can be made the day before and stored in the refrigerator in separate plastic bags.

6½- or 8-inch quiche pan with removable bottom
Serves 4 to 6

> *Tart Crust, page 170*
> *Thin Cake Layer, page 38*
> *Apricot Jam Glaze, page 178*
> *Marzipan Topping, page 45*

1. Make the tart dough and place it in the refrigerator for 45 minutes.

2. While the tart dough is chilling in the refrigerator, make and bake the thin cake layer, following the recipe directions. Set aside. (See *Note.*)

3. When the tart dough has chilled, roll it out. Line the buttered quiche pan and bake the shell according to the recipe directions for a shell with an unbaked filling. (You will have leftover dough.)

4. Make the apricot jam glaze following the recipe directions for the 8-inch cake; for the 6½-inch cake, use ¾ the recipe ingredients given.

5. Prepare the marzipan topping just before putting the cake together.

6. Trim the thin cake layer so that it will fit inside the tart pastry shell.

To Assemble:

1. Spread all but 2 tablespoons of the apricot jam glaze on the bottom of the cooled 6½-inch tart pastry shell, smoothing the glaze up the sides of the shell; for the 8-inch shell, reserve 3 tablespoons of the glaze.

2. Put the trimmed thin cake layer in place over the glaze, bottom side up. Spread the reserved glaze over the surface of the thin cake layer.

3. Preheat the oven to 450°.

4. Scoop up the marzipan topping into a pastry bag fitted with a cone that has a ½-inch slit opening, toothed on one side. Pipe out parallel lines over the top of the glaze on the thin cake layer, making a little wavelike bump every 1½ inches.

5. Put the cake/tart in the oven for 5 to 10 minutes to set the marzipan topping, then put it under the broiler to lightly brown the top. Watch it every second because it can burn quickly!

6. Remove the pan from the oven and place it on a cake rack. Allow the cake/tart to cool in the pan. To serve, remove the cake/tart from the pan, slip off the bottom metal disk, and place the cake/tart on a serving dish.

Note: There may be enough batter left from the Thin Cake Layer batter to bake an extra very thin 6½-inch layer. This extra layer can be put in a plastic bag and frozen for another dessert.

Meringue Cake (Parma)

Parma's center city, dense with twelfth- and fifteenth-century buildings facing spacious squares, is one of our favorite places. (And yes, they still sell Parma Violet perfume, that beloved perfume of the Edwardian ladies.) Just off the broad pedestrians-only square in front of the cathedral is the elegantly appointed Angiol d'Or restaurant where we stopped for a long lunch after the cathedral and museums had closed for the noon-to-three-o'clock break. Our lunch ended with a meringue confection: two layers of crisp, dry meringue with a one-half-inch-thick filling of vanilla-flavored custard lightened with whipped cream, the custard sprinkled with Amaretti crumbs.

For a special occasion, or just any day that deserves a treat, this is a spectacular but simple cake to make. The separate components can be made the day before and assembled shortly before starting dinner preparations; the response by your guests and family will be fantastic compliments.

11-x-17-inch baking pan
Serves 6 to 8

> *Basic Baked Meringues, page 35; double the recipe*
> *Egg Custard, page 237; or Time-Saver Custard, page 240,*
> *double the recipe*
> *½ cup heavy cream*
> *½ to ¾ cup Amaretti or vanilla cookie crumbs (see* Note)

1. Preheat the oven to 225°.
2. Cover the baking pan with a sheet of aluminum foil. With a pencil or blunt instrument trace two 8-inch circles on the foil, using a plate, a cake pan, or a pot cover as a pattern.
3. Prepare the meringue mixture and spoon it into a pastry bag fitted with a plain ½-inch tube. Cover 1 circle on the foil with a ½-inch-deep spiraled layer of meringue; smooth the surface with a plastic or rubber spatula. Pipe small ½-inch rounds almost touching one another around the drawn edge of the other circle so they are half inside and half outside the line. Fill in the rest of the circle with a ½-inch-deep spiraled layer of meringue, touching the inner edges of the small rounds. Do not smooth the top of this circle; leave the spiral ridges in place.
4. Bake the meringue layers for 45 minutes in the preheated oven. Turn off the oven heat and allow the layers to remain in the oven for 20 to 30 minutes. Remove the pan from the oven and carefully slip the foil out of the pan and onto 2 cake racks placed side by side. Delicately remove the meringue layers from the foil and cool them on cake racks.
5. While the meringue layers are baking, make either custard. Pour the custard into a bowl and cover the top with a circle of wax paper to prevent a skin from forming on the top. Place the bowl in the refrigerator until the custard is needed.
6. Whip the heavy cream. Remove the custard from the re-

frigerator and fold in the whipped cream. Taste for sweetness and flavor and correct if necessary.

To Assemble:

1. Place the plain meringue layer on a serving plate. Cover its top with less than half the crumbs. Spoon the custard smoothly over the crumbs to the same depth as the meringue layer. Cover the top and sides of the custard with the remaining crumbs.

2. Put the top layer in place, being careful not to knock off any of the knobs of meringue around the edge.

3. Place the cake in the refrigerator. Remove it 30 minutes before serving so it will not be too chilled. Cut the cake into narrow wedges with a sharp knife.

Note: Amaretti di Saronno Biscotti can be bought in gourmet shops and Italian grocery stores.

Meringue Layers with Whipped Cream
Florentine Cavour

In Florence, one lunchtime, we ended our meal with a delicate sweet. The lightest of dry meringue layers were sandwiched together with sweetened whipped cream studded with small pieces of chocolate and chestnuts preserved in syrup. The "Cavour" was served in wedges cut from a large circle.

11-x-17-inch baking pan
Serves 6 to 8

> *2 Basic Baked Meringue layers, 8 or 9 inches in diameter,*
> *page 35; double the recipe*
> *3 heaping tablespoons chestnuts preserved in syrup (drained)*
> *1 cup heavy cream*
> *2 teaspoons sugar, or to taste*

¾ teaspoon vanilla extract
3 heaping tablespoons chocolate mini-chips
Vanilla-Flavored Confectioners' Sugar, page 40

1. Preheat the oven to 225°.
2. Lightly oil a baking pan, smooth on a sheet of wax paper, but do not oil paper. Draw two circles on the wax paper, by tracing around a 8- or 9-inch pan or plate with the point of a knife.
3. Make batter for 2 meringue layers, doubling the amount given in the recipe.
4. Put the meringue in a pastry bag with a ½-inch plain tip, and fill in the 2 outlines with concentric circles. To give the bottom layer a rimmed edge, pipe an extra layer of meringue on top of the outer circle of one round. Or simply spoon an equal amount of meringue within the circles and smooth with a spatula into thin layers.
5. Bake in the preheated oven for 45 to 50 minutes; room temperature and humidity play an important part in the baking of meringues, so check them at 35 minutes to see if they are crisp enough. When crisp, turn off the heat and allow the meringue layers to stay in the oven for 20 minutes.
6. Remove the pan from the oven. Place the meringue layers on a cake rack, carefully removing the paper. Let cool.

To Assemble:
1. Make and add the filling to the meringue layers shortly before serving, so they will stay crisp. Drain and cut the chestnuts into approximately ⅜-inch pieces and set aside in a small bowl.
2. Whip the heavy cream until soft peaks form. Add the sugar and vanilla and beat until the cream is smooth and stiff.
3. Fold in the chestnut pieces and chocolate mini-chips.
4. Spread the filling evenly over the rimmed bottom layer, and gently put the top layer in place. Dust with the vanilla-flavored confectioners' sugar. Cut into portions with a sharp knife, point down.

Nut-Meringue Whipped Cream Cake (Vigoreto)

Our favorite Parco Cappuccini, just outside Sabionetta, is a small yellow-painted villa with an inner courtyard reached by a narrow arched driveway, and stables and barns flanking two sides. Inside the villa there is a country smell of wood fires and wax-polished floor tiles. Dark wainscoting and flowered wallpaper surround the dining room. A mixture of family-size tables and small tables are scattered through the room, with salad and dessert tables just inside the entrance door.

One of several cakes we tried at the Parco Cappuccini was light and delicate—nothing more than three thin layers of a special nut-meringue with a filling of stiffened whipped cream. The Swiss call this type of meringue *broyage,* but for some unknown reason the Italians call it Giapponese (Japanese). These nut-meringue layers were mocha colored from the addition of small amounts of unsweetened cocoa powder and instant espresso coffee powder.

Serves 6 to 8

> *Nut-Meringue Layers for Cakes, page 36, using almonds,*
> *making 3 layers, and adding the following: 1 teaspoon*
> *unsweetened cocoa powder, 1 teaspoon instant espresso*
> *coffee powder, and 1 teaspoon almond extract*
> *Stiffened Whipped Cream, page 46*

1. Preheat the oven to 225°.

2. Follow the directions for making the nut-meringue layers, adding the cocoa powder and coffee powder to the sugar-cornstarch mixture and substituting almond extract for vanilla.

3. While the meringues are baking and cooling in the oven, make the stiffened whipped cream and place it in the refrigerator to chill and stiffen.

4. When the meringue layers are cool, spread the stiffened whipped cream between the layers, leaving the top plain. (The

spiral pattern of the meringue serves as decoration.) Return the cake to the refrigerator until just before serving. Serve cut in narrow wedges.

Note: You can also use plain, sweetened whipped cream, beating the cream and filling the meringue layers 30 minutes to 1 hour before serving. You will need 1¼ to 1½ cups of heavy cream, ¾ teaspoon of vanilla extract, and 4 to 6 teaspoons of sugar, or to taste.

Orange Cake (Urbino)

For years we have admired in the Uffizi in Florence the double portraits by Piero della Francesca of the Duke of Urbino and his wife. We finally spent a day in Urbino—all too short a time to absorb the fantastic warm-brick Renaissance Ducal Palace, both inside and out; the adjoining cathedral; and the up-and-down streets of the town. With its cool, well-proportioned rooms, carved fireplaces and doors, paintings that include two by Piero della Francesca, and the duke's own amazing study in trompe l'oeil inlaid wood, the palace is a place to return to time after time.

At the noontime closing we walked across the wide courtyard and found a restaurant where we could look at the palace and cathedral. Lunch was eaten at an outside table set at the edge of the downhill road. We finished with a wedge of a crumbly, buttery, plain orange cake well browned on the outside, a perfect foil for our chilled white wine.

9-inch quiche pan with removable bottom
Serves 6 to 8

> *8 tablespoons (1 stick) unsalted butter*
> *Zest of ½ orange (approximately)*

⅔ cup cake flour
¾ teaspoon baking powder
Pinch of salt
2 eggs
⅔ cup sugar
¾ teaspoon orange extract
1 tablespoon rum
Vanilla-Flavored Confectioners' Sugar, page 40 (optional)

1. Preheat the oven to 350°.
2. Butter the quiche pan, lining the bottom and sides with wax paper; butter the paper and dust with flour.
3. Slice the butter into a bowl and soften to room temperature. When soft, beat the butter until it is the consistency of mayonnaise. Set aside.
4. Grate the zest of half a thick-skinned orange, or enough for 3 packed tablespoons. Set aside.
5. Measure the flour, baking powder, and salt into a sifter and set aside.
6. In a mixing bowl, beat the eggs with a wire whisk until fluffy. Gradually add the sugar alternately with the orange extract and rum, beating constantly. Stir in the grated orange zest.
7. Mix 3 tablespoons of the egg-sugar mixture into the softened butter, working them together until creamy, then blend this butter with the remaining egg-sugar mixture. Beat with a wire whisk until light. Sift the flour and baking powder gradually into this mixture, blending all together with the wire whisk.
8. Pour the batter into the quiche pan and bake for 30 minutes, or until a thin skewer inserted into the center of the cake comes out clean. Allow the cake to cool on a cake rack for 10 minutes, then remove from the pan. Carefully remove the wax paper and turn the cake right side up to finish cooling.
9. Serve plain or dusted with vanilla-flavored confectioners' sugar.

Orange Marzipan Cake (Vigoreto)

In this delicious confection, a round, flat, 1½-inch-high Génoise cake is cut into three layers, and apricot jam is spread between them. The top layer is soaked with a strongly flavored orange liqueur or orange-flavored syrup. The orange liqueur used in Italy seems to be unavailable in this country, so a mixture of rum, orange extract, and corn syrup is substituted. The top layer, with its "basket weave" pattern of marzipan brushed with orange-flavored syrup, is baked briefly and then browned under the broiler to give it a glossy sherry color.

11-x-17-inch baking pan
6½- to 7-inch springform pan
Serves 4 to 6

> *Génoise, page 29; double the recipe*
> *Marzipan Topping, page 45*
> *¼ cup light corn syrup*
> *2 tablespoons rum*
> *1 teaspoon orange extract, or to taste*
> *10 to 12 ounces apricot jam*

1. Make and bake the Génoise cake and let it cool. It can be made the day before serving and refrigerated in a plastic bag.
2. Prepare the marzipan topping and set it aside.
3. Make the syrup for the top of the cake by mixing the corn syrup, rum, and orange extract together. Set aside.
4. Melt the apricot jam in a saucepan over low heat. When it has melted, press it through a fine sieve, then set aside.

To Assemble:
1. If there is a hump in the center of the cake, level it off. Turn the cake over and cut it into 3 layers, making a vertical notch on one side so the layers can be matched as they are filled. Spread

the layers out on cake racks. Place the bottom layer on the lightly buttered upturned bottom of a baking pan.

2. Spread half of the strained jam on the cut surface of the bottom layer (formerly the top of the cake) and cover with the middle layer. Spread this layer with the rest of the jam and cover with the flat top layer.

3. Thickly brush the orange-flavored syrup over the top layer and side of cake, reserving enough to lightly brush the marzipan topping.

4. Preheat the oven to 450°.

5. Attach a ½-inch-slit-opening tip with one serrated edge to a pastry bag and spoon the marzipan topping into the bag. Cover the top of the cake with side-by-side parallel strips of marzipan, then add spaced-out cross strips. You can make a true basket weave top, but it requires a planned stop-and-go series of short strips of marzipan to give the over-and-under effect of weaving. Lightly brush the marzipan with the reserved syrup. Put the cake in the oven for 5 to 10 minutes to set the marzipan topping, then put it under the broiler to brown. Watch it every second because it can burn quickly.

6. Remove the cake from the broiler and cool on the baking pan. When cold, transfer the cake to a serving dish.

Panettone

In Milan and other areas of northern Italy, panettone is the sweet bread served at Christmastime; each region has its own variation of this basic, sweet, yeast-risen dough. It is frequently packaged and sent abroad, but the dry commercial variety has little resemblance to a freshly baked round loaf gloriously studded with dried fruits. In spite of tradition, panettone, like all good coffee cakes, can be eaten at any time of the year.

After the first rising, the dough is kept in the refrigerator overnight; the next day it is formed and put into a tube pan, set in a warm place to rise a second time, and then baked.

Deep tube pan or kugelhopf pan, 7¾ inches in diameter
Makes 30 to 32 slices

> 5 tablespoons unsalted butter
> 1½ teaspoons plus 2 tablespoons sugar
> 2 tablespoons warm water
> 1 tablespoon dry yeast
> 4 tablespoons bread flour
> 2 eggs
> 1 egg yolk
> 1½ cups bread flour, plus ¼ cup for the board
> ¼ teaspoon salt
> 1 teaspoon lemon extract
> 1 teaspoon vanilla extract
> 1¼ ounces citron, cut into ¾-inch dice
> ¼ cup dark raisins
> ¼ cup golden raisins
> 2 tablespoons diced Candied Orange Peel, page 51

1. Cut the butter into slices and then into quarters; put on a plate to soften.

2. Mix 1½ teaspoons of sugar and 2 tablespoons of warm water together in a small bowl. Sprinkle the yeast on top and set the bowl in a warm place until the yeast is foamy. Add the 4 tablespoons of bread flour and stir until the mixture forms a ball. Brush the top lightly with warm water, cover with a clean towel, and put in a warm place to rise until double in bulk, approximately 45 minutes.

3. Beat the eggs and egg yolk together. Reserve 3 tablespoons of the beaten egg in a small ramekin for brushing on the top of the dough before and during baking. Cover the ramekin and store it in the refrigerator until the panettone is ready for the oven the next day.

4. Sift the 1½ cups of flour and the salt into a bowl. Mix in the 2 tablespoons of sugar and the remaining beaten eggs, mixed with the lemon and vanilla extracts. Beat with a wooden spoon, adding the softened butter a little at a time. When well mixed, add the yeast mixture and beat again with a spoon.

5. Turn the dough out onto a pastry board floured with part of the extra ¼ cup of flour. Knead the dough for 12 minutes, adding a little more flour from the ¼ cup, but do not add any more than the ¼ cup. Finally, knead in the citron, raisins, and candied orange peel.

6. Oil a straight-sided bowl. Put in the dough, turn it over so all sides are oiled, and cover the bowl with a clean towel. Put the bowl in a warm place for 1 to 1½ hours, or until the dough is double in bulk.

7. Turn out the dough, punch down, and knead it for about 1 minute. Re-oil the bowl lightly and put the dough back in. Cover the bowl with a piece of clear plastic wrap and place the bowl in the refrigerator overnight.

8. The next day, turn out the dough on a lightly floured board, punch it down, then roll it out to a 5½-x-15-inch rectangle. Roll it up starting on the long side. Tuck in any exposed raisins (so they won't burn in the baking). Curve the rolled-up dough into the buttered tube or kugelhopf pan. Cover the pan with a clean towel and let the dough rise in a warm place until double in bulk, approximately 1 hour.

9. Preheat the oven to 400°.

10. Brush the top of the panettone with half of the reserved beaten egg. Be sure not to get egg on the side walls of the pan because this would prevent the dough from rising. Bake in the preheated oven for 12 minutes; turn down the heat to 350° and bake 25 minutes more. Brush the top again with the egg after 20 minutes. At the end of the baking time, slip the panettone out of its pan and put it back in the oven without the pan for 5 to 10 minutes to crisp the crust on the sides and bottom. Remove from the oven and cool on a cake rack. Do not overcook because it will get too dry. Serve cut in thin slices.

Panforte di Siena

We spent an early spring morning at the museum in the Palazzo Publico at the edge of the large square in Siena. Turning from the fourteenth-century paintings of that same square to look through the gallery window, nothing seemed to have changed—including the faces of the people, though their clothes were different—except that automobiles had intruded into the classic scene.

We drifted across the piazza, our eyes still filled with paintings in the museum, and settled at an outside table of a trattoria. We ate lunch sitting in the sun, immersed in the circle of buildings. For dessert: panforte di Siena, the classic "cake" of Siena that is more like a very compact nut and fruit honey-brittle.

We had often bought this fruitcake in Italian stores in New York City, usually at Christmastime. It was always rock-hard and had to be enclosed in a tin with a wet, crumpled piece of paper towel to soften it. But the panforte that came to our table was a revelation: softly crisp but freshly flavored, and the thin sheet of rice paper on the bottom kept the wedge from sticking to the plate.

2 round cake pans 5½ x 1 to 1½ inches or 1 round cake pan 10 x 1 to
    1½ inches
Baker's rice paper, 2 to 3 sheets 8 x 11 inches
Serves 10 to 12

> *3 ounces Almonds, Blanched and Toasted, page 48*
> *3 ounces Toasted Hazelnuts, page 49*
> *2½ ounces candied cherries*
> *3½ ounces candied citron*
> *1 ounce Candied Orange Peel, page 51, diced*
> *1 ounce Candied Lemon Peel, page 50, diced*
> *5 tablespoons flour*
> *3 tablespoons unsweetened cocoa powder*
> *¼ teaspoon coarsely ground black pepper*
> *½ teaspoon freshly grated nutmeg*

½ teaspoon ground cinnamon
½ cup plus 1½ teaspoons sugar
½ cup plus 2 tablespoons dark honey
¼ teaspoon each orange and lemon extracts (optional; see
    Step 8)
Vanilla-Flavored Confectioners' Sugar, page 40

1. Preheat the oven to 300°.

2. Butter the bottom and sides of the pans or pan. To line the bottom and sides, cut a matching circle and strip from the baker's rice paper. Put the circle in place on the bottom of the pan. Break the strip into 3-inch lengths and press them against the side wall, overlapping the separate pieces. Cut another equal-size circle to protect the top of the panforte while it is baking.

3. Cut the almonds in half crosswise.

4. Split the hazelnuts in half lengthwise.

5. Place the candied cherries in a bowl and cover with boiling water. Stir to wash the sticky surface off the cherries, then dry them on paper towels. Cut some cherries in half and others in quarters.

6. Cut the candied citron into ⅜- to ½-inch dice. If you are using your own candied orange and lemon peel, they will already be cut into dice; for store-bought peel, cut into ¼- to ⅜-inch dice.

7. In a bowl, mix together the almonds, hazelnuts, and candied fruit. In a small bowl, mix together the flour, cocoa, and spices. Sift the mixture over the nuts and fruits, turning and blending everything together. Set aside.

8. Put the sugar and honey into a saucepan (rub a little plain salad oil on the inside of the cup and tablespoon to keep the honey from sticking). Stir together, then put the saucepan over medium heat. Bring to a boil, stirring constantly. Lower the heat a little and continue to stir to keep the syrup from burning. Cook for approximately 2 minutes, or until a drop of the syrup forms a soft ball when placed in ½ cup of cold water. Immediately remove the saucepan from the heat. If you have used store-bought candied orange and lemon peel, taste the fruit-nut mixture for strength. If the flavor is weak, add the orange and lemon extracts to the syrup.

9. Gradually stir ½ of the syrup into the fruit-nut mixture, adding only a small amount at a time and immediately blending it in; too much syrup added at once will sink through the mixture and harden on the bottom of the bowl.

10. Transfer the contents of the bowl to the paper-lined pan or pans, spreading out the mixture to a smooth top; spoon the rest of the syrup evenly over the top. Press the second round of rice paper against the top surface to keep it from burning in the oven.

11. Bake the panforte in the preheated oven for 40 minutes. When done, remove the pan from the oven and place it on a cake rack to cool. Loosen the sides with the point of a small knife if any of the filling has oozed over the paper. When cold, remove the panforte from the pan, leaving the bottom and side paper in place. Trim the side paper level with the top and discard the top round of paper. Baker's rice paper is edible and melts in the mouth.

12. Heavily dust the top with vanilla-flavored confectioners' sugar just before serving. Cut in narrow wedges to serve.

Pineapple Marzipan Cake (Chioggia)

Chioggia, a fishing town in the southern part of the Venetian lagoon, is known as Little Venice, and many of the houses lining its canals are Venetian in design. The narrow canals are lined with fishing trawlers festooned with nets and working gear, and the large square at the end of the main street looks out on seemingly endless water. Over a long bridge from Chioggia is the seashore area of the mainland, its wide beaches crowded with umbrellas and cabanas, and lined with hotels.

In the window of a small pastry shop we saw a pineapple-topped cake with marzipan swirls decorating the sides. We looked at each other and immediately entered the shop to acquire this enchanting pastry with its delicate combination of flavors.

Slant-sided pie plate 1 inch deep and 8 inches in diameter
Serves 6 to 8

> *Génoise, page 29; double the recipe*
> *Marzipan Topping, page 45*
> *Apricot Jam Glaze, page 178*
> *Apple Jelly Glaze, page 177*
> *5 slices canned pineapple*

1. Make the Génoise according to the recipe directions. Remove the cake from the pan and cool, top side up, on a cake rack.

2. Prepare the marzipan topping and set it aside.

3. Prepare the apricot jam glaze and set it aside to cool until it begins to thicken.

4. Make the apple jelly glaze and set it aside to cool until it begins to thicken.

5. Slip the cooled cake under a preheated broiler to crisp the top because Génoise does get sticky on top as it cools. Remove the cake from the broiler when the top is slightly brown and crisp, and let it cool on a cake rack.

6. When cool, turn the cake upside down (the bottom now becomes the top) on the upended bottom of a baking pan. Spread the top with apricot jam glaze.

7. Fit a pastry bag with a ½-inch star tip and spoon the marzipan topping into the bag. Cover the sides of the cake with an up-and-down continuous line, curved top and bottom. Follow the recipe for baking the marzipan, brushing the surface with the remainder of the beaten egg mixed with a little cold water.

8. Remove the cake from the oven and allow it to cool; the apricot glaze will have developed a thin skin.

9. While the cake is cooling, drain the 5 slices of pineapple and place them on paper towels to dry. Cut 4 of the slices in half and 1 of the halves into quarters; cut the remaining slice into quarters.

10. Arrange the pineapple slices in a pattern on top of the apricot glaze: 4 halves around the edge, with the curved sides of

the slices along the edge of the cake; the next row has 3 halves; 2 quarters will fill the center, and the remaining 4 quarters are tucked in among the outer row of 4 halves.

11. Spread the apple jelly glaze over the pineapple and place the cake in the refrigerator until 30 minutes before serving.

Plum Cake (Pisa)

In Pisa we stayed at the Victoria, with its cavernous and dimly lighted reception rooms and a marble bust of Queen Victoria at the head of the wide stairway. Decorating the center of the ceiling over our bed was a scene of a gray and misty moor complete with stag that could only have been painted by a homesick Scottish artist. A few doors away on the Lungarno, that lovely street along the Arno River with its Renaissance houses, was a small pastry shop. Here we bought a small buttery loaf cake full of currants and candied fruit, crisp and brown on the outside. This was our picnic dessert for several days until every flavorful crumb was gone. It took us several years of trying different formulas before we matched the plum cake. Here it is.

4-cup loaf pan, 3½ x 9 x 2¾ inches
Makes approximately 18 slices

> *9 rounded tablespoons currants or chopped raisins*
> *2 tablespoons rum*
> *12 tablespoons (1½ sticks) unsalted butter*
> *1 cup flour, plus extra for dusting*
> *¼ cup cornstarch*
> *Pinch of salt*
> *1 teaspoon baking powder*
> *3 ounces citron*
> *Zest of 1 lemon*
> *2 tablespoons honey*

⅔ cup sugar
1 egg
1 egg yolk
2 tablespoons dry Marsala
¼ teaspoon lemon extract
1 teaspoon vanilla extract

1. Preheat the oven to 350°.

2. Butter the loaf pan and cover the bottom with wax paper. Butter the paper and dust the bottom and sides with flour.

3. Put the currants or chopped raisins in a small bowl, add the rum, and let soak for 30 minutes.

4. Cut the butter into slices and allow to soften in a large mixing bowl.

5. Sift the 1 cup flour, cornstarch, salt, and baking powder into a small bowl and set aside.

6. If using a chunk of citron, weigh, slice, and cut the slices into ¼-inch cubes. Put the cubes on a piece of wax paper and dust with flour to keep them separated.

7. Grate the lemon zest and set aside in a small bowl.

8. Cream the softened butter with a wooden spoon until it is smooth. Blend in the honey and beat well. Beat in the sugar with the spoon. Add the egg and egg yolk, and with a wire whisk beat the butter-sugar mixture until it is a light lemon color.

9. Add the Marsala, lemon and vanilla extracts, and grated lemon zest, beating after each addition. Drain the currants or raisins and add the rum to the mixture.

10. Fold in the sifted flour mixture, ⅓ at a time, until just blended.

11. Spread ⅓ of the batter on the bottom of the buttered and floured loaf pan. Lightly mix the citron and the drained currants or chopped raisins into the remaining dough and scrape into the pan. This method will keep all the fruit from sinking to the bottom of the cake during baking.

12. Put the pan in the oven for 60 to 80 minutes, or until a thin skewer inserted into the center of the cake comes out clean.

Remove from the oven and run a thin-bladed knife around the edge of the cake. Allow the cake to cool for 5 minutes. Turn the cake out on a baking rack and remove the paper from the bottom. Turn the cake right side up to finish cooling.

VARIATION

About halfway through baking or once the cake has risen, add a line of 6 glacéed cherry halves down the center, curved sides up.

Strawberry Sherbet Cake

On a late afternoon we came to the road that skirts the Ionian Sea. We had been on our way down that seemingly endless serpentine road from the high mountains in the interior of Calabria, an area that in winter is a ski resort and in spring is a meadowland interspersed with evergreen forests and chalets. In late afternoon we reached the shore road that had been in sight for several tantalizing hours of our downward trip and continued along it looking for a place to spend the night. Finally we saw a long complex of old buildings and a sign, Motel Capanello, and by sheer luck they had a vacant room high above the sea and with a wisteria-draped balcony. On one wall was a framed facsimile of a poem written by Garibaldi on February 8, 1880; it was to a former owner of the villa in memory of his stay there.

Once settled, we went downstairs to locate the restaurant and found there was none, only a sort of snack bar and, since it was Sunday evening, it was closed. We started off for the nearest town, Catanzaro, on its three hills. It started to rain as we climbed and circled through the nearly deserted streets with darkened restaurant signs. Then we spotted the welcomed lighted sign of Hosteria. We entered a series of warm, stuccoed rooms, some walls curving cave-like up to the low ceiling. In this softly lighted haven we had a good dinner and slices of a fabulous dessert of sherbet that was the essence of strawberry flavor with a center of frozen whipped cream and covered top and bottom with a thin cake layer. The sherbet, frozen whipped cream, and thin cake layer can be made the day before serving.

3½-x-7½-x-2-inch straight-sided loaf pan as a mold
8-inch square pan for Thin Cake Layer
Serves 6 to 8

> *Strawberry Sherbet, page 273*
> *Frozen Whipped Cream, page 262*
> *Thin Cake Layer, page 38*

1. Make and freeze the strawberry sherbet according to the recipe directions.

2. Make and freeze the frozen whipped cream according to the recipe directions.

3. Make the thin cake layer using the 8-inch square pan and bake according to the recipe directions.

4. While the cake is baking and cooling, measure and cut out 2 wax paper patterns, one to fit the inside bottom and the other the inside top of the loaf pan mold.

To Assemble:

1. Smoothly line the loaf pan with aluminum foil, allowing 1 inch of foil to extend above the pan's top edge; fold over this margin to the outside.

2. Put the thin cake layer, sugared side up, on a cutting board. Place the 2 wax paper patterns on the top surface of the cake and cut out both rectangles with a sharp knife. Fit 1 layer into the bottom of the foil-lined loaf pan and place it in the freezer. Wrap the other layer in foil and place it in the freezer.

3. Remove the sherbet from the freezer and allow to soften just enough to be spooned out. Remove the loaf pan mold from the freezer and quickly skim off shallow tablespoons of sherbet from the container, spooning it on top of the cake layer. Press the sherbet against the 2 long sides, about ¾ inch thick and to within

½ inch of the top of the pan. Fill around the corners and about ¼ of the way along each side of the two short sides, leaving the *center* area free. This will leave an irregular trough in the center of the sherbet approximately 2 inches wide and 1 inch deep the length of the loaf pan mold. You will use almost 2 cups of sherbet.

4. Cover the loaf pan with aluminum foil and return to the freezer for 3½ to 4 hours to stiffen the sherbet. The center of frozen whipped cream will be softened and added later.

5. About 45 minutes before serving, remove the frozen whipped cream from the freezer and allow it to soften at room temperature. When it is no longer frozen hard, beat it with a small wire whisk to a smooth but still stiff consistency. Spread it in the center trough of the mold, leveling the top. Remove the second cake layer from the freezer and press it into position on top of the molded sherbet and frozen cream. Put the mold into the refrigerator, not the freezer, for about 30 minutes. You will have to experiment with the amount of time needed depending on the temperature of your refrigerator. At the same time, place the serving dishes in the refrigerator to chill and place an oval serving platter in the freezer.

6. When ready to serve, remove the mold and serving dishes from the refrigerator and the serving platter from the freezer. Lift the strawberry sherbet cake out of the mold by grasping the extra foil on the long sides and peel the foil away from the sides and bottom. Place the cake on the oval serving platter. To serve, cut the cake into 8 slices approximately ⅞ inch wide or 6 slices approximately 1⅛ inches wide.

Torta Margherita (Brenta Canal)

At the Ristorante Margherita on the Brenta Canal road, our enthusiastic young waiter talked us into trying their special cake, sight unseen. Two generous wedges of a snow-white confection arrived with a flourish. The bottom layer was crisp meringue and the top layer a light Génoise. The filling was sweetened vanilla-flavored whipped cream lightly tossed with scattered dice of fresh fruit: peaches, apricots, pineapples, and cherries. The top and sides were covered with plain sweetened whipped cream, just enough to hold in place the angled chunks of broken-up meringue pressed helter-skelter all over the top and sides of the cake.

6½-inch quiche pan with removable bottom
10-x-15-inch baking pan
Serves 4 to 6

> *Génoise, page 29*
> *2 Basic Baked Meringue layers, page 35; double the recipe*
> *Stiffened Whipped Cream, page 46*
> *½ to ¾ cup of diced mixed fresh fruit*

1. Make and bake the Génoise layer and set it aside to cool on a cake rack. Turn down the oven to 225°.
2. Mark two 6½-inch circles on a sheet of aluminum foil covering the baking pan. Prepare the meringue batter. Fill a pastry bag fitted with a ½-inch plain tube and pipe the meringue within the 2 circles; or spoon the meringue within the 2 circles and spread with a narrow spatula. Bake and cool the meringue according to the recipe directions.
3. Make the stiffened whipped cream and place it in the refrigerator in a covered bowl to chill and thicken.
4. Drain the prepared diced fruit and mix it with ⅓ of the whipped cream.

To Assemble:
1. Crumble 1 meringue layer into sharp-angled pieces from ½ to 1 inch in size.
2. Place the other meringue layer on a serving plate and cover evenly with the whipped cream—fruit mixture. Top with the Génoise layer.
3. Spread the plain whipped cream over the top and sides of

the cake. Press the meringue pieces all over the top and sides, not flat but sticking out at angles with some pieces partially flat so there is an "icy" look to the cake.

4. Put the cake in the refrigerator until just before serving.

Note: Both the Génoise layer and the 2 meringue layers can be made the day before and kept in the refrigerator in plastic bags.

VARIATION
Use an Almond Cake layer (page 33) in place of the Génoise layer.

Whipped Cream Cake
Taverna Eolia Torta

Out in the countryside of the Veneto on a day when we were searching for Palladian villas, we came upon the charming Taverna Eolia at Costozza di Longare, just south of Vicenza, in an area noted for its mushroom-growing caves. Galileo was supposed to have spent much time in the cave wine cellars under the taverna and was said never to have recovered from rheumatism contracted there.

It was lunchtime when we arrived, and it was also Mother's Day. Outside, the charming garden was in bloom, and the white chairs and tables were occupied by family groups. Inside, in the informal, paneled dining room, sun streamed in the windows that looked out onto the garden. A large room upstairs featured a fanciful ceiling painted by Zelotti, who did the magnificent frescoes on the interior walls of Palladio's Villa Emo.

We settled in the sunny dining room that was comfortably crowded although the tables were far apart. There was no menu, but the waiter told us what the open kitchen was serving, including the intensely flavored local mushrooms. We spotted another waiter going by with a fantastic whipped cream cake creation, and we immediately asked our waiter to set aside two slices for us.

A little later we saw twelve cakes lined up on the counter in front of the open kitchen and decided this was the "specialty of the house." These cakes were quickly cut up or were carried as whole cakes to family tables. By the time we had finished our lunch, we were glad we had reserved those two slices; otherwise, we would never have experienced an ambrosial end to our sunny luncheon.

The cake is a magnificent contrast of textures and flavors (a super St. Honore): a thin, crisp bottom layer topped with apricot jam and chocolate sprills or grated chocolate, covered with a thicker Génoise layer sprinkled with a mixture of rum and banana extract, the whole thing covered with whipped cream and decorated with small custard-filled cream puffs, alternating with same-size mounds of whipped cream.

9-inch springform pan
Serves 8

> *Génoise, page 29*
> *Thin Cake Layer, page 38*
> *Cream Puff Dough, page 118*
> *Stiffened Whipped Cream, page 46*
> *Egg Custard, page 237, half the recipe; or Time-Saver*
> *   Custard, page 240, full recipe*
> *Apricot jam*
> *Banana extract*
> *Rum*
> *2 to 3 tablespoons chocolate sprills, or grated unsweetened*
> *   chocolate mixed with ½ teaspoon cocoa, or to taste*
> *Vanilla-Flavored Confectioners' Sugar, page 40*

1. Prepare the Génoise cake. This can be done the day before.
2. Make and bake the 9-inch thin cake layer.
3. Prepare the cream puff dough, form, and bake. (See *Note.*) The puffs can be made the day before.
4. Prepare the stiffened whipped cream and place it in the refrigerator.

5. Make the custard filling.

6. In a small pot over low heat melt 6 to 8 tablespoons of the apricot jam. When melted press through a sieve.

7. In a small bowl, mix ¼ teaspoon of banana extract with 2 tablespoons of rum.

To Assemble:

1. Place the thin cake layer in the center of a serving plate, sugared side down. Brush the top surface with warm sieved apricot jam and sprinkle the chocolate sprills or grated chocolate over the jam.

2. Cover with the Génoise layer, placing its original top against the jam so that the flat "bottom" side is upward. Sprinkle the rum–banana extract mixture over the top of this layer.

3. Cover the top of the Génoise with a 1-inch layer of stiff-

ened whipped cream. Cover the sides lightly with the whipped cream, reserving enough for top decorations.

4. Fill the cream puffs with custard and dust lightly with vanilla-flavored confectioners' sugar. Carefully space the puffs around the edge of the cake.

5. Add equal-size mounds of whipped cream between the cream puffs. Add any leftover cream to the sides of the cake.

6. Place the cake in the refrigerator until ready to serve. When serving, cut the cake so that each wedge has a mound of whipped cream and a cream puff.

Note: Since the full recipe makes 12 puffs, 1½ inches in diameter, and only 8 puffs are needed for the cake, freeze the 4 extra puffs for another dessert. You might consider doubling the recipe, which gives 16 puffs to freeze for later use as profiteroles.

Whipped Cream Cake with Meringue Chips (Mantua)

In the dairy-rich areas of northern Italy there is a visible lack of cows in the fields, yet there is an abundance of whipped cream cakes and rich ice creams throughout the area. The secret? The cows are kept in large stone barns surrounded by fields of closely planted grass that is cut, dried, and baled as hay to be stored in the barns as fodder.

In Mantua, at a favorite restaurant near the cathedral, we sampled an opulent whipped cream cake as the final touch to a sumptuous dinner. This was one variation of a popular north Italian cake that consists of either cake or meringue layers, or a combination of the two, with custard or whipped cream fillings; you will find several recipes in this book. The Mantua one was a blending of flavors that makes a wholly satisfying sweet at the end of a dinner or with coffee during an evening.

The sponge layers are held together with an egg custard filling;

the whipped cream topping is covered with broken pieces of meringue. The cake, the custard, and the meringue can be made the day before serving, with the cake and custard kept in the refrigerator.

6-x-1¾-inch round cake pan
Serves 4 to 6

> *Sponge Cake, page 32*
> *Basic Baked Meringue layer, page 35*
> *Egg Custard, page 237, half the recipe; or Time-Saver*
>   *Custard, page 240, full recipe*
> *Stiffened Whipped Cream, page 46, or 1½ cups heavy*
>   *cream*
> *Apricot Jam or Butter Glaze, page 178*
> *4 tablespoons dark rum*
> *Sugar*
> *Vanilla extract*

1. Make the Sponge Cake according to the recipe directions (see *Note*).

2. Make the meringue and bake in 5 thin rectangles, 3 x 4 x ⅛ inch, in a 225° oven.

3. Make the egg custard. Pour into a bowl and cover the top of the custard with a circle of wax paper to prevent a skin from forming. Place the bowl of custard in the refrigerator to cool.

4. On the day you are putting the cake together, make the stiffened whipped cream ahead of time and keep it in the refrigerator to stiffen. As an alternate, you can whip the cream 1 hour before serving, and then you do not need the gelatin.

5. Prepare the apricot jam or butter glaze. Spread it on the layers while it is still slightly warm.

To Assemble:

1. If the top of the cake has a center hump, cut it away with a sharp knife. Turn the cake over; the flat bottom will now be the

top of the cake. Split the cake in half horizontally with a thin, sharp knife. Cut a very shallow vertical notch on the side of the cake so you can match the 2 halves when putting them back together again. Place the 2 halves side by side on a cake rack.

2. Mix the rum with 2 tablespoons of water. Sprinkle or brush this mixture, using a pastry brush or pastry feathers, over the 2 cut surfaces, reserving some for the top of the cake.

3. Brush the warm apricot jam or butter glaze over the 2 cut surfaces and the outside edge of the cake.

4. Spread the custard filling about ⅜ inch deep over the bottom layer and add the top layer. Sprinkle or brush the top with the remaining rum-water mixture. Slide the cake onto a serving dish and place it in the refrigerator until 1½ hours before serving.

5. At that time, remove the cake from the refrigerator. Break up the 5 meringue sheets into irregularly shaped pieces about ½ inch or less in size. If you have prepared stiffened whipped cream, remove it from the refrigerator and, if needed, freshen it with a beater; otherwise, whip the 1½ cups of heavy cream until it holds stiff peaks and flavor it with sugar and vanilla extract to taste.

6. Spread most of the whipped cream on top of the cake, smoothing it up into a dome shape. Thinly cover the sides with the rest of the whipped cream. Cover the top and sides of the whipped cream with the meringue pieces, lightly pressing them into the whipped cream with the back of a broad spatula to make a semi-smooth surface. Return the cake to the refrigerator until almost time to serve.

Note: When making the Sponge Cake there will be enough batter left over for small cupcakes or a single, 7-x-4¼-inch rectangular layer that can be cut in half for the Fantastic Pear dessert for 2 (page 281).

*Small Cakes
and Cookies*

In all the pasticcerias

in Italy there are sumptuous displays of small cakes and cookies for which we were always grateful, because we could not carry large cakes or tarts with us in the car. The small, very transportable goodies were a satisfying end to a meadow, mountain, or seashore picnic including ham, one of the many sliced sausages, cheese, salads, olives, bread or rolls, and wine or mineral water—all usually bought in the morning at local stores.

The types of small cakes and cookies varied according to the part of Italy we were in: tiny fruit tarts and rice pastries in the north, to the southern Moorish and marzipan varieties influenced by North Africa, to the flaky doughs and almond pastries of the southern Adriatic in the style of Greece across the way, and Turkey just beyond.

Certain cities seem to specialize in a lavish assortment, as we found out in Ravenna and Verona in the north, and Lecce in the southeast. But no matter where we were, we never lacked for a choice from the several pasticcerias in each place, and yet we left behind many untried varieties for future trips.

Cream Puff Dough
Pasta Sfinge (or Bigne)

This classic dough is called *pasta sfinge* in Italy, *pâte à chou* in France, and *cream puff dough* in the United States and England.

11-x-17-inch baking pan

> ½ *cup water*
> 4 *tablespoons unsalted butter*
> ½ *cup flour*
> *Pinch of salt*
> 2 *eggs*
> 1½ *teaspoons sugar*
> ¼ *teaspoon vanilla or lemon extract*

1. Preheat the oven to 425°.
2. In a saucepan, bring the water and butter to a boil, then turn down the heat a little.
3. Add the flour and salt all at once and stir with a wooden spoon until the mixture forms a ball. Remove from the heat.
4. Add the eggs, 1 at a time, beating after each addition. Add the sugar and vanilla or lemon extract.
5. Spoon the dough into a pastry bag fitted with a ⅝-inch tube. Squeeze out the dough, in amounts according to the individual recipe, onto an ungreased aluminum foil-covered baking pan. Or drop round or long ovals from a tablespoon.
6. Place in the preheated oven. Baking time varies depending on the size of the puff. The first 10 to 15 minutes are at 425° and the next 20 to 30 minutes are at 375°. Follow individual recipes for timing.
7. Remove the pan from the oven and place the puffs on a cake rack. When cool, cut in half horizontally, remove any dough left inside, and return the halves to a 400° oven for 3 to 5 minutes to crisp. Fill just before serving.

Note: This amount of dough will make approximately 18 small fingers; fourteen 2-inch puffs using a rounded tablespoon; 8 fingers 4½ x 1 inch; 8 puffs 2½ inches in diameter; 16 to 18 profiteroles. All dimensions are the cooked sizes. See individual recipes for exact directions.

Ladyfingers
Savoiardi

These light, small cakes that we call Ladyfingers are known in Italian as Savoiardi and in French as Biscuit de Savoie; so we often believe they were a specialty of the Savoy/Piedmont area of Italy, a province on the northwestern corner bordering France and Switzerland. The young princess of Savoy traveled to France in 1696 to be married to the young Duc de Bourgogne, grandson of Louis the Fourteenth, as part of a settlement after a border war. Perhaps it was her chef who brought along this delicacy from her homeland since the specially shaped pans for the cakes are also known as Savoy pans in France.

Two 9¼-x-12½-inch ladyfinger pans with 12 compartments each
    or an 11-x-17-inch baking pan
Makes 20 to 24 ladyfingers

>   *2 eggs, separated*
>   *⅛ teaspoon cream of tartar*
>   *¼ cup plus 1 tablespoon sugar*
>   *1 teaspoon vanilla extract or ½ teaspoon lemon extract*
>   *4 tablespoons flour*
>   *2 tablespoons cornstarch*
>   *Pinch of salt*
>   *Superfine sugar*
>   *Vanilla-Flavored Confectioners' Sugar, page 40 (optional)*

1. Preheat the oven to 350°.
2. Butter the pans and dust with cornstarch.
3. Beat the egg whites with the cream of tartar. When soft peaks form, add 1 tablespoon of sugar and beat until the whites are stiff. Set aside.
4. Beat the egg yolks with a wire whisk, slowly beating in the remaining ¼ cup of sugar until the mixture is lemon-colored and fluffy. Beat in the vanilla or lemon extract.
5. Mix the flour, cornstarch, and salt together in a small bowl, then pour into a sifter.
6. Gradually sift in the flours over the egg-sugar mixture, blending in thoroughly.
7. Freshen the egg white and mix 2 tablespoons into the batter to soften it. Add the rest of the egg white to the batter and fold it in with a rubber or plastic spatula. When just mixed, fill the ladyfinger compartments of the pan ⅔ full, or spoon round-ended rectangles 3½ x ¾ inch onto the baking pan, adding an extra ½ teaspoon of batter on top of each end. Sprinkle the top surface of the batter with superfine sugar. Bake the ladyfingers in the pre-heated oven for 10 to 12 minutes.

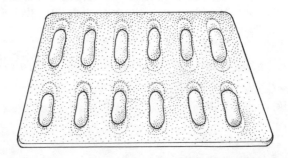

8. Remove the baked ladyfingers from the pan to a cake rack and dust with vanilla-flavored confectioners' sugar. If they are to be used as part of a dessert, then do not dust with confectioners' sugar.

Note: In Italy, the flavoring is often grated lemon or orange rind to taste, or orange flower water.

Chocolate Mousse

This rich, dark chocolate mousse is ideal for filling rolled piz-zelle, puff pastry squares, and tiny profiteroles, or between plain sugar cookies.

Makes about ¾ cup

>5 *ounces unsweetened chocolate*
>1 *ounce semisweet chocolate*
>2 *tablespoons sugar*
>1 *teaspoon instant espresso coffee powder*
>3 *tablespoons unsalted butter, sliced*
>2 *egg yolks, beaten*
>1 *tablespoon Amaretto liqueur*

1. Break the chocolate into small pieces and melt in the top of a double boiler over simmering water.

2. Mix the sugar and the espresso coffee powder together in a small bowl.

3. When the chocolate has melted, stir in the sugar-coffee mixture with a fork until the sugar has melted.

4. Stir in the butter slices until melted.

5. When the butter has melted, remove the pan from the heat and in a slow stream pour the beaten egg yolks into the hot chocolate mixture, stirring with a spoon until well mixed. Stir in the Amaretto liqueur.

6. Cool the chocolate mixture in the pan for 1 hour at room temperature. Do not refrigerate or the mousse will get too thick and hard. Use the same day.

Chocolate Sauce

This popular sweet dessert sauce is made of chocolate and cocoa powder with underlying flavors of coffee and rum. It is poured over profiteroles or ice cream, or used to mask squares of sponge cake, Génoise, or ladyfingers—with or without a filling of ice cream.

Yields 1 cup

> 1½ tablespoons sugar
> 2 tablespoons unsweetened cocoa powder
> 3 tablespoons strong coffee
> 5 tablespoons water
> 1 teaspoon instant espresso coffee powder
> 2 ounces semisweet or unsweetened chocolate
> ½ teaspoon vanilla extract
> 1½ teaspoons dark rum
> 1 tablespoon unsalted butter
> Pinch of salt

1. Mix the sugar and cocoa powder together in the top of a double boiler. Add the liquid coffee and water slowly, stirring to prevent lumps. Add the espresso coffee powder and let it melt while breaking up the chocolate into small pieces. Add the pieces of chocolate to the pan.

2. Place the pan over simmering hot water until the chocolate has melted and the mixture is smooth.

3. Take the top of the double boiler off the heat and cool for 10 minutes. Add the vanilla extract and the rum. Stir in small pieces of butter a few at a time, stirring until the butter melts. Add salt to taste.

4. Set the sauce aside to cool completely before using. It can be stored in a jar in the refrigerator for up to 1 week.

Almond Cakes (Verona)

At our favorite pasticceria in Verona we bought an assortment of small cakes, each with a different topping. We took these with us to Asolo where we picnicked in a flower-filled meadow halfway up the road to Mount Grappa.

A buttery almond cake batter is baked in small, shallow, round or oval fluted pans. The cakes are decorated with glacéed cherries, strips of candied orange peel, and toasted sliced almonds.

½-inch-deep fluted pans, either 2-inch rounds or 4¼-x-2-inch ovals
11-x-17-inch baking pan
Makes 10 small cakes

> 2 ounces Almonds, Blanched and Toasted, page 48
> 2 eggs
> 5 tablespoons unsalted butter
> 5 tablespoons sugar
> 1½ teaspoons almond extract
> ⅔ cup cake flour
> 1 teaspoon baking powder
> Pinch of salt, or to taste
> Glacéed cherries, Candied Orange Peel strips (page 51),
>   preserved orange slices, toasted sliced almonds
> Vanilla-Flavored Confectioners' Sugar, page 40

1. Preheat the oven to 400°.

2. Butter the small fluted pans. Place an upturned baking pan in the oven to heat.

3. Grind the toasted almonds in a food processor or Mouli grater to a fine powder.

4. Beat the 2 eggs together in a small bowl. Set aside 1½ tablespoons of the beaten egg in a small ramekin for brushing on the surface of the cakes.

5. Cream the butter, add the sugar, and beat them together.

Add the beaten egg and the almond extract. Beat the mixture together with a wire whisk until light in color.

6. Fold in the ground almonds. Mix the flour with the baking powder and the salt. Sift over the batter in small quantities, mixing in after each addition.

7. Fill the pans ¾ full (2 level tablespoons per pan) and spread the batter to fill the pans.

8. Garnish the tops in various ways before baking: Cut the glacéed cherries in thirds and put 3 pieces down the center of the oval cakes. Cover the tops of the cakes with slightly toasted sliced almonds. Place a serpentine-curved strip of candied orange peel down the center of an oval cake with a piece of glacéed cherry at each curve. Curve a strip of candied orange peel in a circle on top of a round cake and center it with a piece of glacéed cherry or a slice of almond. Lay a ¼ slice of preserved orange on top of a round cake with a piece of glacéed cherry at the point.

9. Place the cake-filled pans on the heated baking pan in the preheated oven and bake for 20 minutes. After 10 minutes of baking, brush the tops of the cakes with the reserved beaten egg.

10. When baked, remove from the oven to a cake rack. After 5 minutes remove the cakes from the pans and allow to cool before serving. Dust the almond-covered cakes with vanilla-flavored confectioners' sugar. The cakes should be eaten the day of baking because the crisp surface will soften by the next day.

Chocolate Cake and Shortbread Squares

We have always found it impossible to buy only one pastry in a pasticceria in Italy, especially when it is one we have never been in before and many of the pastries are new to us. And so it was at Ascoli Piceno, up a long valley from the Adriatic Sea, a town dating from Roman times. Its breathtaking Piazza del Popolo is bordered by thirteenth- and sixteenth-century buildings.

One choice was chocolate rectangles, two inches by two and one-half inches, for the chocoholic of the family. A crisp, hauntingly rum-flavored shortbread forms the base, and rising from the base is a chocolate-almond cake heavily dusted with vanilla-flavored confectioners' sugar.

8-x-8-x-2-inch pan
Makes 12 pieces

> *8 tablespoons (1 stick) butter*
> *¼ cup confectioners' sugar*
> *2 teaspoons dark rum*
> *¼ teaspoon baking powder*
> *Pinch of salt*
> *1 cup flour*
> *Chocolate-Almond Loaf Cake, page 72*
> *Vanilla-Flavored Confectioners' Sugar, page 40*

1. Preheat the oven to 350°.
2. Butter the pan and dust with flour.
3. For the shortbread, cream the butter and add the sifted confectioners' sugar, mixing well. Blend in the rum.
4. Mix together the baking powder, salt, and flour, and sift over the butter-sugar mixture, ¼ cup at a time, stirring until blended.
5. Pat the dough into the bottom of the buttered pan.
6. Bake in the preheated oven for 10 minutes. Remove from the oven and set aside. Reset the oven to 375°.
7. Make the chocolate-almond loaf cake. Spoon the batter evenly over the shortbread. Return the pan to the oven and bake for 45 to 50 minutes, or until a thin skewer inserted into the center of the cake comes out clean.
7. Remove from the oven and cool in the pan on a cake rack. When cool, cut into 16 pieces, 2 inches square, or 12 pieces slightly more than 2⅝ inches square. Slip each one out of the pan with a

broad spatula. Dust the tops heavily with vanilla-flavored confectioners' sugar.

Note: Before cutting the cake into squares, top with Soft Chocolate Glaze, page 44, instead of Vanilla-Flavored Confectioners' Sugar.

Cream Puff Fingers (Pisa)

One evening in Pisa, after an early dinner, we decided to have coffee and dessert at a pasticceria cum espresso coffee bar, but we were unsuccessful in putting pastry and coffee together in one place. The pasticceria was open but had not begun the evening's serving at small tables. At the regular counter we bought small, finger-shaped cream puffs, heavily sprinkled with crystals of sugar, and took them back to the hotel. On the way we stopped for a quick espresso.

11-x-17-inch baking pan
Makes 16 to 20 fingers

> *Cream Puff Dough, page 118*
> *Clear sugar crystals*
> *Egg Custard, page 237, half the recipe; or Time-Saver Custard, page 240, full recipe. Substitute for the vanilla extract 1 tablespoon Amaretto liqueur or 1 tablespoon dark rum mixed with ¼ to ½ teaspoon almond extract.*

1. Preheat the oven to 425°.
2. Make the cream puff dough. Spoon the dough into a pastry bag fitted with a ⅝-inch plain tip. Squeeze out fingers 2½ inches long by ¾ inch wide, or form with a tablespoon. Sprinkle the tops with the sugar crystals. Bake in the oven for 10 minutes, then lower the heat to 375° and bake 20 minutes more. Remove from the oven and set aside on a cake rack to cool.

3. While the puff fingers are baking, make the custard filling, substituting the Amaretto liqueur for the vanilla extract. If Amaretto liqueur is not available, mix the rum and almond extract together.

4. The custard may be made ahead of time and stored in the refrigerator until 1 hour (or less) before serving. Filling the puffs earlier will soften the crust, and you want them to be crisp. Split the puffs in half, crisp them in the oven, and cool. Slightly mound the custard on the lower halves of the puffs, then cover with the upper halves.

Little Surprise Cakes (Taranto)

As we explored Taranto one warm spring day, we made mental notes of pasticcerias that looked interesting because we knew that the next day we would be driving across the countryside to Lecce and picnicking at midday. At one shop the cakes and tarts looked yummy, but we needed something more transportable. The understanding lady behind the counter pointed to cupcakes in a glass-fronted display case and told us they were filled, not plain. We bought four, and she liberally dusted them with confectioners' sugar before putting them into a small box that she tied with a red, white, and green ribbon.

The filling of the feather-light sponge cakes was a not-too-sweet jelly containing dried currants and a small, round, dull-red berry that we did not recognize and have never identified. The tops were covered with a thin almond-flavored icing on which was centered a small dollop of the filling. In re-creating the filling we substituted an English jam of whole black currants and added dried currants.

Muffin pans with openings 2½ inches wide x 1¼ inches deep
Makes 16 small cakes

6 tablespoons dried currants
1 tablespoon dry Marsala
6 rounded tablespoons black currant jam
Sponge Cake, page 32
Almond Icing, page 41

1. Measure the currants into a small bowl and add the Marsala. Soak the currants for 15 minutes, then stir in the black currant jam. Set aside.

2. Butter only the bottom of the muffin cups. Cover each bottom with a circle of wax paper, butter the paper, and set the pans aside.

3. Prepare the sponge cake batter following the recipe directions.

4. Spoon 2 tablespoons of the batter into each muffin cup. Place 1 teaspoon of currant filling in the center of the batter. Cover the filling with ½ tablespoon of batter and gently smooth the top to cover the filling. There should be about 4 teaspoons of currant filling left over to decorate the tops of the finished cakes.

5. Place the pans in the oven and bake for 20 minutes. Remove the pans from the oven and place under the broiler until the tops are a light brown. They will brown *very* quickly, so watch them carefully.

6. Remove the pans from the broiler and loosen the edges of the cakes with the point of a sharp knife. Let the cakes cool in the pans for 10 minutes. Run a small sharp knife blade firmly around the edges and remove the cakes onto a cake rack. Remove the wax paper from the bottoms and allow the cakes to cool completely before icing them.

7. Prepare the almond icing. The icing consistency has to be thin enough to spread on the tops of the cakes, but not so thin as to run over the edge. You may need to add either more liquid or more sugar; if adding liquid, taste the icing to decide whether to add more wine or Amaretto liqueur.

8. After spreading the icing smoothly on the little cakes, add a small dollop of the reserved currant filling on the top of each cake.

Meringues with Chocolate Glaze (Ferrara)

There is an elegant row of shops lining the sidewalk backed by the Castle of Este and the Palazzo Communale in Ferrara, their windows and the sidewalk shaded with curved awnings. One, a pasticceria/coffee shop, had prominently displayed large double rosettes of meringue held together on their facing flat sides by a thick chocolate filling. We bought two and brought them home to our apartment in Igea Marina on the Adriatic Sea, north of Rimini.

11-x-17-inch baking pan
7-x-10-inch muffin pan with 2⅝-inch openings
Serves 4, 2 meringues per person

> *Basic Baked Meringues, page 35*
> *Soft Chocolate Glaze, page 44*

1. Make, then form 8 meringues into peaked swirls using a pastry bag with a star tube. For more than 4 servings, double or triple the basic recipe depending on how many meringues you need. Bake according to the recipe.

2. When the oven is turned off and the meringues are drying in the slowly cooling oven, make the soft chocolate glaze. Let it cool, then place the pot in the refrigerator until the glaze is thick enough to spread and hold its position without running.

3. When the chocolate glaze is thick, support *half* the cooled meringues, flat bottoms up, in the deep cups of a muffin pan and spread approximately ⅜ to ½ inch of glaze over the flat bottoms of these meringues. Lightly press the bottom of the second set of meringues against the glaze. Put the muffin pan containing the meringues in the refrigerator until ready to serve.

Moorish Pastries (Reggio di Calabria)
Morettos

One year on the way to Sicily we stayed overnight in Reggio di Calabria before taking the ferry the next day for Messina. After settling into our hotel, we went down the street to the local super-mercado to buy bottled water, instant coffee powder, and a few other things for the next day's picnic. During this time Italy was having difficulty providing enough small coins for change. In line at the checkout counter we felt perfectly at home; the faces around reminded us of New York's Little Italy, and everyone helped us to make change, with coins and bills passed from hand to hand rapidly until we had the exact amount for the cashier.

We ate that evening at a small restaurant near the hotel and our dessert, *Moretto* (which means Moorish), made us realize how far south we were and how many centuries of close ties there were between southern Italy and North Africa. Morettos are rounds of chocolate cake, three inches in diameter and one inch thick, topped by an opulent swirl of sweetened whipped cream and covered with shaved unsweetened chocolate.

6½-x-10-x-1½-inch baking pan
3-inch cookie cutter
Makes 6 pastries

> *Chocolate Torta, page 74*
> *2 ounces unsweetened chocolate, or to taste*
> *1½ cups heavy cream*
> *4 or 5 teaspoons sugar, or to taste*
> *1 teaspoon vanilla extract, or to taste*

1. Butter the cake pan, line the bottom with wax paper, butter it, and dust the bottom and sides with flour.
2. Make the chocolate cake following the recipe directions.

When baked, turn the cake out on a cake rack, remove the wax paper from the bottom, and turn the cake upright to cool.

3. When the cake has cooled, cut it into 6 circles with the 3-inch cookie cutter.

4. One hour before serving, shave the chocolate with a sharp knife and set the shavings aside on a small plate. Whip the cream, adding sugar and vanilla extract to taste. Spoon the cream into a pastry bag fitted with a ½-inch star tip and pipe a high swirl over the top of each cake round, or mound the whipped cream on the cakes with a tablespoon. Place the pastries in the refrigerator until just before serving.

5. Before serving, heavily sprinkle the whipped cream rosettes with chocolate shavings. Place the pastries on individual dessert plates and serve.

Profiteroles

We have eaten profiteroles in several areas of Italy, and the fillings and chocolate sauce thickness have varied. In the south, the filling is usually ice cream and the sauce is thin. In the north, Ravenna in particular, the filling is an egg custard and the sauce is very thick, masking the puffs and not flowing into the dessert dish. Our sauce recipe is halfway between these two varieties.

Any or all of the components, except the whipped cream, may be made the day before serving.

11-x-17-inch baking pan
Serves 6, 3 puffs per person

> *Cream Puff Dough, page 118*
> *Coffee Ice Cream, page 264, or use commercial coffee ice*
> *cream*
> *Chocolate Sauce, page 122; 1½ times the recipe*

¾ cup heavy cream
3 teaspoons sugar, or to taste
6 drops almond extract, or to taste

1. Bake 18 small puffs 1½ to 2 inches in diameter in a 425° oven for 15 minutes, then at 375° for 10 minutes. When they are cold, cut each one in half with a sharp knife; scrape out any soft dough inside with a teaspoon. Return the shells to a 400° oven on the upturned bottom of a baking pan. Bake for 5 to 10 minutes, until the shells are crisp. Remove the shells to a cake rack to cool. If the puffs are made the day before, cut and crisp them the next day.

2. Make and freeze the coffee ice cream.

3. Make the chocolate sauce and let it cool in the top of a double boiler. If it is made the day before, store the sauce in a covered glass jar in the refrigerator. Remove the jar from the refrigerator at least 2 hours before using the sauce.

4. About 1 hour before serving, whip the heavy cream. When it holds soft peaks, add the sugar and almond extract. Adjust the sweetening and flavoring if necessary.

5. In order to keep the profiterole shells crisp, fill each one with 2 heaping teaspoons of slightly softened ice cream as near to serving time as possible. Arrange 3 filled shells on each shallow dessert dish. Spoon 1 tablespoon of chocolate sauce over each profiterole and 1 teaspoon or more in the dish. Add 1 heaping teaspoon of whipped cream on top of each profiterole and serve.

Puff Pastry Folded Squares (Rimini)

Rimini was just a few kilometers south of our home base at Igea Marina, and we often explored the city on foot and shopped at the open market. One day, wanting a light dessert for dinner, we settled on puff pastries displayed in the window of a pasticceria.

They were an excellent choice to accompany espresso coffee as we sat on our balcony watching the *passéggio* below—the tourists and townspeople spilling out of their hotels or homes for an evening stroll.

Opposite points of the appetizingly brown puff pastry were folded over chopped almonds. When baked, the exposed point on one side was covered with vanilla egg custard, and on the other side with chocolate egg custard.

11-x-17-inch baking pan
Notched-wheel cutter
Makes 8 pastries

> *3 tablespoons Almonds, Blanched and Toasted, page 48*
> *Puff Pastry, page 174, or 2 frozen commercial sheets 9½ x*
>   *10½ inches*
> *1 egg yolk*
> *1 teaspoon cold water*
> *Egg Custard, page 237, half the recipe; or Time-Saver*
>   *Custard, page 240, full recipe*
> *Chocolate Egg Custard, page 239*

1. Preheat the oven to 425°.
2. Chop the almonds into coarse pieces.
3. Follow the recipe directions for making puff pastry or use the commercial puff pastry, following the manufacturer's directions for defrosting; do not roll out any thinner.
4. If using your own pastry, roll it into a 10-x-20-x-¼-inch sheet and cut eight 5-inch squares. If using commercial puff pastry, cut each 10-inch-square sheet into quarters. In both cases use a notched-wheel cutter.
5. Beat the egg yolk with the cold water.
6. Sprinkle the center of each square with ½ teaspoon of chopped almonds. Fold over the opposite points and overlap them in the center, covering the almonds. Hold the points in place with

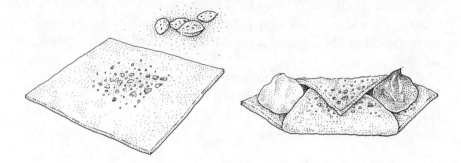

a brushing of beaten egg yolk between the points. Add a sprinkling of almonds on top of the center folded points. Brush the top surface of the dough with the egg yolk glaze and bake in the oven for 30 minutes.

7. While the pastry is baking, make both the vanilla-flavored egg custard and the chocolate-flavored egg custard. Put each one in a separate bowl and cover the tops with a circle of wax paper to prevent a skin from forming. Refrigerate the custards to chill and thicken.

8. One hour before serving, remove the custards from the refrigerator. Place 1 tablespoon of vanilla custard on one flat exposed end of the pastry and 1 tablespoon of chocolate custard on the other exposed end.

Note: Custard flavored with almond extract may be substituted for vanilla-flavored Egg Custard. Chocolate Mousse (page 121) may be substituted for Chocolate Egg Custard.

Red-Edged Apricot Pastries (Igea Marina)

In Emilia-Romagna, a brilliant red coloring is used on many cakes and puddings. It stains the tops and sides of cakes and turns a zuppa inglese into a fiery bowl of custard and cake. One baker we talked to described the stain as kermes mixed with spirits, and kermes is a designation of a special red color in commercial food coloring. We are certain that originally a more interesting and flavorful coloring matter must have been used, such as pomegranate or cherry juice, which would have been seasonally limited. We have substituted grenadine syrup mixed with maraschino liqueur, which we think approaches the original in color and is more delectable than red dye.

In these pastries, round disks three and one-half to four inches are cut from a one-half-inch-thick sheet of Génoise. Or you can use disks made of the leftover dough from Strawberry Cake/Tart (page 206). The edges are brushed with the grenadine mixture, and the cake is topped with apricot jam and three stewed apricot halves that are lightly brushed with jam. Whipped cream is piped on top of the disk between the apricot halves and around the edge of the cake.

8-x-8-inch square pan
Tart or muffin ring, 3½ to 4 inches in diameter
Serves 4

> *Génoise, page 29*
> *6 whole or 12 halves dried apricots*
> *4 rounded tablespoons apricot jam*
> *2 tablespoons grenadine syrup*
> *2 tablespoons maraschino liqueur*
> *1 cup heavy cream*
> *4 teaspoons sugar, plus sugar to taste*
> *¼ teaspoon almond extract*

1. Make and bake the Génoise in the 8-x-8-inch pan following the recipe directions. When baked, put under the broiler to crisp the top. Unmold on a cake rack, remove the wax paper, and cool with the top side up.
2. Cook the dried apricots in water to barely cover them, sugaring them to taste. Drain well and cool. When cool, place on paper towels to drain.

3. Heat the apricot jam but do not sieve; chop up any large pieces of fruit.

4. In a small bowl, mix together the grenadine syrup and the maraschino liqueur.

5. Beat the heavy cream and, when thickened, add the sugar and the almond extract and beat until thick.

To Assemble (1½ hours before serving):

1. Cut the cake into 4 circles with the tart or muffin ring. Place the circles top side down on a cake rack.

2. Brush the sides of each cake disk with the grenadine-maraschino mixture, letting the liquid soak in.

3. Spread the warm apricot jam on the surface of each cake disk, reserving enough to brush the apricot tops lightly after they are in place.

4. Pile 3 apricot halves in the center of each disk. Brush the apricot tops with a light coating of melted jam.

5. Fit a pastry bag with a ½-inch star tube, then fill the bag with the whipped cream. Pipe the cream around the edge of each disk, then pipe a second row inside the edging to fill the space up to the apricots. Place all the disks in the refrigerator until 30 minutes before serving. They should not be served ice cold.

Sweet Ravioli (Sperlonga)

One of the ever-recurring desserts found well south of Rome is a sweet ravioli sometimes called tortelli or calcionetti (little balls). There are several tempting varieties depending on the type of dough and the fillings, and whether the raviolis are baked in the oven or deep fried in oil.

In a small hotel on the edge of the beach at Sperlonga, on the Golfo di Gaeta near the grotto of Tiberio and the ruins of his palace, we feasted on fettuccine vongole followed by langouste on

ver a wood fire in the sprawling old-fashioned
old copper pots. For dessert we chose small,
baked sweet ravioli stuffed with nuts, pureed
e, still slightly warm from the oven. Some were
h vanilla-flavored confectioners' sugar; others
were topped with a thin lemon-flavored white icing.

11-x-17-inch baking pan
Notched-wheel cutter
Makes 24 pieces

> *Puff Pastry, 1 sheet 10 x 9½ x ⅛ inches, page 174, or*
>   *commercial puff pastry*
> *1 egg white*
> *1 teaspoon cold water*
> *1 green apple, 2¾ inches in diameter*
> *2 ounces Toasted Hazelnuts, page 49*
> *1 tablespoon unsalted butter*
> *1 ounce semisweet chocolate*
> *3 tablespoons sugar, or to taste*
> *Simple Icing, page 40, using lemon flavoring*
> *Vanilla-Flavored Confectioners' Sugar, page 40 (optional)*

1. Preheat the oven to 375°.

2. If using frozen commercial puff pastry, defrost it for 20 minutes or follow the manufacturer's directions.

3. Add the water to the egg white and beat with a fork to mix. Set aside.

4. Peel, core, and cut the apple into dice. Melt the butter in a small saucepan and mix in the apple dice. Cover the pan and, *over low heat,* cook the apple dice until they are soft. Remove the cover and stir the apple dice until a little of the juice has evaporated. Scrape the apple into a small bowl to cool.

5. Coarsely grind the toasted hazelnuts in a food processor; do not reduce the nuts to a powder.

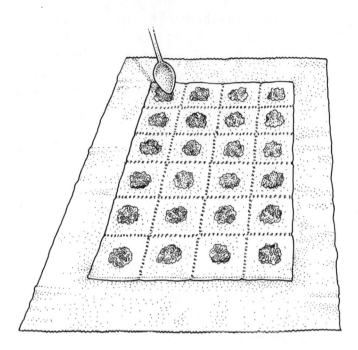

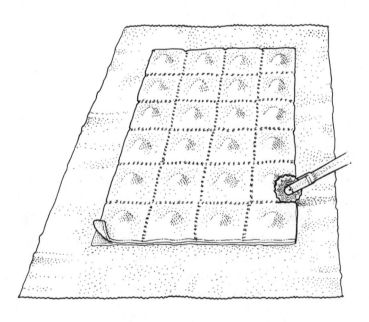

6. Sieve the cooled apple dice into a small mixing bowl, pressing almost all of the solids through the mesh. Stir in the ground nuts.

7. Melt the broken-up pieces of chocolate over simmering hot water. When melted, stir into the apple-nut mixture. Blend in the sugar and then set the bowl aside.

8. Unfold the puff pastry sheet and spread it out on a floured sheet of wax paper on a pastry board. Cut the pastry sheet in half and set one half aside. Flour a second sheet of wax paper and place it over the puff pastry on the board; roll out the pastry to an 8-x-12-inch rectangle. Remove the top sheet of wax paper. With a notched-wheel cutter, lightly mark off 24 squares 2 x 2 inches each, but do not cut through the dough. Transfer the wax paper with the marked sheet of dough to another work surface.

9. Roll out the other sheet of puff pastry between floured sheets of wax paper and do the same as the first half.

10. Heap 1 teaspoon of the filling in the center of each square of this second sheet of pastry; if there is any filling left over, divide it among the squares. Brush all the margins of dough around the fillings with the egg white.

11. Lay the first sheet of pastry, marked side up, over the filled sheet of pastry. Starting in the center, press the 2 sheets of dough together between the humps of filling, gradually working out to the edge, as you do so pressing out any air pockets caught between the 2 sheets of pastry. Cut the squares apart with the notched-wheel cutter. Press together any edges that look loose so the filling does not escape.

12. Transfer the squares to the ungreased baking pan. Brush the tops of the pastries with the egg white. Prick the center of each square once with the tines of a fork, then place the baking pan in the oven. After 10 minutes, brush the tops again with the egg white; 5 minutes later, brush them again. When the squares are done, a total of 20 to 25 minutes, slip the pan under the broiler until the tops of the ravioli turn golden.

13. Remove the pan from the broiler and transfer the squares

to a cake rack to cool. When cool, cover the tops with simple icing, or dust heavily with vanilla-flavored confectioners' sugar.

VARIATIONS

The fillings for sweet ravioli fascinated us as we tried many varieties. You can balance the ingredients listed below according to taste, which is what an Italian cook does. Here are several suggestions for fillings: almonds substituted for the hazelnuts in this recipe; a thick, cooked custard flavored with maraschino liqueur (or with Marsala) and mixed with ricotta cheese plus diced candied orange peel; plain ricotta cheese mixed with both lemon and orange zest (or just one) and flavored with dark rum; ricotta cheese mixed with assorted candied fruits and flavored with cinnamon. Sweeteners for the fillings are either sugar or honey.

Three-Cornered Hats (Verona)

Another small picnic pastry was part of our "loot" from the Pasticceria Castelvecchio in Verona where we bought cakes and cookies whenever we were shopping in town. All the small cakes and cookies accompanied us on picnics into the countryside, when we were photographing villas, or into the high mountains surrounding Lake Garda, as we searched for wildflowers to photograph.

This one was a small crisp pastry, a little more than two inches across at the points, with a filling of finely chopped apple and dried currants, held together with a dark jam. The Verona baker probably used a boiled-down, tawny-flavored grape jam made from wine grapes. One can sometimes buy jars of this jam from Montepulciano in specialty stores, but it is generally hard to find in this country. We've substituted jams available in the United States.

11-x-17-inch baking pan
3-inch fluted or plain cookie cutter
Makes 16 to 18 small pastries

> *Tart Crust dough, page 170*
> *5 tablespoons dried currants*
> *1 tablespoon plus 1 teaspoon dry Marsala*
> *1 green apple, approximately 2½ inches in diameter*
> *1 teaspoon unsalted butter*
> *2 tablespoons black currant jam*
> *1 tablespoon grape jam*
> *2 teaspoons sugar*

1. Spread aluminum foil on the baking pan and lightly butter the foil.

2. Make and chill the tart dough following the recipe directions.

3. While the dough is chilling in the refrigerator, put the dried currants in a small bowl and add 1 tablespoon of dry Marsala. Soak the currants for 5 to 10 minutes.

4. Peel, core, and cut the apple into ¼-inch dice. Melt the butter in a small saucepan. Add the apple dice and the dried currants with Marsala. Cover and cook over low heat until the apple dice are soft, about 15 minutes.

5. Remove the pan from the heat. Add the black currant and grape jams, sugar, and remaining 1 teaspoon of Marsala. Put the pan back on the heat for 5 minutes to dry out the mixture, stirring all the time. Remove from the heat, spoon the mixture into a small bowl, and place in the refrigerator to chill.

6. Preheat the oven to 400°.

7. Remove the tart dough from the refrigerator and with the heel of your hand press it into a rectangular shape, pinching together any cracks that develop around the sides. Place the dough in the center of the board between the sheets of wax paper. Roll out to approximately 13½ x 9 x ⅛ inch thick.

8. Stamp out as many rounds as you can with the fluted or plain cutter, placing them on the aluminum foil–covered baking pan. Gather up the scraps of dough, re-form, and reroll. Stamp out with the cutter and repeat until all the dough is used.

9. Put 1 teaspoon of the fruit filling in the center of each circle. Bring the surrounding dough up and pinch into three angled points, leaving about ½ inch of filling exposed in the center. Bake for 15 minutes, then place under the hot broiler for about 30 seconds or until the edges and surface of the dough are an appetizing light brown. Remove the pastries to a cake rack to cool. Store in an airtight container overnight; they are much better the next day.

Zuppette Napoleone (Naples)

We bought Zuppette Napoleone squares in a pastry shop in Naples to take with us on a picnic at Paestum, where the golden Greek temples are silhouetted against a dark mountain and a blue sky overhead. Terrestrial bee orchids and other wildflowers bloom in the grass, and at the end of the fields is the Gulf of Salerno.

These square, layered pastries have a thin flaky puff paste top and bottom; each inner side is spread with apricot glaze, and enclosed is a Génoise layer heavily sprinkled with rum. Confectioners' sugar is dusted over the top and then slightly crisped under a broiler.

It is always interesting to speculate on the origin of a pastry's name; in many cases it is impossible, for the meaning is totally lost in time. The French Napolitain is a cake of several crisp layers held together with jelly or jam; the rum-sprinkled Génoise layer accounts for the *zuppette* (soaked). Or perhaps the cake was first named in that period when Napoleon had conquered much of Italy and his name was attached to many things.

11-x-17-inch baking pan
8-x-8-inch cake pan
Makes sixteen 2-inch squares or nine 2⅝-inch squares

> *Puff Pastry, page 174, or a commercial frozen sheet*
> *Génoise, page 29*
> *Apricot Jam or Butter Glaze, page 178; double the recipe*
> *Dark rum to taste*
> *Confectioners' sugar*

1. Preheat the oven to 425°.
2. Roll out a sheet of puff pastry dough to a 12-x-17-x-⅛-inch rectangle. Cut two 8-x-8-inch squares and place them on the ungreased baking pan. (Return the rest of the pastry to the freezer for another use.)
3. Bake the puff pastry squares in the oven for 15 to 20 minutes, or until puffed, crisp, and lightly browned. Remove them from the oven and transfer to cake racks to cool.
4. Make and bake a Génoise layer in the 8-x-8-inch cake pan prepared following the recipe directions. When done, transfer to a cake rack to cool.
5. When the 2 puff pastry squares and the Génoise square have cooled, make the apricot jam or butter glaze. Cool until the glaze starts to thicken.

To Assemble:
1. Place 1 square of puff pastry on the baking pan. Cover the top surface with half of the apricot glaze. Place the Génoise layer on top of the glaze. Generously sprinkle it with rum, then spread its top surface with the rest of the apricot glaze. Cover the glazed Génoise with the second square of puff pastry.
2. Heavily dust the top of the pastry with confectioners' sugar and place it under the broiler to slightly harden the sugar but not to melt or caramelize it. Remove from the broiler and transfer the cake to a serving dish. Serve at room temperature, cutting the cake into squares and adding more confectioners' sugar if needed.

Almond Cookies (Lecce)
Amaretti

A golden glow permeates Lecce, and nowhere is it more apparent than in the large square where the sun reflects off the amber stone of the buildings. It was at a shop in this square that we bought cookies, trying to make a practical choice between how long the cookies would keep on our way east and north and all the new varieties we wanted to try. There were almond-based crisp cookies, butter cookies rolled in confectioners' sugar similar to the Greek courambiades, and flaky, stuffed small pillows like small Greek trigonas. Lecce is truly at the crossroads of the east and west.

These crisp almond cookies are not to be confused with the commercially packaged Italian Amaretti cookies.

11-x-17-inch baking pan
Makes 21 to 24 cookies, 2½ inches in diameter

> *6 ounces (1¼ cups) full unskinned almonds*
> *¾ cup sugar*
> *2 egg whites (less 2 tablespoons)*
> *1¾ teaspoons almond extract*
> *Pinch of salt*

1. Preheat the oven to 300°.
2. Cover the bottom of the baking pan with aluminum foil, and butter and flour the foil.
3. Blanch and toast 2 ounces (⅓ cup) of the almonds (page 48). When cool, put them into a food processor fitted with a steel blade, along with the remaining unskinned almonds and the sugar. Spin until the mixture climbs the wall of the processor. Scrape down with a plastic spatula, then turn on the processor again and spin until the almonds are as finely cut as possible without turning into a paste.

4. Remove the almond-sugar mixture to a bowl. Mix in the unbeaten egg whites, almond extract, and salt.

5. Scoop out rounded teaspoons of the dough and place them on the foil-covered baking pan, 1½ to 2 inches apart. Bake the cookies for 25 minutes—no longer or they will become too hard when cool. If not brown enough, put under a preheated broiler for a maximum of 3 minutes. Remove the pan from the heat and slip the foil off the pan onto a baking rack. Remove the almond cookies from the foil when they have cooled.

Almond Horseshoe Cookies (Ravenna)

We bought cookies like these at the pastry shop opposite the duomo in Ravenna at the same time that we bought the Marzipan Cherry Cookies. We found that the dough was very similar but a little stiffer.

11-x-17-inch baking pan
Makes 18 cookies

> *3 or 4 ounces (½ to ¾ cup) Almonds, Blanched and Toasted, page 48*
> *Marzipan Cherry Cookie dough, page 151, with 3 additional tablespoons flour*
> *1 egg white*
> *1 teaspoon cold water*
> *Vanilla-Flavored Confectioners' Sugar, page 40*

1. Preheat the oven to 375°.

2. Chop the toasted nuts into small pieces and spread them on a sheet of wax paper. Set aside.

3. Make the cookie dough following the recipe directions but adding the 3 tablespoons of flour for a stiffer dough. Chill in the refrigerator for 15 minutes.

4. While the dough is chilling, beat the egg white slightly (just enough to break it up), mixing in the cold water.

5. On a floured pastry board, form the dough into a roll 1 inch in diameter. Cut it into 18 equal pieces and form each piece into a 3½-inch-long roll. Dip each piece in the almonds, on one side only. Form each small roll into a horseshoe shape, slightly pressing the nuts on top into the dough. The inner sides should not touch. Place each cookie on the ungreased baking pan, plain side down. Lightly brush the nutted tops and sides with egg white.

6. Bake the cookies in the preheated oven for 10 to 12 minutes. Remove the pan from the oven and transfer the cookies to a cake rack to cool. Just before serving, heavily dust the horseshoes with the vanilla-flavored confectioners' sugar.

Basic Butter Cookies

This crisp, buttery cookie becomes slightly chewy as it ages. This recipe is written without flavoring because it is the basis for several cookies that have their own flavors and decorations. If you wish, you can add vanilla, lemon, orange, or almond extract to taste if you want to make a plain cookie. Also see Filled Finger Slices (page 149), Pepper Cookies (page 154), and Pine Nut Cookies (page 157).

11-x-17-inch baking pan
3-inch cookie cutter
Makes 18 to 20 cookies

> *3½ tablespoons unsalted butter*
> *¾ cup plus 2 tablespoons flour*
> *½ teaspoon baking powder*
> *⅛ teaspoon salt*
> *1 egg*

½ cup sugar
1½ teaspoons half-and-half
Vanilla, lemon, orange, or almond extract to taste

1. Preheat the oven to 350°.
2. Butter the baking pan and set it aside.
3. Cut the butter into thin slices and allow to stand in a mixing bowl until slightly soft.
4. Put the flour into a sifter placed on a small plate and add the baking powder and salt. Set aside.
5. Beat the egg in a small bowl. Set aside.
6. Cream the softened butter, add the sugar, and beat until the mixture is lemon-colored and fluffy. Add the half-and-half and choice of flavoring to taste, beating after each addition. Add 1 tablespoon plus 1 teaspoon of the egg and beat in vigorously.
7. Sift ⅓ of the flour–baking powder over the mixture and beat thoroughly. Sift and beat in another ⅓. Add the rest of the flour and mix until it is well incorporated.
8. Form the soft dough into a 3-x-5-inch rectangle. Put it on a plate and set it, uncovered, in the refrigerator to chill for 30 to 40 minutes.
9. Roll out the dough between sheets of floured wax paper to an 8½-x-11-inch rectangle approximately ³⁄₁₆ inch thick. Stamp out the cookies and transfer to the baking pan with a cake turner. Brush the tops with the remainder of the beaten egg and put in the oven for 12 minutes. Transfer the baking pan to a preheated broiler and brown the tops of the cookies.
10. Remove the cookies to a cake rack to cool.

VARIATIONS

See the other cookie recipes for additions and directions for decorations and baking.

Festival Meringues (Amalfi)

At the Pasticceria Bar Savoia in Amalfi, these meringues were piled high on the counter. Red and green slivers of glacéed cherries were stuck into the faintly ivory-colored meringues, with ground nuts or perhaps almond brittle sprinkled in circles around the cherries.

Makes 8 large meringues (see Note*)*

> *Basic Baked Meringues, page 35*
> *4 red and 4 green glacéed cherries (or 8 red glacéed cherries*
> *if you cannot get green ones)*
> *2 tablespoons ground Almonds, Blanched and Toasted, page*
> *48, or ground Almond Brittle, page 52*

1. Make the meringues, following the recipe through Step 4, plus Step 7.
2. If the cherries are packaged in a sticky syrup, wash them off in hot water and then dry them with paper towels. Cut each cherry into 4 pieces.
3. Before baking the meringues, sprinkle the ground almonds or brittle in 4 small circles on each meringue top. Poke the pointed end of a cherry piece into the center of each circle, alternating green and red cherries on each meringue.
4. Put the meringues in the oven and bake according to the directions given in the recipe.

Note: If more than 8 large meringues are desired, double or triple the recipe for Basic Baked Meringues and the number of cherries and almonds accordingly.

VARIATIONS

Make small meringues of slightly heaping teaspoons of the basic mixture. Use the same amount of cherries, cut in smaller pieces, adding a general sprinkling of ground almonds or brittle on the top of each meringue.

Filled Finger Slices (Lecce)

This is another enchanting cookie from the fabulous assortment we bought in Lecce, an inland town on the eastern side of the "heel" of Italy that is sometimes called the Florence of Apulia.

These are finger-width pastries made of a buttery almond-flavored dough rolled around a filling of quince or apricot butter and toasted almonds. They are both crisp and chewy, reminiscent of the Near East with their combination of quince and almond so typical in the "heel" of Italy. The jam available in that area is a thick puree with no visible pieces of fruit.

11-x-17-inch baking pan
Makes 24 finger-width slices

> *Basic Butter Cookies dough, page 146, using 1 teaspoon*
> *   almond extract*
> *30 (approximately 1½ ounces) Almonds, Blanched and*
> *   Toasted, page 48*
> *12 tablespoons quince jam or apricot butter*
> *2 teaspoons dark rum*
> *1 egg, beaten*

1. Butter the baking pan and set it aside.
2. Make the butter cookie dough, then chill it uncovered on a small plate in the refrigerator for 30 to 40 minutes.
3. Coarsely chop the toasted almonds. Set them aside in a small bowl.
4. Heat the quince jam or apricot butter with the rum and boil for a few minutes to thicken the mixture. Set aside to cool slightly. If it stiffens too much before you use it, reheat to soften.

5. Preheat the oven to 350°.

6. Remove the dough from the refrigerator and divide it into 2 equal-size pieces. Roll 1 piece between floured sheets of wax paper into a 6-x-12-inch sheet. Spread with half the jam, leaving a ½-inch margin along 1 long edge. Sprinkle the jam with half of the chopped almonds. Starting at the long "jammed" edge, fold over 1 inch of the dough and continue folding (not rolling) just up to the "unjammed" edge. Brush this edge with some of the beaten egg to seal and flop the roll over. It will be 1¾ to 2 inches wide and ¾ inch high.

7. Transfer the roll to the baking pan. Repeat with the other piece of dough and the remainder of the jam and nuts. Transfer the second roll to the baking pan, leaving generous space between them because the rolls spread to 2¾ or 3 inches wide and 1½ inches high. Brush both rolls with the remaining beaten egg.

8. Bake the rolls in the oven for 15 minutes, then brown the tops under a preheated broiler.

9. Remove the baking pan from the broiler and place on a cake rack until the baked rolls are cold. *They should not be removed* from the pan until cold. When cold, cut the rolls with a sharp knife across the narrow width into 1-inch-wide slices. Store in an airtight container.

Hazelnut Cookies (Lecce)
Biscottino Nocciola

With its past history of conquests by Greeks, Romans, and Normans, all of whom left their mark in the form of buildings and culture, Lecce has a special mood of its own. But the New York "conquest" of Lecce is not mentioned in the guidebooks: We stayed at the Astor, ate at the Plaza down the street, and observed a mod dress and jeans shop nearby called Woodstock.

Our Lecce cookies went north with us as we drove first to Brindisi and then on to Alberobello in Trulli country. They were consumed at a picnic on a low hillside looking down at the open fields below, dotted with olive trees and those round, almost pre-historic stone Trulli houses, some splashed with white paint designs on their curved peaks. This was a fairyland scene that hardly seemed real. One expected to see gnomes emerge from the low doorways.

This crisp, flavorsome cookie is a keeper, if you have will-power, and is wonderful served with coffee or chocolate ice cream.

11-x-17-inch baking pan
Makes approximately 36 cookies

> *Hazelnut Pasta Frolla, page 172*
> *³/₈-inch candied citron dice, 1 piece for each cookie*

1. Butter the baking pan and set it aside.
2. Make the hazelnut pasta frolla dough and chill it.
3. After the dough has been chilled in the refrigerator, remove it to a pastry board. Preheat the oven to 375°. Break off walnut-size pieces and roll them into balls between the palms of your hands. Make an indentation in the top of each ball with a thumb, flattening the ball slightly. Circle the sides with thumb and forefinger of one hand to squeeze the cracks together.
4. Place each cookie on the baking pan and press a piece of candied citron into the indentation.
5. Bake on the center rack of the oven for 15 minutes; the tops will not get brown. Remove the baking pan from the oven. With a broad spatula remove the cookies to a baking rack to cool. When cool, transfer to an airtight container for 24 hours before eating.

Marzipan Cherry Cookies (Ravenna)

While waiting for the duomo and the baptistry with its brilliant mosaics to open after the midday closing, we wandered around the wide square facing the duomo, looking in all the shop windows to pass the time. The pastry shop across the way had several varieties of cookies piled on stands in the window, among them cherry-centered spritz cookies and horseshoe-shaped cookies covered with chopped almonds and confectioners' sugar. Later on we bought some of each to be enjoyed later with the pure white, frozen "whipped cream" bought at a beach ice-cream bar at Igea Marina.

These cookies are crisp, strongly flavored with almond, and with marzipan in the dough. To make the spritz shape we use a crank cookie gun, adding a swirl-pattern disk, but the cookie dough can be squeezed out from a pastry bag through a large star tip.

11-x-17-inch baking pan
Cookie gun or pastry bag with star tip
Makes 18 to 20 cookies

> *4 tablespoons unsalted butter*
> *⅔ cup plus 1 tablespoon flour*
> *¼ teaspoon baking powder*
> *Pinch of salt*
> *9 to 10 glacéed red cherries*
> *1 egg*
> *4 tablespoons sugar*
> *1 ounce marzipan or almond paste*
> *¼ teaspoon lemon extract*
> *1 teaspoon almond extract*

1. Cut the butter into slices and set aside to soften in a mixing bowl.

2. Mix together with a fork the flour, baking powder, and salt. Pour into a flour sifter placed on a small plate and set aside.

3. Drop the cherries into a bowl of hot water and wash off the sticky surface. Dry them on paper towels, then cut each one in half, turning the cut side down to drain on the towels. Set aside.

4. Beat the egg in a small bowl. Set aside.

5. Cream the softened butter with a wooden spoon and slowly add the sugar, beating constantly with the spoon. Break the marzipan into small pieces and add to the butter-sugar mixture. Thoroughly smooth and blend in the marzipan, using the side of the spoon. Add the lemon and almond extracts. Mix well, then add 1½ tablespoons of the beaten egg. Stir and beat the dough until fluffy.

6. Sift ¼ of the flour mixture over the butter-sugar mixture and blend. Add another ¼ and blend. Follow this procedure until all the flour has been incorporated.

7. Dust a small plate with flour. Spoon the soft dough onto the plate, forming it into a roll a little narrower than the interior of the cookie gun. Lightly dust the top and sides with more flour. Place the plate with the dough into the refrigerator for 15 minutes to chill and stiffen.

8. When chilled, remove the dough from the refrigerator and transfer the roll to the cookie gun, adding the swirled rosette disk. Preheat the oven to 375°. Turn the handle of the cookie gun ½ to 1 full turn while holding the gun almost upright; the braces at one side should touch the baking pan. Give the gun a half turn as you lift it up. Repeat until all the dough is used. Add ½ cherry in the center of each cookie, rounded side up. (As an alternative, transfer the dough to a pastry bag with a large star tip and squeeze out swirled rosettes, then add the halved cherries.)

9. Put the baking pan on the center rack of the oven and bake for 10 to 12 minutes. The bottoms and edges will be brown, but the rest will be pale. Place the baking pan under the broiler for 30 seconds to 1 minute, until the tops are lightly golden. Transfer the cookies to a cake rack while still hot and allow to cool. Store in an airtight container.

Note: You might consider making Almond Horseshoe Cookies (page 145) at the same time by doubling the ingredients of this recipe and using some of the leftover beaten egg. The amount of flour called for in that recipe will then be added to half the dough. Or you may want to make double or triple the amount of marzipan cherry cookies by doubling or tripling the ingredients.

Pepper Cookies (Veneto)

Long ago, in Apicius' book of Imperial Roman cookery, pepper was listed as a flavoring for sweet preparations. Through the centuries, translators and editors of this book have interpreted "pepper" as an all-encompassing word for unspecified spices. However, we have run across its use today in Italy, particularly in sugar cookies. It adds an exotic fragrance to the dough, and the "peppery" bite is barely noticeable. Pepper-flavored cookies are particular favorites in north Italy in the Veneto region.

11-x-17-inch baking pan
2½-inch round, fluted cookie cutter
Makes 18 to 20 cookies

> *Basic Butter Cookie dough, page 146, adding ½ teaspoon*
> *coarsely ground black pepper and ½ teaspoon vanilla*
> *extract*
> *Crystal sugar granules (Demerara raw cane sugar)*

1. Butter the baking pan and set it aside.
2. Make the dough for Basic Butter Cookies, adding the pepper and vanilla extract. Chill the dough, uncovered, on a small plate in the refrigerator for 30 to 40 minutes. The remaining beaten egg will be used to brush the cookie tops before sprinkling them with sugar granules.
3. Preheat the oven to 350°.
4. Remove the dough from the refrigerator and roll out between 2 floured sheets of wax paper into a 9-x-16-x-⅛-inch rectangle. Cut into rounds with the cookie cutter and transfer them to

the baking pan. Re-form the scraps and roll out, cutting more rounds; continue until all the dough is used.

5. Brush the cookies with the reserved beaten egg and thickly sprinkle with the sugar granules, pressing them lightly into place. Bake in the oven for 12 minutes. Remove the pan from the oven and transfer the cookies to a cake rack to cool. Store in an airtight container.

Sweet Piadina Fritto (Emilia-Romagna)

Driving along the autostrada A14 that parallels the Adriatic Sea from Rimini southward, we were often fascinated by brief glimpses of a castle perched high on a hill near Cattolica. One day, determined to find the castle but not knowing its name, we took a local road and, keeping our eyes on the hill, kept switching to roads that took us in that direction. Finally, climbing the last one that wound around the hill, we came to Castello Gradara, a reconstructed castle and walled town—a pure fun tourist trap! We parked under some olive trees across from the castle wall and wandered through the few sloping streets, looking in ceramic shops, toy shops filled with crossbows of all sizes from six inches up, and shops displaying garish plastic souvenir items.

Just as we drove back down the hill we passed the more formal parking lot with an ice-cream stand to one side and a piadina fritto stand on the other. We had seen people eating thin, crisp, golden-brown disks twelve inches across and dusted with granulated sugar, but we did not know where they had bought them. We bought four of the disks to take home with us for dinner desserts and in-between nibbles, plus one to eat on the spot, leaning slightly over so the sugar drifted to the ground.

We knew that thin, *unsweetened* piadina, much like flour tortillas with their spots of brown against a white surface, were sold along the roadsides from blue-and-white-striped piadina stands. They are the ancient, local bread of Emilia-Romagna. Reheated on a grill they are folded over prosciutto, salami, or cheese and served as a "sandwich." But the sweet crisp piadina was an enchanting discovery. Ours are only four inches in diameter, which is easier to handle.

Makes 5 or 6 piadina disks

> *1 tablespoon unsalted butter*
> *1 egg*
> *2 tablespoons heavy cream*
> *Pinch of salt*
> *1 cup less 2 tablespoons flour*
> *2 teaspoons sugar*
> *Oil for frying*
> *Superfine sugar for dusting*

1. Melt the butter and set it aside.
2. Beat the egg in a small bowl, then beat in the cream and salt.
3. Sift the flour and sugar into a mixing bowl, and make a well in the center. Pour in the egg-cream mixture and the melted butter. Mix together until all the ingredients are blended. If the dough does not hold together, add a little more cream; if it is too moist, add a little more flour.
4. Cover the dough with a towel and let it stand for 30 minutes.
5. Divide the dough into 5 or 6 pieces. Roll out each piece between sheets of floured wax paper to a 4-inch-diameter thin disk. Brush off the excess flour from the surfaces of the disks.
6. Heat ½ to ¾ inch of oil in a frying pan to 350° to 365°, or until a 1-inch cube of bread browns in 60 seconds. Fry the disks until golden on both sides. Drain on paper towels and sprinkle heavily on both sides with superfine sugar while hot. Serve at room temperature. Just before serving, you may want to sprinkle more sugar on the piadina.

VARIATION

This dough is very similar to one made farther south that is used to make Gli Struffoli, literally the Heap of Shreds. The dough is cut into short strips or small irregular pieces, fried in oil, drained, then dropped into boiling honey and water. The pieces are removed, drained, and piled into a ring mold to cool. The top of the pile is sprinkled with multicolored nonpareils while sticky, or with confectioners' sugar when cold.

Pine Nut Cookies (Viterbo)

We made our base for a few days in medieval Viterbo, fifty or so miles north of Rome. We not only wanted to visit the city but we wanted to be near both Bomarzo and Bagnaia—Bomarzo, with its slightly mad, gargantuan statues carved out of huge boulders and its partially troglodytic village on the cliffs above, and Bagnaia, the site of the princely Villa Lante and its gardens reflecting the elegant side of the Renaissance world. Not knowing what we would find in the way of restaurants at Bomarzo, we planned to picnic among the monstrous statues scattered under the trees, and so we went shopping early in the morning for panino, thinly sliced ham, cheese, olives, wine, and cookies. As is the custom, we gathered our supplies as we walked from store to store.

These oval, double cookies are buttery and lemon-flavored. They are put together with a thick apricot jam, and the tops are well covered with toasted pine nuts. They were substantial enough for our picnic, and they are also ideal at the end of a hearty dinner to nibble with espresso coffee or a sweet white wine.

11-x-17-inch baking pan
Oval cookie cutter, 1¾ x 3 inches
Makes 18 to 20 single cookies or 9 to 10 double cookies

Basic Butter Cookie dough, page 146, adding 1 teaspoon
lemon juice and ¾ teaspoon lemon extract
4 tablespoons pine nuts
10 tablespoons apricot jam
1 tablespoon dark rum
Confectioners' sugar (optional)

1. Butter the baking pan and set it aside.

2. Make the butter cookie dough, adding the lemon juice and lemon extract (as flavoring) to the butter-sugar mixture. Add only 1 tablespoon of the beaten egg in the original recipe because of the extra liquid of the lemon juice. Chill the dough, following the recipe directions.

3. While the dough is chilling, toast the pine nuts in a small baking pan in a 350° oven until light tan, about 10 minutes. Take care—they burn easily. Leave the oven on because the cookies are baked in a preheated 350° oven.

4. Roll out the dough between sheets of floured wax paper to an 8½-x-11-inch rectangle approximately ³⁄₁₆ inch thick. Cut out an even number of cookies and, with a broad cake turner, place them on the buttered baking pan. Gather up the leftover scraps and reroll and cut out the dough again, adding the cookies to the baking pan. You should have 18 to 20 cookies in all.

5. Brush the top surface of all the cookies with the remaining beaten egg. Cover the surface of half the cookies with the toasted pine nuts, slightly pressing them into the dough. Put the baking pan into the preheated oven for 12 minutes. When the cookies are done, transfer the baking pan to a preheated broiler and brown the tops.

6. Remove the cookies to cake racks to cool. While they are cooling, make the filling.

7. Place the jam in a small saucepan, stir in the rum, and put the pan over moderate heat. Bring to a boil and cook for 4 or 5 minutes, stirring constantly.

8. Remove from the heat and strain through a sieve into a

small bowl. Allow the jam to cool; you may have to place it in the refrigerator until it thickens.

9. Turn the plain cookies over and spread the flat bottom sides with the apricot jam. Press the flat bottom sides of the pine nut–covered cookies over the jam and gently press the 2 cookies together. Store in an airtight container. The cookies can be dusted with confectioners' sugar, if desired, just before serving.

Pizzelle

In southern Italy, from Naples on one coast to Bari on the other, crisp wafers impressed with a raised design are made in a round form that is held over either a gas or electric burner (probably originally over wood or charcoal). Rolled pizzelle are the forerunners of the commercial ice-cream cone. They are so crisp and flavorful that they can be eaten plain as a flat wafer or cut into quarters and the points stuck into a serving of ice cream. Sweet fillings can be squeezed into cone shapes with a pastry bag or spooned in with a long-handled iced-tea spoon.

Our iron is a two-sided aluminum disk about five inches across with long metal and wooden handles. There are several styles of designs and even electric ones that make two pizzelle at a time.

Iron for making pizzelle (see above)
Makes 10 pizzelle wafers

> *4 tablespoons unsalted butter*
> *½ cup plus 1 tablespoon flour*
> *½ rounded teaspoon baking powder*
> *1 egg*
> *¼ cup sugar*
> *1 teaspoon vanilla extract*
> *¼ teaspoon lemon extract*

1. Melt 3 tablespoons of butter in a small pan and set aside to cool a bit.

2. Sift the flour and baking powder together into a small bowl and set aside.

3. Beat the egg in a mixing bowl and gradually add the sugar, beating until light-colored and fluffy. Beat in the vanilla and lemon extracts. Add the melted butter in a thin stream, beating all the while.

4. Put the iron on a stove burner over low heat. Put the remaining 1 tablespoon of butter in the small pan to melt over low heat.

5. Add about ⅓ of the sifted flour to the egg-sugar mixture and fold in. Add the next ⅓ and fold in and then add the last of the flour. This will be a rather stiff dough.

6. Turn the iron over while you are mixing the flour. When the mixing is complete, check the iron for heat: If a drop of water sizzles on the open iron, make the first pizzelle as a test.

7. Brush both sides of the iron with the melted butter. Add a slightly heaping tablespoon of dough ¾ of the way to the back hinge of the iron, forming it quickly into a crosswise oblong roll. Close the iron slowly to push the dough backward and forward evenly and squeeze the iron shut, cutting off any batter that shows along the edges. Cook for 30 seconds *only,* then turn the iron over and cook for 30 seconds *only.* Take the iron off the heat, open it, and with the flat side of a table knife lift out the soft wafer onto a plate. The wafer will be golden brown and limp but will crisp up quickly. Depending on the color of this first pizzelle, either lower or raise the heat of the burner.

8. Repeat brushing both sides of the iron with melted butter and continue until all the dough is used. The wafers will stay crisp for 3 or 4 days in a covered container or closed plastic bag, with no need to refrigerate.

VARIATIONS

Rounds can be sandwiched together with whipped cream that is mixed with chopped, sweetened berries or fruit; apple slices cooked in butter and brown sugar; ice cream; chocolate mousse; or whipped cream and toasted nuts. The plain wafer rounds are very good served with coffee or sweet white wine, with ice cream, and especially with Lemon Ice (page 269).

Filled Pizzelle Cones:

To make the cones, remove the wafers from the iron onto a clean, folded dish towel. Quickly position a metal cone or small wire whisk at 1 side of the wafer. Curl the edge up onto the cone or wire whisk, lifting the towel and wafer together as you roll the wafer and the cone or wire whisk over. Let the wafer cool with the seam at the bottom. While it is cooling, make the next wafer, using the same mold for forming.

Pizzelle cones are filled with plain whipped cream, with whipped cream to which fruit or nuts have been added, or with ice cream. Chocolate or fruit and rum sauce can be spooned over the filled cones. Serve the cones crisp on the first day of making them, or better still, put them into a plastic bag for 3 days at room temperature. After 3 days the cones will lose just enough crispness so they can be eaten with a fork without shattering into pieces and will blend with a soft filling.

Strawberries and Whipped Cream:

Proportion the strawberries and whipped cream to suit your own taste. Thinly slice the strawberries into a bowl, sprinkling each layer with light corn syrup and sugar. Allow to stand for 1 hour. Whip the heavy cream, sweeten it slightly with sugar, and flavor it with 2 or 3 drops of almond extract. Lightly toss together the strawberries, juice, and whipped cream. Place the cones on individual dessert plates and, with a teaspoon, fill them with the strawberry–whipped cream mixture, allowing some of the filling to spill out of the cone onto the dessert plate.

Other fruits can be used: peaches, nectarines, bananas, blueberries, stewed dried figs, and stewed dried apricots. Toast and chop almonds or hazelnuts and add to the whipped cream. Chestnuts in syrup and chestnut puree are also good choices to add to the whipped cream.

Chocolate Croccante Africano (Sorrento)

The ubiquitous, south-of-Naples pizzelle turned up in Sorrento, this time filled with a dark chocolate mousse. "Africano," said the proprietor of the small, rustic restaurant off the square. And very good it was, with its tantalizing contrast of crunchy brown outside and soft tangy chocolate inside.

Chocolate Mousse, page 121
6 Pizzelle, page 159, rolled into tubes with an outside
measurement of approximately 1¼ inches in diameter
Vanilla-Flavored Confectioners' Sugar, page 40

1. Prepare the chocolate mousse, then cool in the pan for 1 hour at room temperature. Do not refrigerate.

2. While the mousse is cooling, prepare the pizzelle.

3. Divide the cooled mousse into 6 equal portions. Fill each rolled tube with 1 portion of the mousse. Set aside until serving time. Dust each croccante with vanilla-flavored confectioners' sugar just before serving.

Shortbread Cookies (Brindisi)

In a pastry shop window in Brindisi, we saw small domed cookies covered with confectioners' sugar and with a clove stuck in the middle of each one. Yes, they were just like Greek courambiades. Of course we went into the shop to buy a dozen to have in the car for nibbling on our way north along the Adriatic.

Brindisi straddles the two worlds of West and East. The Appian Way—the highway of Imperial Rome—ended here, and two columns from the period still stand in the quay. Ships going to and from the eastern Mediterranean dock in Brindisi's harbor, so it was no surprise to find Greek cookies in this eastern Italian port.

These must be started a day in advance.

11-x-17-inch baking pan
Makes 24 cookies

> *8 tablespoons (1 stick) unsalted butter*
> *1 teaspoon solid vegetable shortening or lard*
> *1 teaspoon almond extract or Rose Essence Concentrated*
>   *(see* Note*)*
> *¾ cup flour*
> *¼ teaspoon baking powder*
> *2 teaspoons light cream or half-and-half*
> *¾ cup confectioners' sugar*
> *24 cloves*

1. The day before baking, cut the butter into slices and allow to stand in a bowl for 1 hour, then cream until fluffy. Add the solid vegetable shortening or lard and blend it in thoroughly. Stir in ½ teaspoon of almond extract or rose essence.

2. Mix together the flour and baking powder, and sift over the butter mixture, alternating with the cream or half-and-half. Mix well into a very soft dough, then cover the mixing bowl with clear plastic and place it in the refrigerator overnight so the dough will stiffen.

3. The next day, before taking the bowl out of the refrigerator, sift the confectioners' sugar into a bowl and sprinkle with the remaining ½ teaspoon of almond extract or rose essence, stirring with a fork to mix in the flavoring. Let stand for 15 to 20 minutes to dry.

4. Preheat the oven to 400°.

5. Cut a 12-x-18-inch-long piece of aluminum foil and place it on a flat surface, turning up ½ inch all around the edges. Put the flavored confectioners' sugar into a sieve and cover the surface of the foil with the sifted sugar to a depth of ⅛ inch. You"ll have sugar left over to be used later.

6. Butter the baking pan and take the dough out of the refrigerator.

7. Scoop out the dough with the large end of a melon scoop, the dough slightly rounded. Place the mounds of dough on the baking pan about 1 inch apart. Slightly smooth the surface of the mounds and stick a clove in the center of each one. When the pan is filled, place it in the preheated oven for 12 minutes or until the bottom of each cookie is brown; the tops will not be brown.

8. Remove the baking pan from the oven and immediately but *carefully* transfer the cookies to the sugared aluminum foil with a broad cake turner. Sift the remaining sugar over the tops of the cookies. Let them stand until cold; they will break if moved while they are still warm.

9. When cold, remove the cookies from the foil and place them on a cake rack. Scrape the sugar from the foil into the sifter. Place the cleaned foil under the cake rack and sift the sugar over

the cookies. Pack them away in an airtight container with wax paper between the layers. They are best if kept for a day.

10. Resift the remaining confectioners' sugar on the foil under the rack and put it into a plastic storage bag. Dust the sugar over the cookies just before serving.

Note: Rose Essence Concentrated is an oil-based rose flavoring imported from India; it is much stronger than rose water and has a truer flavor.

Tarts and Pies

The delight

of large Italian tarts and pies is the crunchy goodness of the dough. It is made to be eaten and enjoyed for its own sake, not merely a vessel for fillings. Tart Crust Pasta Frolla (page 170), lemon-flavored, is crisp. Hazelnut Pasta Frolla (page 172) is a splendid foil for fruit or custard fillings. The Cake/Tart Crust (page 39) is a thicker, cakelike crust that adds a delicate balance of textures and flavor. And Puff Pastry (page 174) is light and airy.

Tart fillings vary—from the lavish use of fruits in northern and middle Italy, where orchards flourish, to ricotta in the south. Fillings and crust are combined as open tarts or as latticework-topped fillings. The ricotta mixtures with solid top coverings are referred to as pies.

Don't eat your heart out for a nonmelting jelly covering on a fruit tart, one that lasts more than a day before turning runny and disappearing into the fruit. Those shiny, solid jelly tops on bakery tarts that last two or three days are formed from "boughten" commercial jelly that is just about indestructible, to which the baker adds a little apricot or currant jelly for flavor and color. In Italy we used a product called Tortagel, a grainy powder that is sold in thirteen-gram packets (just enough to cover a tart). It is available both clear and red; mixed with water, wine, or fruit syrup, plus sugar, it is brought to a boil, then poured over the fruit tart, which is then placed in the refrigerator until the gel stiffens. Lacking this, we've listed jam and jelly glazes.

In making a precooked large or small tart shell, there is no need to use dried beans, rice, or metal pellets to weight the dough during baking. Just make sure the top edge of the dough is "hooked" over the outside rim of the pan and the bottom and sides are well pricked with a fork before placing the pan in the oven. After five minutes of baking, open the oven door and again prick the dough with a fork, breaking any bubbles that have formed; make a second check five minutes later and prick any new bubbles. Finish baking the pastry shell.

Tart Crust
Pasta Frolla

Pasta frolla, literally tender paste, sweet and flavored, is the standard crust for most tarts, tartlets, pies, some filled cookies, and turnovers. It is a crust that is meant to be enjoyed along with the filling, as an essential part of an elegantly thin tart.

6½- to 8-inch quiche pan with removable bottom

> *4²/₃ tablespoons unsalted butter*
> *1 egg*
> *Zest of ½ thick-skinned lemon*
> *1 cup less 2 tablespoons flour*
> *Pinch of salt*
> *4²/₃ tablespoons sugar*

1. Remove butter from refrigerator half an hour before using. Cut the butter into slices and then into quarters on a piece of wax paper. Allow to soften to room temperature.
2. Beat the egg in a small bowl and set it aside.
3. Grate the lemon zest onto a small plate, cover with plastic wrap, and set aside.
4. When the butter is soft, sift the flour and salt into a cone (Italians use the word "volcano," which is much more expressive) on a dinner plate or small platter, or directly onto the work surface. (Using the plate may make it easier to keep the ingredients from spreading all over the work surface.) Make a well in the center of

the cone and add the sugar and lemon zest. Mix and re-form the cone, then make another well. Add the softened butter and top it with 3 tablespoons of the beaten egg. Work quickly, using fingertips, until all the ingredients are blended, but do not overwork the dough.

5. Form the dough into a 4-inch-wide flattened round. Wrap in wax paper or clear plastic wrap and put in the refrigerator (not the freezer) for 45 minutes. *Never allow Pasta Frolla to remain in the refrigerator more than 1 hour, or it may become too stiff to roll.*

6. Butter the quiche pan.

7. Preheat the oven to 375°.

8. Remove the dough from the refrigerator and roll out into a 9½-inch circle between 2 sheets of floured wax paper. Mark a circle on the top sheet with a knife point drawn around the edge of the quiche pan to serve as a guide, then roll out the additional width. Dust the wax paper with more flour as needed to keep the dough from sticking. When finished, carefully lift off the top sheet of wax paper, roll the dough onto the rolling pin, and transfer it to the pan, dough side down. Remove the other sheet of wax paper.

9. Press the dough gently into place. The excess dough, draped over the edge of the pan, may split here and there along the edge. Cut the excess dough to ¾ inch wide, then fold it over the inside edge, doubling and reinforcing the sides. Bring the dough slightly over the metal edge to hold the dough in place as it bakes. Make diagonal lines on the top rim of dough, using the back of a knife blade.

10. Brush the inside of the shell with leftover beaten egg and prick the sides and bottom with a fork. Put the pan on the middle rack of the oven. In 5 minutes check the shell and prick any bubbles with a fork; repeat in another 5 minutes. Press the side with the back of a teaspoon if it is slipping down. If the shell will contain a filling to be baked it should be only partially cooked—bake the crust 2 or 3 minutes more. If the shell is to be filled with a filling that does not require baking, bake the crust 10 to 15 minutes more. While the shell is still hot, loosen the edge with the point of a small knife to make it easier to remove it from the metal pan when the

tart is ready to serve. If the shell is to be used for a baked filling, do not loosen the edge until the tart has been completely baked.

11. All tarts are cooled in their pans and removed from the pans just before serving.

Note: There will be dough left over when using a 6- or 7-inch pan.

Hazelnut Pasta Frolla

This is a crisp and subtly flavored tart crust that is especially fine with fruits, both fresh and cooked. It is also the dough for one of the fabulous cookies of Lecce (see *Note*).

6½- to 8-inch quiche pan with removable bottom

> 4½ tablespoons unsalted butter
> 2 ounces Toasted Hazelnuts, page 49
> 5 tablespoons sugar
> Zest of 1 lemon
> ⅞ cup flour
> Pinch of salt
> 1 egg yolk

1. Butter the quiche pan and set it aside.

2. Cut the butter into small pieces and set aside on a plate to soften.

3. Put the toasted nuts in a food processor fitted with a steel blade, adding a little sugar from time to time (up to 3 tablespoons in all). Process until the nuts and sugar are finely ground. (Or use a Mouli nut grater attached to a table edge. Grind the hazelnuts onto a dinner plate, transfer to a small bowl, and smooth in the 3 tablespoons of sugar with the back of a large spoon.) Set aside.

4. Grate the lemon zest and set it aside.

5. Sift the flour into a cone shape on a large plate or platter,

then make a well in the center. Pour in the ground nuts, remaining 2 tablespoons of sugar, grated lemon zest, and salt. Mix together well, then form into a cone again and make another well in the center.

6. Add the small pieces of softened butter to the center of the cone and drop in the egg yolk. Mix together with the fingertips, incorporating all the dry ingredients. Form the dough into a ball, wrap it in clear plastic wrap or wax paper, and put in the refrigerator for 1 hour before using.

7. When the dough is chilled, remove from the refrigerator. Preheat the oven to 375°. Break off small pieces of dough and press them into the quiche pan with the fingertips to a thickness of ⅛ inch on the bottom and nearly ¼ inch on the side. Press the dough a little above and slightly over the edge of the pan to hold the dough in place as it bakes. With a fork prick the bottom in several places and all around the side.

8. Put the pan on the middle rack of the oven. In 5 minutes check the shell and prick any bubbles with a fork; repeat in another 5 minutes. Press the side with the back of a teaspoon if it is slipping down. If the shell will contain a filling to be baked, it should be only partially cooked—bake the crust 2 to 3 minutes more. If the shell is to be filled with a filling that does not require baking, then bake the crust 10 to 15 minutes more.

9. When the crust is done, remove it from the oven and place the pan on a cake rack to cool. Loosen the edge with a small knife point and cut away the overhanging dough. Do not remove from the pan until after the shell has been filled.

Note: There will be dough left over when making a 6½-inch tart. It can be used to make 7 or 8 small Hazelnut cookies, page 150.

Wherever Tart Crust (Pasta Frolla) is called for, you can substitute Hazelnut Pasta Frolla.

Puff Pastry
Pasta Sfogliata

The literal translation of *pasta sfogliata* is leaf pastry, as is the French name *feuilletage,* but in English it is known as *puff pastry.*

Making puff pastry is a sort of tour de force, like the graduation project of a student pastry chef. It is an all-day process because of the number of rolling-outs, foldings, and chillings of the dough. Unless one is going to use the dough the next day, it is best to freeze it to keep the butter layers stiff. For this reason we have come more and more to use commercial puff pastry, both here and in Italy where it is found in the frozen food section at supermarkets and butcher shops.

Pan sizes and shapes according to separate recipes
Makes about 1 pound of pastry

Enfolding dough:
1½ cups plus 2 tablespoons flour
1 teaspoon salt
4 tablespoons unsalted butter
1 egg yolk
½ cup cold water

Butter dough:
6 tablespoons flour
20 tablespoons (2½ sticks) unsalted butter

1. To make the enfolding dough, sift the flour and salt into a bowl. Cut in the butter with 2 knives until the mixture is like coarse meal. Beat the yolk in a small bowl, then beat in the cold water. Make a well in the center of the flour and pour in the egg-water mixture, blending the flour and liquid with a fork and then mixing it together with your fingertips. The dough should hold together and not be crumbly. Add a little more water if needed to make a

soft but not wet dough. Gather the dough into a ball, wrap it in floured wax paper or foil, and place it in the refrigerator for 30 minutes.

2. To make the butter dough, spread a sheet of wax paper over a pastry board. Place the flour in a fine sieve and dust about 1 tablespoon over the center of the paper. Cut the sticks of butter in half lengthwise and place over the flour. Dust the tops with flour and mash together with a fork. With a broad spatula, scrape and turn the butter over, adding more flour until all the flour has been incorporated into the butter. Blend it in with the heel of your hand. Work as quickly as possible so that the butter does not soften too much. Form it into a 4½-inch square, wrap it in wax paper or foil, and place it in the refrigerator to chill.

3. Remove the 2 dough packages from the refrigerator. Between 2 sheets of lightly floured wax paper, roll the enfolding dough into a 10-inch square. Remove the top sheet of wax paper and place the square of butter dough in the center of the rolled-out dough. Fold the corners of the dough over the butter square, slightly overlapping the edges of the triangles on top. Make a seal with a thin line of water between the overlapping edges, rolling the pin over the top to gently press the edges together so that the butter will not escape during the next rolling.

4. Lift up the square, lightly flour the wax paper underneath, replace the square, and flour its top. Cover with the second sheet of floured wax paper and carefully roll out the square into a 6½-x-13-inch rectangle. Do not roll the pin off the edges because this will squeeze the butter out from its dough envelope. Remove the wax paper from the top and brush off any excess flour from the dough. Fold over ⅓ of the dough, brush off the flour, then fold the other ⅓ on top, just like folding a sheet of letter paper. You will end up with a rectangle approximately 4⅜ x 6½ inches.

5. Swing the rectangle around so the open long edge of that top flap is at your right. Roll the dough again into a 6½-x-13-inch rectangle between the 2 sheets of floured wax paper. Remove the top sheet of wax paper, brush off the extra flour, and again fold the dough into thirds. Press 2 dimples into the top of the dough with

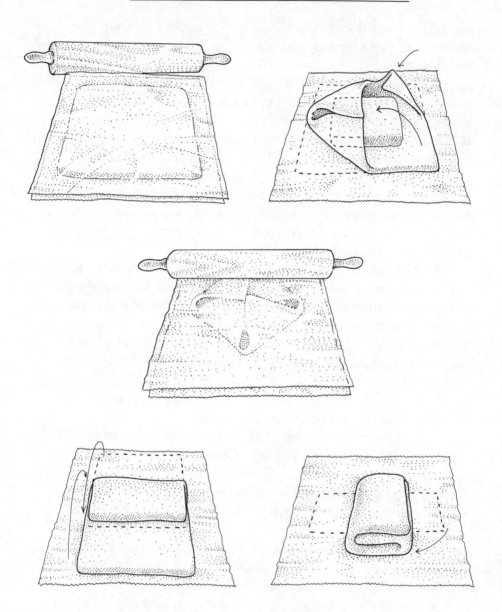

the knuckle of your index finger so that you will know you have made 2 "turns." You will be making 6 turns in all before incorporating the dough into the final recipe.

6. Wrap the dough in wax paper or foil, put it on a plate, and place it in the refrigerator for 1 hour.

7. Remove the dough from the refrigerator. Roll out the third and fourth turns, repeating the process in Steps 4 and 5. Press 4 dimples into the top of the dough. Wrap the dough in wax paper or foil and put it back into the refrigerator for 1 hour. If you are not going to use the dough right away, then wrap it in foil and freeze; the 4 dimples on top will remind you that 4 turns have been made. When ready to use the dough, defrost it in the refrigerator.

8. Whether using the dough right away or working with defrosted dough, repeat Steps 4 and 5 for the fifth and sixth turns, adding 6 dimples. Wrap and return the dough to the refrigerator for 1 hour before forming the dough for the final baking process.

Jelly Glazes

Fruit tarts are enhanced with a sparkling clear topping that adds its own flavor and texture to the fruit and the crisp crust. Here are four different recipes for glazes that are used on fruit tarts as well as for cake fillings, or as a thin spread between cake and icing to keep the icing moisture from being absorbed by the cake.

Use a well-flavored, good-quality jelly that is stiff in the jar. The jam should have body and flavor and contain chunks of fruit. Apricot butter is smooth and very thick, and also is a superior product to most apricot jams.

Apple or Currant Jelly Glaze

This is the simplest of all glazes since both jellies are very solid. For a 6-inch fruit tart, place 6 tablespoons of jelly in a small saucepan over very low heat. Let the jelly melt slowly, breaking up the chunks with a tablespoon. When just melted, remove the pan from the heat.

Spread about 2 tablespoons of melted jelly over the finished tart as it is removed from the oven. Return the tart to the oven for 3 minutes. Remove the tart from the oven and cool on a baking rack. When cool, remelt the jelly in the saucepan and spread over the cooled tart. Let the jelly set before serving.

For a 10- to 12-inch tart, use 12 tablespoons of jelly.

Apricot Jam or Apricot Butter Glaze

Both apricot jam and apricot butter are thicker than jelly and need added liquid during the melting process.

Put 8 tablespoons of apricot jam or butter in a small saucepan with either water, dark rum, or Bianco Cinzano in the following amounts: 2 teaspoons for the jam and 4 tablespoons for the butter because it is very stiff and solid. We prefer water, or water and rum, since the apricot flavor is very delicate and delicious, and sometimes pure rum or Cinzano tends to overpower this flavor.

Place the pan over low heat and stir the contents constantly so the mixture will not burn. When melted, remove from the heat, and, if using jam, press it through a fine sieve to remove the solid fibers. The apricot butter is a sieved product, so it is ready to use when melted.

Stiffened Glaze for Fresh Fruit Tarts

Often the glaze for a fresh fruit tart needs to be stiffer than for cooked fruit because the juice in fresh fruit tends to thin out the glaze.

For a 6½-inch tart of fresh fruit, melt 6 ounces of clear apple jelly in a small saucepan over low heat. While it is melting, sprinkle

2 teaspoons of plain gelatin over 1 tablespoon of rum or Amaretto liqueur in a small bowl or ramekin. When the gelatin has softened, put the bowl or ramekin in a pan of just boiled water (with the heat turned off under the pan) until the gelatin is liquid and clear. Add to the melted jelly and stir for 1 minute.

Remove the pan from the heat and brush the glaze over the top of the fresh fruit in the tart shell. Such fruits as strawberries often are brushed individually with glaze before being placed in the baked tart shell. Pour the rest of the glaze over the top of the fruit so that all the spaces between the pieces of fruit are filled and the top is a levelly-glazed surface (that is, if the fruit surface is level, such as sliced peaches, apricots, or small berries).

Place the tart in the refrigerator until the glaze hardens. Remove 30 minutes to 1 hour before serving to bring the tart to room temperature. This glaze will soften overnight, even in the refrigerator, since the fresh fruit juices dilute the jelly.

Lemon Jelly Glaze

This is a fresh-tasting glaze that adds a piquant flavor to the fruit in a tart or strip, and yet it does not change the color of the fruit since it is a clear glaze.

> *3 tablespoons water*
> *1½ teaspoons unflavored gelatin*
> *1 lemon*
> *6 tablespoons sugar*
> *¾ cup water*
> *1 tablespoon rum*

1. Measure 3 tablespoons of water into a small bowl and sprinkle the surface with the gelatin. Set aside to soften the gelatin.

2. Grate the lemon zest into a small bowl and cover with plastic wrap. Squeeze the lemon juice into a bowl.

3. Mix the sugar and the remaining ¾ cup of water together in a small stainless steel saucepan. Bring to a boil and boil for 5 minutes. Add the grated lemon zest and boil gently 5 minutes more.

4. Take the saucepan off the heat and stir in the lemon juice and rum. Strain the mixture into a bowl through a fine plastic sieve (a metal sieve might taint the lemon), pressing the liquid from the grated zest. Rinse the pot and return the liquid to the pot, placing it over low heat.

5. Add 1 or 2 tablespoons of the liquid to the softened gelatin and mix. Scrape the gelatin into the lemon liquid. Simmer until the gelatin is melted, approximately 1 minute. If foam rises to the surface, skim it off with a spoon. Remove from the heat and pour into a small bowl to cool.

6. The jelly should become semithick but not completely jellied. If not thick enough when almost ready to use, place it in the refrigerator to hasten thickening. If it is too stiff to spread evenly, then place the bowl in a pan of hot water and stir the jelly with a fork to break it up until the mixture is smooth.

7. It is best to put a a thin, even coat of glaze over the fruit, stiffen it in the refrigerator, and then add a second coat using the remainder of the lemon jelly.

Apple Strip (Verona)

After a morning of strolling along the automobile-free shopping streets of Verona, leading to the market in the Piazza delle Erbe, where we bought supplies (small plumlike loquats, red cherries, lettuce Brasiliana or iceberg lettuce, and fresh herbs), we picked an outdoor table in the warm sun at the Pizzeria Imperio/Tavola Calda in the Piazza Dei Signori. We ordered a lunch of spaghetti alla carbonara and a mixed salad that was really an antipasto over crisp, fresh greens. We planned our afternoon's exploration of the countryside as we watched the people crossing the square with a statue of Dante in the center.

We couldn't resist a rectangular slice of apple strip with a crisscrossed top crust and a thick, sharp lemon jelly over all.

10-x-15-x-½-inch baking pan

> *Tart Crust, page 170*
> *Lemon Jelly Glaze, page 179*
> *2 green apples, 2¾ to 3 inches in diameter*
> *Juice of ½ lemon (you can use ½ lemon whose zest was*
> *   grated for the Tart Crust)*
> *2 tablespoons sugar*
> *1 tablespoon cornstarch*
> *3 or 4 gratings of nutmeg*

1. Make the tart dough and form it into a 3-x-5-inch rectangle. Put it in the refrigerator for 45 minutes.

2. While the tart dough is in the refrigerator, make the lemon jelly glaze and set it aside to cool and thicken at room temperature. The glaze can be placed in the refrigerator for approximately 15 minutes just before it is brushed onto the cold apple strip.

3. Pare, cut in quarters, and core the apples. Cut in even-width thin slices (slightly less than ¼ inch thick). Put the sliced quarters on a dinner plate and sprinkle the exposed surfaces with lemon juice to keep them from turning brown.

4. Mix the sugar, cornstarch, and nutmeg together in a small bowl. Set aside.

5. Line the baking pan with aluminum foil and lightly butter the foil.

6. Preheat oven to 400°.

7. Remove the dough from the refrigerator and place ¾ of the rectangle between 2 floured sheets of wax paper on a pastry board. The other ¼ is reserved for the top strips. Roll the dough into a 6½-x-10-inch rectangle barely ¼ inch thick. During the

rolling, carefully lift up the wax paper to lightly reflour the dough and straighten the edges of the dough with the sides of the hands.

8. Carefully remove the top sheet of wax paper, dust flour on the dough, and roll it up on the rolling pin. Transfer the dough to the baking pan, wax paper side up. Remove the wax paper and lightly dust the dough with flour. With the point of a small knife, draw a shallow line 1 inch in from the 4 sides of the rectangle. This margin will be folded over the apple filling. Sprinkle ½ of the sugar-cornstarch mixture over the dough.

9. Cover part of the dough between the drawn lines with a double or triple row of overlapping apple slices down each long side, the curved sides of the apple slices facing the lines. Leave a center section of dough, the width of an apple slice, uncovered.

10. In the center space, arrange a row of tightly overlapping apple slices with the curved sides facing one short edge of the rectangle. Sprinkle the surface of the apple slices with the rest of the sugar-cornstarch mixture.

11. Turn the 1-inch margin of dough over the first row of apples, pinching the corners and smoothing any cracks that develop along the turned edge. Do not press the margin tightly against the apples but leave a little space between the margin of dough and the apples to contain the juice.

12. Put the apple strip in the refrigerator while rolling out the reserved ¼ piece of dough for the top strips. Roll the dough into a 3¾-x-5¼-inch rectangle between well floured sheets of wax paper. With the point of a paring knife, divide the dough lengthwise into 6 strips.

13. Remove the pan from the refrigerator. Brush all edges of the dough with beaten egg (left over from making the tart dough). With a wide spatula, carefully lift up 1 dough strip at a time and put in place, forming 3 X's down the length of the apple strip. Hold the ends in place on the dough margin with brushed-on egg and also brush the tops of the X's, adding a second coat of egg to the dough margin. Wipe away any flour or egg that falls on the aluminum foil.

14. Put the apple strip into the oven for 10 minutes, then

turn down the temperature to 375° for 30 minutes more. When done, remove from the oven, allow to cool on the pan for 15 minutes, then transfer to a baking rack to finish cooling. When cold, place in the refrigerator to chill a bit before heavily brushing the thickened lemon jelly over the apples and into all the hollows. Some jelly will flow over part of the X strips. Return the apple strip to the refrigerator to stiffen the jelly. Add extra jelly if the first coat sinks completely into the apples. Remove from the refrigerator about 1 hour before serving so the strip will not be too cold.

Apricot Tart I (Arcugnano)

On a day when we were driving in the countryside south of Vicenza looking for Palladian and other villas to photograph, we passed a low farmhouselike building halfway down the hill to Villa

Pasini. At the road's edge we saw a sign, Trattoria allo Storione, so we drove into the parking area that faced the broad, small-paned, curved-top windows on the lower floor. Inside was a large sun-filled dining room with appetizing odors emanating from the stainless steel hot carts being wheeled from table to table. The pasta was freshly cooked and surrounded by metal bowls of sauce from which one picked a combination. Another cart held a choice of several meats including guinea hen. There were vegetable and salad choices plus polenta. For dessert, both of us picked a golden apricot tart from the display shelves at the entrance to the dining room.

It was a simple tart with a glorious contrast of flavors and textures: crisp, lemon-flavored crust and not overly sweet apricots topped with a glaze of rum-flavored apricot jam.

6½-inch quiche pan with removable bottom
Serves 4 or 5

> *Tart Crust, page 170*
> *8 to 10 fresh ripe apricots*
> *1½ teaspoons cornstarch*
> *3 tablespoons sugar*
> *4 tablespoons apricot jam*
> *1 teaspoon dark rum*

1. Follow directions for making and baking a partially cooked 6½-inch tart crust shell. Remove the shell from the oven and allow to cool for 5 to 10 minutes.

2. While the pastry shell is baking and cooling, wash and dry the apricots. Cut the apricots in half and remove the pits, but do not remove the skins.

3. Mix the cornstarch and 1 tablespoon of sugar together in a small bowl. When the pastry shell has partially cooled, sprinkle the cornstarch-sugar mixture over the inside bottom of the pastry shell. Place the apricot halves on top, side by side, cut side down, forming a tight circle against the wall of the shell. Fill the center with a closely packed circle of halves. Brush the tops of the apricots with

plain water, then sprinkle them with the remaining 2 tablespoons of sugar. Return the apricot-filled shell to the oven and bake for 35 to 40 minutes; the tops of the apricots will be slightly browned in patches.

4. While the tart is baking, spoon the apricot jam into a small saucepan and add the rum. Place the saucepan over low heat until the jam has melted. Remove from the heat and force the jam through a strainer; discard the solids left in the strainer. Put the strained jam back into the saucepan and, just before the tart is done, bring the glaze to a gentle boil for 1 or 2 minutes, stirring to prevent the jam from burning.

5. Remove the tart from the oven when done. Brush the hot apricot glaze generously over the fruit and over the edge of the crust; use up all the glaze, filling in the spaces between the fruit. Return the tart to the oven for 3 or 4 minutes to set the glaze.

6. Take the tart out of the oven and place it on a baking rack to cool. Immediately loosen the top edge of the crust with the point of a small paring knife, to prevent it from sticking to the pan. When the tart has cooled to room temperature, remove the sides of the pan. The tart is left on the metal bottom of the pan and placed on a serving plate.

Apricot Tart II (Vicenza)

Wandering through Vicenza's streets after absorbing the beauty of Palladio's sixteenth-century Teatro Olimpico, we found the city's buildings reminiscent of the teatro's permanent stage set. When passing a pasticceria we were reminded that we live in this century and had no dinner dessert at home. We carefully chose a golden pureed apricot tart that was as good to eat as it was satisfying to look at.

The thick puree of cooked dried apricots was covered with a pasta frolla latticework and baked in a shallow pasta frolla shell.

6½-inch quiche pan with removable bottom
Serves 4

> Tart Crust, page 170
> 25 dried apricots
> ½ cup sugar
> 1½ teaspoons dark rum

1. Make the tart dough and put it into the refrigerator for 45 minutes. While the dough is chilling, make the apricot filling.

2. Wash the apricots and put them in a small saucepan with ¼ cup of the sugar. Barely cover with water, bring to a boil, then simmer until the fruit is tender but not mushy, about 30 to 40 minutes. Turn off the heat, put a cover on the pan, and allow the fruit to cool in the liquid.

3. Pour the fruit and liquid into a fine mesh sieve placed over a bowl. Reserve the liquid. Cut each apricot in half and put into a food processor fitted with a steel blade. Puree with 2 tablespoons of the apricot liquid.

4. Scrape the puree into a bowl, adding 4 more tablespoons of apricot juice, and up to 4 tablespoons of the remaining sugar, or to taste, and the dark rum. Mix well and set aside.

5. Remove the dough from the refrigerator and set aside ⅓ of the dough for the lattice top. Roll out the remaining dough and line the buttered pan. Add a strip around the side to reinforce the side wall so that the tart can be easily unmolded from the pan when cooled.

6. Fill the crust with the apricot puree, smoothing to a level top. Preheat the oven to 375°.

7. Roll the reserved dough into a strip 4 or 5 inches wide and about 8 inches long. Cut into ⅜-inch-wide strips (10 strips) with a knife or pastry wheel. Separate each strip with a long narrow spatula and pinch each strip lengthwise so it is slightly triangular in shape. Lay 5 strips across the top of the apricot puree, lifting each strip with the narrow spatula (the dough is so short that the strips will break if moved by hand). Lay the remaining strips across the

first set to form a latticework. Cut off the excess dough around the edge and press the ends against the side walls of the pastry shell. Add a decoration of small balls or pinchings of dough at each strip crossing and at each joining around the outside wall.

8. Place the tart in the oven for 1 hour or until the crust is brown. Remove from the oven to a cake rack and loosen around the edge with the point of a small knife. Allow the tart to cool. When cool, remove from the pan and place on the rack until serving time.

Chocolate Mousse Tart (Perugia)

After driving up the road to Perugia on top of its isolated hill, we spent a drizzly morning climbing the streets of this solidly built town of Etruscan, Roman, and medieval buildings, all very exciting in spite of the weather. At noontime, knowing that the buildings would be closed, we found a no-nonsense trattoria and warmed ourselves first with hot soup and then with satisfying pasta. Since Perugia is also linked to chocolate, we chose a dessert that was a pure confection of chocolate cum chocolate.

This seductive sweet combines a crisp pasta frolla shell and a rich, smooth chocolate mousse, topped by a thin cake wafer glazed with unsweetened chocolate.

8-inch quiche pan with removable bottom (for Tart Crust)
8-inch cake pan (for Thin Cake Layer)
Serves 6 to 8

> Tart Crust, page 170, adding ½ to ¾ teaspoon almond
>   extract, or to taste
> Thin Cake Layer, page 38
> Chocolate Mousse, page 121; double the recipe
> ½ cup heavy cream
> Hard Chocolate Glaze, page 43

1. Make the tart dough, adding the almond extract in addition to the lemon zest, and then chill it.

2. While the tart dough is chilling, make and bake an 8-inch thin cake layer. The batter should not be more than ¼ inch thick, if that. When the layer is baked, set it aside to cool on a cake rack.

3. Remove the chilled tart dough from the refrigerator, roll it out to line the 8-inch quiche pan, and bake for the longer time specified for an unbaked filling. When done, remove from the oven and cool on a cake rack.

4. While the tart shell is baking and cooling, make a double quantity of chocolate mousse. Cool it at room temperature for 1 hour.

5. When the chocolate mousse is cool, whip the heavy cream and fold it into the mousse, blending to an even color. Place in the refrigerator.

6. Make the chocolate glaze. Allow it to cool slightly or until it just begins to thicken.

To Assemble:

1. Put the thin layer on a cake rack placed over a sheet of wax paper. Trim the edge if necessary to fit inside the pastry shell. Pour the chocolate glaze over the top of the thin layer and put it in the refrigerator to harden the glaze.

2. Fill the tart shell with the chocolate mousse, allowing enough space at the top for the thin cake layer. Remove the cake layer from the refrigerator and place it on top of the mousse filling.

3. Return the tart to the refrigerator until 20 minutes before serving.

Coconut Custard Tart (Ferrara)

On a warm June day, when Ferrara's sprawling castle and unshaded squares baked in the noontime sun, we sought the elegant awning-shaded outdoor tables of a small restaurant that looked out on a narrow tree-covered park off the big square. After a leisurely lunch of cool salads, we ended with a smooth coconut custard tart. The crisp pasta frolla shell was filled with a strongly flavored vanilla egg custard, and the top was lightly covered with very thin "angel hair" strings of coconut that had been toasted under the broiler.

Coconut adds a touch of the exotic to an Italian summer. We remember the coconut stands in Venice—the slices speared on metal points with cool water running over them, and the musical call of "cocobella" by the vendor, walking along the Adriatic beach of Igea Marina with his water-filled pail of coconut slices swinging from one hand.

6½- to 7-inch quiche pan with removable bottom
Serves 4 or 5

> *Tart Crust, page 170*
> *Egg Custard, page 237; or Time-Saver Custard, page 240,*
> *   double the recipe*
> *Apricot Jam or Butter Glaze, page 178*
> *Shredded coconut*

1. Make and bake the tart crust following the recipe directions for an unbaked filling. When baked, cool the shell on a cake rack.
2. While the shell is baking and cooling, make the custard. Pour it into a bowl and cover the surface with a circle of wax paper or clear plastic wrap to prevent a skin from forming. Allow to cool.
3. Make the apricot jam or butter glaze. Brush it over the inside of the cooled pastry shell to keep it crisp.
4. Spoon the cooked cooled custard into the shell and smooth the top. Lightly sprinkle the shredded coconut over the top. Place the tart under a preheated broiler and brown the coconut. Remove from the broiler and cool on a cake rack. Place the tart in the refrigerator until 30 minutes before serving.

Custard and Mixed Fruit Tart (Ravenna)

At La Gardela Ristorante in Ravenna, one of us gorged on crisp profiteroles filled with smooth vanilla-flavored custard and covered with a super-thick chocolate sauce served from a silver tray, while the other chose a wedge cut from a sparkling, springlike tart with fruits and custard nicely balanced against a crisp cakelike crust.

The delectable crust was filled with smooth egg custard, topped with circles of three fruits: plump cooked dried apricots, wedges of pineapple slices, and sliced strawberries, all covered with an apricot jam glaze.

8-x-1-inch raised center flan pan ("Mary Ann")
Serves 6

> *12 small dried apricot halves or attached wholes*
> *Sugar*
> *Cake/Tart Crust, page 39*
> *Egg Custard, page 237; or Time-Saver Custard, page 240,*
> *   double the recipe*
> *Apricot Jam Glaze, page 178*
> *1 slice canned pineapple*
> *5 medium strawberries*

1. Cook 12 dried apricots in enough water to cover, adding sugar to taste. (Some dried apricots are definite halves while others are whole apricots with slits where the pit has been removed; leave these whole and treat them as halves.) When cooked, 30 to 45 minutes, depending on their size and thickness, drain the apricots in a small mesh sieve. Let them cool in the sieve suspended over a small bowl to drain. You can always find a good use for the tasty apricot juice. When cool, place the apricots on a plate covered with paper towels to absorb the moisture and put in the refrigerator to chill.

2. Butter the flan pan. Fit a circle of wax paper on the raised center of the pan; butter this and dust the whole pan with flour.

3. Preheat the oven to 350°.

4. Make the cake/pie crust and spoon it into the pan to ¼ inch from the top rim, leveling off the surface. Bake for 25 minutes, or until a thin skewer inserted in the outside edge (the thickest part) and into the center comes out clean. Remove the pan from the oven and place it on a cake rack. Loosen the scalloped edge with the point of a small knife and turn the cake out onto the rack. Remove the wax paper from the center section and allow the cake to cool, hollow side up.

5. While the cake is baking, make the custard. Spoon the prepared custard into a bowl, cover the top with a circle of wax paper to prevent a skin from forming, and place in the refrigerator to cool.

6. Make the apricot jam glaze and let it cool and thicken a bit.

7. Cut the slice of canned pineapple into 6 wedges; trim off the narrow ends so the wedges are 1¼ inches long. Drain the wedges on paper towels and place in the refrigerator to chill.

8. Wash and hull the strawberries. Remove a thin slice on opposite sides of each of 4 strawberries, just enough to flatten the 2 sides. Cut each strawberry into 3 lengthwise slices; the remaining strawberry is left whole.

To Assemble:

1. Remove the custard from the refrigerator and fill the hollow in the crust almost to the top edge, smoothing the surface with a plastic or rubber spatula.

2. Place the apricots close together around the outside edge of the custard. Make a circle of the 6 pineapple wedges, with the broad edges just touching the apricots. Circle the strawberry slices into a double-row rosette in the center, with the outer layer overlapping the narrow ends of the pineapple wedges.

3. Dip the whole strawberry into the apricot glaze and set it aside. Cover the rest of the fruit with the glaze, then stand the single strawberry upright in the center of the tart. Place the tart in the refrigerator until 30 minutes before serving.

Flaky Apple Roll (Adriatic)

Along the Italian Adriatic Sea coast all the way down to the "heel" and across to the tip of the "toe," puff pastry is a favorite "wrap" for fruits, nuts and chocolate, ricotta cheese and candied fruit; the pastries are either baked or fried in oil. This type of sweet drifted from Greece, Turkey, and North Africa long ago and was adopted by those living on the opposite coast. Sometimes the pastry is the standard butter-flaky puff pastry; other times it is thin, layered filo sheets with melted butter brushed in between each sheet. Both doughs are available here ready-made, as they are in Italy, in the supermarket's frozen pastry section. Puff pastry or filo made from scratch is a long process, and the frozen variety is very good.

3-x-17-x-2-inch half round French bread pan
10-inch-long apple roll
Serves 4

> *3 green apples, 2³/₄ to 3 inches in diameter*
> *¹/₂ cup white wine*
> *2 tablespoons dark honey*
> *¹/₈ teaspoon powdered cinnamon*
> *3 tablespoons sugar*
> *³/₄ teaspoon gelatin*
> *2¹/₂ teaspoons cold water*
> *Puff Pastry, page 174, or a frozen commercial sheet 9 x 10 inches*
> *1 egg*

1. Peel, quarter, and core the apples. Cut each quarter into 3 slices and each slice into 3 pieces.
2. Put the pieces in a small saucepan, add the white wine, honey, powdered cinnamon, and sugar. Bring to a boil, then sim-

mer until the apples are soft but still hold their shape, 3 or 4 minutes. Remove the pan from the heat and pour the contents into a sieve placed over a bowl. Shake the sieve slightly to drain the apples, then place it on a plate with the apples still in the sieve to continue draining.

3. Soften the gelatin in 1½ teaspoons of cold water.

4. Measure the apple juice; if necessary, return it to the pan and lightly boil it to reduce to ⅓ cup. Watch the pan constantly so the liquid does not burn. When reduced, add 2 tablespoons of the hot liquid to the softened gelatin, stir, then return the mixture to the pan. Stir until the gelatin is completely melted and incorporated into the hot syrup.

5. Transfer the apple pieces from the sieve to a small bowl. Pour the hot liquid over the apples and stir lightly with a fork. Place the bowl in the refrigerator to chill the apples and thicken the syrup.

6. While the apples are chilling, defrost the frozen sheet of puff pastry for 20 minutes. Roll out on a floured board into a 12-x-11-inch rectangle. Cut a 7-x-12-inch rectangle, two 2-inch-diameter circles, and a ¾-x-10-inch strip. The leftover dough can be refrozen for another use.

7. Beat the egg with the remaining 1 teaspoon of cold water in a small bowl.

8. Lay the large rectangle of pastry lengthwise in the open-ended French bread pan, near one open end. Overlap and fold about ¾ to 1 inch of pastry on each end, holding the folds together with brushed-on egg glaze, so you have an open-top trough closed at each end and a little over 10 inches long. Be sure that there are no splits or openings at each end; smooth all seams with the blade of a small knife.

9. Remove the apples from the refrigerator, stir them, and check for sweetness, adding more sugar if needed. Carefully spoon the apples into the pastry trough, making sure that you have enough pastry on each long side to cover the apples with a ¾-inch overlap at the top. Distribute the thickened juice over the apples, making your own decision as to how much to add. Bring the pastry

edges up over the apple filling. Brush the facing edges with egg glaze and smooth them together into a tight seal using the blade of a small knife. Press the tines of a fork the full length of the joined edge as a final seal.

10. Preheat the oven to 375°.

11. To both seal and keep the cylindrical form, brush the outside of each folded and sealed end of the apple roll with egg glaze and brush 1 side of each round of pastry with the egg glaze. Put a round at each end, with the glazed sides pressed together. Seal the edges by smoothing them with the flat blade of a small knife, then press the tines of a fork all around the circle as a final sealing.

12. Brush the outside of the apple roll and the ends with the egg glaze. Twist and pull the ¾-inch strip of pastry to the length of the roll. Place it along the center top of the roll. Brush with the egg glaze to hold it in place and to color it in baking. Prick the top of the roll in 4 places to let out steam.

13. Put the pan into the preheated oven and bake for 30 to 35 minutes. If the top is not brown enough, place the pan under the broiler for a few seconds; watch it carefully so that the roll does not burn.

14. Place the pan on a cake rack and allow the apple roll to cool for 10 to 15 minutes, or until it has stiffened and feels luke-warm to the touch. Slide the roll carefully out of the pan and onto the cake rack to continue cooling. If any juice has leaked out be-tween the end of the apple roll and the open end of the pan, scrape it away before sliding the roll out of the pan.

15. Just before serving, if the apple roll has cooled completely, reheat it to crisp the pastry and slightly warm the filling. Serve, cut in 2½- to 3-inch-wide slices, either plain or with a dollop of sweet-ened, vanilla-flavored whipped cream.

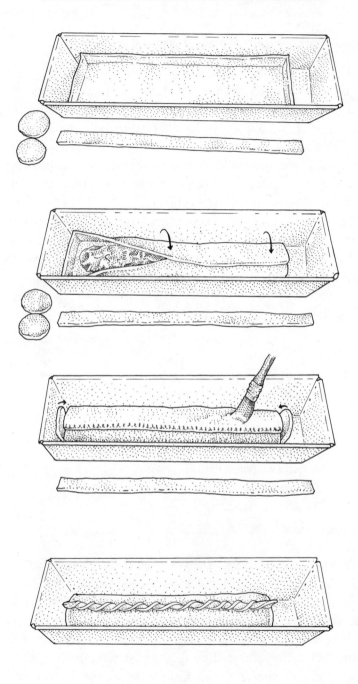

Flower-Patterned Apple Tart (Milan)

For most tourists the industrial city of Milan centers around the railroad station, the airport, and the circling autostradas that spin off the cars to all parts of Italy. For those who stop in the city it is a visit to the cathedral and the museums. But for the residents there are also the local food stores, salumerias, and pasticcerias. It was in one of the pasticcerias that we bought an apple tart that was beautiful to look at and sweet to the taste.

The abstract rose design of this apple tart is formed by overlapping circles of apple slices, their scalloped, curved edges facing the rim of pastry. A shimmering clear apple jelly, stained a light red in the center, covers this flower pattern of apple slices.

6½-inch quiche pan with removable bottom
Serves 4

> *Tart Crust, page 170*
> *Juice of ½ lemon (you can use the*
>   *½ lemon whose zest was grated for the Tart Crust)*
> *4 tablespoons sugar*
> *1 teaspoon cornstarch*
> *⅛ teaspoon powdered cinnamon*
> *3 green apples, 2½ to 3 inches in diameter*
> *6 tablespoons clear apple jelly*
> *Red food coloring*

1. Make and bake a partially cooked 6½-inch tart shell.
2. Squeeze the lemon half and set aside the juice.
3. While the tart shell is partially baking in the oven, prepare the apple filling. Mix together 2 tablespoons of sugar, cornstarch, and cinnamon in a small bowl. Peel, quarter, and core 1 apple, cut into small dice, and add to the sugar-cornstarch mixture.
4. Peel the other 2 apples. Gouge three ⅛-inch-deep grooves

with the point of the swivel peeler around the circumference of each apple: 1 each in the middle, near the top, and near the bottom of the apple. Cut the apples in quarters and remove the cores. Slice the apples into thin, even slices and sprinkle with lemon juice. The curved edge of each slice will be scalloped.

5. Scatter the apple dice mixture over the bottom of the shell, mounding it toward the middle.

6. Raise the oven heat to 400°.

7. To cover the chopped apples with the scalloped slices, start at the inside rim of the crust. Lay the first row of apple slices around the edge, scalloped sides against the crust. Repeat in overlapping circles with the scalloped edges always facing the outer edge of the pastry shell. Finish with 2 slices in the center forming a circle. Sprinkle the top slices with the remaining 2 tablespoons of sugar, or more if the apples are very sour. Put the tart in the oven for 35 to 50 minutes, or until the apples are cooked.

8. When the tart is almost baked, melt 2 heaping tablespoons of apple jelly over very low heat, stirring gently to prevent burning. When the tart is done, remove it from the oven and brush the melted jelly over the surface of the apples. Return the tart to the oven for 3 minutes, remove, and cool on a baking rack.

9. When the tart is completely cold, melt the remaining 4 tablespoons of apple jelly over low heat, stirring just enough to prevent burning; too much stirring will form bubbles. When the jelly is melted, scoop out 1 tablespoon into a small bowl and add the red coloring (about 5 dips of the end of a toothpick) to form a medium red color. Brush the other 3 tablespoons of jelly over the top of the apples, leaving a 2-inch circle in the center of the tart. Cover the center circle with the red jelly, blending it at the edges into the plain jelly. Put the tart into the refrigerator for 30 minutes to set the jelly. Serve the tart at room temperature.

Pear Tart (Vicenza)
Crostata di Pera

We lunched in a *tavola calda* ner Palladio's magnificent basilica in Vicenza, ordering their day's special, baccala and polenta, which was chalked up on a slate just inside the entrance. Since it was a chilly day, we sat in the rear near the pizza charcoal fireplace and watched the chef deftly putting pizzas together, flourishing his copper and brass oil container as he scattered bits of this and that over the thin crusts. For dessert we ordered a pear tart with a hazelnut-flour crust. Its crunchy goodness contrasted with the soft sweet pears.

6½-inch quiche pan with removable bottom
Serves 4

> *Hazelnut Pasta Frolla, page 172*
> *2 pears*
> *¼ cup white wine*
> *¼ cup water*
> *2 tablespoons sugar*
> *3 whole cloves*
> *Apple Jelly Glaze, page 177*
> *9 glacéed cherries*

1. Make the hazelnut pasta frolla dough following the recipe directions and chill.
2. Peel the pears, cut them into quarters, and core. Place the pear sections, curved sides down, in a stainless steel frying pan that is just large enough to hold them in 1 layer. Add the wine, water, sugar, and cloves. Bring to a boil and keep the liquid lightly boiling. Baste the pear sections and, after 2 or 3 minutes, turn them over with a large slotted spoon. Continue to cook 5 to 8 minutes more, basting the pears a few times and keeping the liquid at just

boiling temperature. When the prongs of a table fork easily pierce the pear sections, turn off the heat; the fruit should hold its shape and not be mushy. The liquid will have almost evaporated from the pan.

3. Remove the pear sections from the pan with a slotted spoon. Place them on a dinner plate, curved sides up, to drain and cool. When the sections are cool, transfer to a clean plate and put them in the refrigerator to chill.

4. Preheat the oven to 375°.

5. When the dough is ready, roll it out and line the quiche pan. Bake the shell in the oven for 25 minutes, then cool on a baking rack. Be sure to loosen the edge with the point of a small knife while the crust is still hot.

6. When the baked tart shell is cool and the pears are chilled, prepare the apple jelly glaze and brush part of the hot jelly over the inside of the tart shell.

7. Remove the pears from the refrigerator and pat them dry with paper towels. Brush the apple jelly on all sides of each pear section before putting it in place in the shell, narrow end at the center, thicker end against the side of the shell, and rounded side facing upward. If the pear sections are too long, trim pieces off the narrow ends.

8. Wash the cherries in hot water, dry, and put a cherry between pear sections at the crust edge and 1 in the center. Brush the rest of the jelly over the fruit and between the fruit sections. Put the tart in the refrigerator to set the jelly.

9. One hour before serving, remove the tart from the refrigerator, loosen the edge, and slip the tart out of the pan, leaving the bottom metal circle in place. Transfer the tart to a serving plate.

VARIATION

For an 8-inch quiche pan, use 3 pears and increase the other amounts by half. Serves 6.

Pignolo Tart (Mira)

Ristorante "Da Nalin" is just outside the center of Mira, across the Brenta Canal, facing the road that runs beside a narrow feeder canal. There are several restaurants scattered through this area, and while staying at the Villa Ducale we tried them all. They were all good, each having its own fish and dessert specialties.

Here, a thinly rolled pasta frolla is filled with cooked egg custard that has been subtly flavored with lemon zest or extract. The tart is baked until the top of the custard is a tawny brown; when cooled, the top is sprinkled with toasted pine nuts and heavily coated with vanilla-flavored confectioners' sugar.

6½- to 7-inch quiche pan with removable bottom
Serves 4 or 5

> *Tart Crust, page 170*
> *Egg Custard, page 237; or Time-Saver Custard, page 240,*
> *   double the recipe; substitute for the vanilla or almond*
> *   extract the grated zest of ½ lemon or ¾ teaspoon lemon*
> *   extract*
> *4 to 6 tablespoons pine nuts (pignoli) or blanched slivered*
> *   almonds*
> *Vanilla-Flavored Confectioners' Sugar, page 40*

1. Make and chill the tart crust dough, following the recipe directions.
2. While the dough is chilling, prepare the custard, substituting grated lemon zest or extract for the vanilla or almond extract. When cooked, remove the pan from the heat and transfer the custard to a bowl. Cover the top of the custard with wax paper to prevent a skin from forming.
3. Butter the quiche pan and set it aside.
4. Preheat the oven to 350°. Roll out the chilled tart dough

and line the quiche pan, adding an extra strip of dough around the side for reinforcement. Crimp the top edge with your fingers.

5. Fill the shell with the custard and smooth the top. Put the tart in the oven and bake for 35 to 40 minutes, or until the top of the custard is a toasty brown. If the top is not well browned, put the tart under a preheated broiler, but watch carefully so it does not burn.

6. Remove the tart from the oven and cool on a cake rack. While it is still hot, loosen the edge with the sharp point of a small knife but leave the tart in the pan until cold.

7. Spread the nuts on a small baking pan and brown them in the oven, turning the nuts over once or twice so they will be evenly tan. (This can be done while the tart is baking or after the tart is out of the oven.) Remove the nuts from the oven and pour them into a small bowl to cool.

8. If serving time is several hours away, store the tart in the refrigerator until 1 hour before serving. At that time, remove the tart from the pan and return the tart, with the circle of metal on the bottom, to a cake rack placed over a sheet of wax paper. Sprinkle the nuts over the custard and dust the top heavily with vanilla-flavored confectioners' sugar. Carefully transfer the tart to a serving platter; the metal disk can be left on the bottom or removed.

Attention: When serving, some nuts will roll off the top—just as they did in Mira!

Ricotta Cheese Pie (Palermo)

In Palermo one night we found a restaurant facing a small interior square and well away from the tourist restaurants. It was well lighted, with a long help-yourself antipasto table up front, and the lively dining room in back was popular with young professionals.

Here we had a ricotta pie about one and one-half inches high, full of bits of chocolate, citron, and glazed cherries. The broad strips of latticed dough on top were brown and crunchy.

We had often been put off from making a Sicilian ricotta pie by those recipes that called for a tablespoon or two of chocolate chips and the same of mixed candied fruit for a ten- or twelve-inch pie; it just didn't seem worthwhile. But now we found the answer: Someone who had never eaten the real pie had mistranslated an Italian recipe, thinking that a tablespoon measure in Italy is the same as a tablespoon measure in the United States! To translate spoon designations in Italian recipes, our teaspoon is their coffee spoon, our tablespoon is their dessert spoon, and our large "cooking" tablespoon is an Italian tablespoon (which actually equals three United States tablespoons). This error had been compounded ever after in recipe after recipe.

To also set this pie apart, there was an underlying faint flavor of Parmesan cheese that took away any cloying sweetness.

8- or 9-inch cake pan, 1½ inches deep
Serves 8 to 10

> *Tart Crust, page 170; double the recipe*
> *Ricotta Cheese Pie (Taranto), page 204; see Step 2 below for*
> *   changes*
> *⅓ cup chocolate mini-chips*
> *3 tablespoons grated Parmesan cheese*
> *1 egg*
> *2 teaspoons cold water*

1. Make the tart pastry dough. Form the dough into 2 disks, 1 slightly larger than the other, and put in the refrigerator to chill.

2. Make the ricotta filling according to the recipe directions with the following exceptions: Ignore Step 3. In Step 8, substitute chocolate mini-chips for the golden raisins. In Step 7, mix the grated Parmesan cheese with the ricotta before adding the semolina. Set aside the filling.

3. Butter the pan.

4. Remove the tart dough from the refrigerator and between

2 floured sheets of wax paper roll out the smaller of the 2 disks to a 12-inch circle. Carefully transfer this to the buttered pan. Since it is a very "short" crust, you will have to repair it along the edges. Trim the edge to a ½-inch overhang and fold it over to make a flat rim around the edge.

5. Preheat the oven to 375°. Add the leftover scraps of dough to the larger disk. Roll out between 2 floured sheets of wax paper to a 14-inch circle. Cut the circle into 1-inch-wide strips.

6. Fill the dough-lined pan with the ricotta cheese mixture almost to the top of the pan, leveling it off to an even surface.

7. Beat the egg with the cold water.

8. Brush the flat rim of dough around the edge of the pan with the egg glaze. Cover the ricotta filling with approximately half of the dough strips, transferring the strips with a narrow spatula. Place them all in one direction; they should be about ¼ inch apart. Cut away any excess dough and press the ends against the egg-glazed edge.

9. Brush the egg glaze on a ½-inch-wide edge on the top of the strips. Cross the first set of dough strips with the remaining strips, spacing them at least ½ inch apart to show the under-strips. Cut away the excess dough and press the ends against the glazed margin.

10. Brush the lattice top with the egg glaze, reserving enough glaze for a second brushing. Place the pie in the preheated oven for 50 minutes. After 30 minutes, brush the top of the pie once again with the egg glaze. If the top is not brown enough when the pie is done, slip the pie under a preheated broiler to finish browning the crust.

11. Remove the pie to a cake rack and cool it in the pan. Serve the pie directly from the pan, cut into wedges.

Note: Neither the Apricot Jam Glaze nor the multicolored nonpareils are used for this ricotta pie.

Ricotta Cheese Pie (Taranto)

We walked through Taranto, on the Ionian Sea where the "heel" joins the "boot," on Fair Night. Lights were strung across the streets, and booths were set up in the square. Restaurants were either crowded or not yet open or open and looking coldly lighted and semioccupied. We ended up at The Refuge (in more ways than one), which was warmly lighted and filled with cheerful family groups. The meal was only moderately good, but we finished with their stupendous ricotta cheese pie. This was quite different from the one we had eaten recently in Palermo; it had a complete top crust and no chocolate bits.

An almost cakelike filling studded with golden raisins, candied cherries, and citron was enclosed in a buttery crust and, after baking, brushed with an apricot glaze and sprinkled with multicolored nonpareils, creating a festival mood of confetti and fireworks.

Back in our hotel we fell asleep at about eleven o'clock, only to be awakened by a loud *boom*. Across the bay were fireworks: beautiful combinations of green, red, and white, and squiggly orange and yellow. A spectacular grand finale, low against the far shore, reflected in the waters of the bay.

8- or 9-inch pan, 1½ inches deep
Serves 10 to 12

> *Tart crust, page 170; double the recipe*
> *8 tablespoons (1 stick) butter*
> *2 to 2½ ounces (⅓ cup) golden raisins*
> *2½ ounces (about 12 large) glacéed cherries, approximately*
>   *¾ inch long*
> *3 ounces (⅓ cup) citron (see Note)*
> *2 eggs*
> *Grated zest of 1 lemon or 1 teaspoon lemon extract*
> *1 teaspoon vanilla extract*

Pinch of salt
12½ ounces (1½ cups) ricotta or creamy cottage cheese
5 tablespoons semolina, or white or yellow cornmeal
¾ cup sugar
Apricot Jam or Butter Glaze, page 178
Multicolored nonpareils

1. Make the tart dough and divide it into 2 flattened rounds, 1 slightly larger than the other. Put it into the refrigerator to chill.
2. In a small saucepan, melt the butter over low heat, then set it aside to cool.
3. Soak the raisins in warm water to cover for 5 to 10 minutes, then drain and dry on paper towels.
4. Rinse the glacéed cherries in a bowl of hot water to remove their sticky surface, then drain and dry the cherries with paper towels. Cut large cherries into quarters and small cherries in half.
5. Slice and cut the citron into dice and triangles, ¼ to ⅜ inch.
6. Beat the eggs in a small bowl. Add the grated lemon zest or lemon extract, vanilla extract, and salt. Set aside.
7. Put the ricotta or creamy cottage cheese into a large mixing bowl. Add the semolina or cornmeal and mix with a wooden spoon. Add the sugar and continue to mix.
8. Pour the egg mixture into the cheese mixture and stir until all ingredients are blended. Add the raisins, cherries, and citron. Mix well and set aside.
9. Preheat the oven to 375°. Remove the larger of the 2 pieces of tart dough from the refrigerator. Roll it out between 2 sheets of wax paper to form a 12-inch circle. Carefully transfer to a buttered pan; since this is a very "short" crust, you will have to repair it along the edge. Allow about ½ inch of dough to extend above the edge of the pan.
10. Roll out the other half of the dough in the same way, incorporating the leftover scraps of dough.
11. Fill the dough-lined pan with the cheese-egg mixture to the top of the pan, mounding it slightly in the center. You will not

use all the filling in an 8-inch pan, but the 9-inch pan will be filled evenly.

12. Cover the filling with the second half of rolled-out dough. Cut away the excess dough, leaving a ½-inch overhang. Pinch together the edges of the lower and upper doughs. Roll the edge inward to form an upstanding edge. Cut four ½-inch slits in the center of the top dough. Place the pie in the preheated oven for 50 minutes.

13. Remove the pie from the oven when done and cool in the pan. The upstanding edge will have spread outward.

14. When the pie is cold, spread the top with the hot apricot glaze, then sprinkle with 2 or 3 teaspoons of round multicolored nonpareils.

Note: Buy half a candied citron because it has more flavor than the diced citron sold in plastic jars. Store the citron in a covered glass jar in a cupboard.

Strawberry Cake/Tart (Venice)

It was May—strawberry season—and in a small restaurant on a side street beside a canal bridge we had a thin tart that was a fragrant mixture of textures and flavors: a cakelike crust spread with sliced deep-red strawberries and baked until the flavors were subtly blended. Strawberries in Italy are deep red all the way through, juicy, sweet, and strongly flavored. They come ripe to the market from the surrounding fields where they are picked every day.

6½- to 8½-inch quiche pan with removable bottom
Serves 4 to 6

> *1 container ripe strawberries, 4 x 4 x 2¾ inches, approximately 12 ounces*

Cake/Tart Crust, page 39
1½ or 2 tablespoons sugar, or to taste

1. Butter and flour the quiche pan.

2. Wash, hull, and slice the strawberries into ¼-inch-thick slices. If using a 6½-inch pan, you may need only ½ or ¾ of the container and the whole container for the 8½-inch size pan. Set aside.

3. Make the cake/pie crust batter following the recipe directions.

4. Preheat the oven to 400°.

5. Cover the bottom of the quiche pan with a ⅜-inch-deep layer of the batter, smoothing it with the back of a tablespoon. Add a ⅜-inch-wide "strip" of batter around the edge, almost but not quite reaching to the top edge of the pan. (There will be batter left over if a 6½-inch quiche pan is used. See *Note*.)

6. Spread the sliced strawberries over the batter in a 2-layer pattern or helter-skelter but with an even top. Sprinkle the berries with the sugar. Place the pan in the oven on the center rack for 40 to 45 minutes.

7. When cooked, brown the edges of the crust under the broiler. Remove from the broiler and place on a cake rack. Loosen the edge with the point of a small knife. Allow the cake/tart to cool in the pan on the cake rack. Remove from the pan just before serving.

Note: With any leftover batter, half-fill 3 or 4 English muffin rings or small tart rings placed on a buttered baking sheet. Bake for 15 minutes in the oven at the same time as the Strawberry Cake/Tart.

During the baking, a little of the batter will "leak" out at the bottom of the rings onto the baking sheet. After cooking, remove the sheet from the oven, brace the top of each ring with a hand protected by a mitt or pot holder, and cut away the brown edges at the base of the rings. Lift off the rings and with a wide spatula or cake turner transfer the cake rounds to a cake rack. Allow to cool. If not using the rounds immediately, freeze them in a plastic bag. When ready to use, defrost at room temperature, put them in a 400° oven for a few minutes to freshen, then cool before using.

Use the rounds as the base for the Red-Edged Apricot Pastries, page 134.

Strawberry Tart (Asolo)

We spent a long weekend at the Villa Cipriani, on the hill above the town of Asolo and next door to the villa where Eleonora Duse had lived. The view from the terrace garden is spectacular, with the ghostly Villa Contarini on the facing hill across a small valley. The orangerie, the scene of the murder in Browning's *Pippa Passes,* is still visible to the right of the valley.

We explored the area, its villas and the mountains to the north, and ate well at the Cipriani. The main courses were substantial and the desserts light. One was a heavenly combination of crisp tart shell, refreshing chunks of ripe strawberries, and smooth, sweetened whipped cream.

6½- to 8-inch quiche pan with removable bottom
Serves 4 to 6

> *Tart Crust, page 170, substituting ½ teaspoon almond extract for the lemon zest*
> *1 container ripe strawberries, 4 x 4 x 2¾ inches, approximately 12 ounces*
> *Superfine sugar to taste*
> *1 to 1½ cups heavy cream*
> *½ to 1 teaspoon vanilla extract*

1. Make, chill, and form the tart pastry shell, substituting the almond extract for the lemon zest. Bake the shell the length of time needed for a filling that does not require baking. Remove the shell from the oven, loosen the edge, then cool on a baking rack.

2. Chop the strawberries into chunky pieces and sugar them lightly. Put the bowl of berries, covered with plastic wrap, in the refrigerator until 1 hour before serving. Allow the berries to come to room temperature before putting the tart together.

3. One hour before serving, whip the cream, sweeten it to taste, and add the vanilla extract. Cover the bowl and place it in the refrigerator.

4. Just before serving, remove the pastry shell from the sides of the pan; the metal circle on the bottom can be left in place. Put the shell in the center of a serving plate. Fill the shell almost to the top with the whipped cream and smooth the top. Cover the cream thickly with the berries, using a slotted tablespoon so the berries will be drained. Serve immediately.

Strawberry and Cherry Tart (Igea Marina)

At the pastry shop in the Adriatic seashore resort of Igea Marina, we bought pastry at different times for our dinners at home in the apartment we had rented. One was a variation of a custard and fresh fruit tart, the pasta frolla crust half-filled with an almond-flavored egg custard and the top decorated with circular rows of whole strawberries and pitted cherries. In the center was a cluster of cherries with their stems standing upright like a crown. Currant jelly glaze was brushed over all the fruit except the stemmed cherries in the center.

6 ½- to 8-inch tart pan with removable bottom
Serves 4 to 6

> *Tart Crust, page 170*
> *Egg Custard, page 237, half the recipe; or Time-Saver Custard, page 240, full recipe. Substitute for vanilla extract ½ to ¾ teaspoon almond extract, or to taste.*
> *Currant Jelly Glaze, page 177*

24 to 40 ripe strawberries
Sweet cherries with stems

1. Make and chill the tart crust dough, following the recipe directions.

2. While the dough is chilling, cook the custard you are using, substituting almond extract for the vanilla extract. Spoon the finished custard into a bowl. Cover the surface with a circle of wax paper to prevent a skin from forming. When cooled, place in the refrigerator until ready to put the tart together.

3. After 45 minutes, remove the dough from the refrigerator. Preheat the oven to 375°. Roll out the dough and line the buttered tart pan. Bake the pastry shell following the recipe directions for a filling that does not require baking. When baked, remove from the oven and cool on a cake rack. Loosen the edge with the point of a small knife. Keep the baked shell in the pan until just before serving.

4. Prepare the currant jelly glaze and set it aside to thicken slightly.

5. Wash, dry, and hull the strawberries. Wash and pit the cherries, reserving enough cherries with their stems attached for the center of the pie.

To Assemble:

1. Spoon the custard into the baked tart shell, filling it ½ to ¾ full. Smooth the top.

2. Rim the edge of the custard with a single row of strawberries, pointed end upright. Follow with a circle of pitted cherries and then a circle of strawberries. The number of circles depends on the size of the fruit. Leave a 1½-inch circle in the center and fill it with unpitted cherries, their stems standing upright.

3. Following the recipe directions, glaze the fruit with the currant jelly glaze, except for the center of stemmed cherries. Chill the tart until 30 minutes before serving. At that time, remove the tart from its pan and place it on a serving dish.

Thin Fruit Tart (Ascoli Piceno)

We stopped at the bread and cheese shop in Ascoli Piceno, attracted by a round, crusty, whole-grain bread. In a glass case were several thin fruit tarts of very simple, almost primitive design: A disk of dough was placed on a baking pan, and a layer of fruit was spread on the dough to within an inch of the edge. This edge was turned over the fruit and held in place with crisscrossing strips of dough brushed with egg yolk.

Any fresh fruit of the season can be used; in wintertime, thickly fruited jams or cooked dried fruits are a good substitute.

10-x-15-inch baking pan
Notched-wheel cutter
Serves 5 or 6

> *Tart Crust, page 170*
> *2 large peaches*
> *1 tablespoon cornstarch*
> *2 tablespoons plus 2 teaspoons sugar*

1. Make and chill the tart crust dough following the recipe directions.
2. When the dough has almost finished chilling, peel and thinly slice the 2 peaches. Cut the slices in half crosswise.
3. In a small bowl, mix together the cornstarch and 2 tablespoons of sugar.
4. Cut a sheet of aluminum foil to fit the baking pan. Butter and flour the foil.
5. Preheat the oven to 375°.
6. Remove the dough from the refrigerator, cut off ¼ of the dough, and roll the rest between floured sheets of wax paper into a circle 10 or 11 inches in diameter and ⅛ inch thick. Add extra flour to the top and bottom as needed.

7. Carefully remove the top sheet of wax paper. Roll the dough and the attached bottom sheet of wax paper onto the rolling pin. Transfer to the aluminum foil-covered baking pan, *dough side down*. Remove the sheet of wax paper. Center a 6½-inch cake pan on top of the dough, pressing the rim slightly against the dough— just enough to leave a slight indentation. Cut out a circle of dough with a notched-wheel cutter, *leaving a 1-inch margin all around the outside edge of the indentation,* forming an 8½-inch circle. Remove the extra scraps of dough from the baking pan.

8. Gather up the scraps of dough and knead them into the reserved piece of dough. Roll out a rectangle approximately 6 x 9 inches and ⅛ inch thick. Cut six 9-x-½-inch strips with the notched-wheel cutter. There will be dough left over.

9. Sprinkle the circle in the center of the dough disk with half the cornstarch-sugar mixture and arrange the sliced peaches evenly on the 6½-inch circle. Sprinkle the rest of the cornstarch-sugar mixture and the 2 teaspoons of sugar over the top of the peaches.

10. Carefully fold the 1-inch margin of dough up and over the peaches. Do not press the edge against the peaches but leave the edge raised a little so the juice will be contained during baking. Repair any breaks in the dough. Scoop up each dough strip with a long, narrow spatula and put in position across the peaches: 3 strips one way crossed by 3 strips. Cut the ends of the strips level with the outside edge of the tart and hold them in place with a dab of the beaten egg left over from the tart crust.

11. Put the baking pan into the preheated oven on the lowest shelf. After 15 minutes, brush the exposed dough with half of the reserved beaten egg. Ten to 15 minutes later, brush the dough again with the remaining beaten egg. In all, bake the tart for 35 to 40 minutes, until the crust is well browned. Some of the juice will bubble out onto the foil; scoop it up with a spoon when you first brush the dough with egg, and discard.

12. When the tart is done, remove it from the oven. Slip the foil and tart onto a cake rack and cool for 10 minutes. Carefully remove the tart from the foil to finish cooling.

Three-Fruit Tart (Florence)

One night when we had dinner at Otello's in Florence, we tried a wedge of their shallow, fresh fruit tart that looked like a lustrous Renaissance jewel: circles of tiny wild strawberries, halved apricots, and pitted cherries covered with glistening apple jelly. The crust had just the right crunchiness to contrast with the soft fruit and thin sweet jelly.

Either Hazelnut Pasta Frolla or Tart Crust will add the right crispness. Any three fruits of the season can be used, as long as there is a rich contrast of color. This recipe takes advantage of early summer fruits available in the United States.

6½- to 8-inch quiche pan with removable bottom
Serves 4 to 6

> *Hazelnut Pasta Frolla, page 172, or Tart Crust, page 170*
> *Stiffened Glaze for Fresh Fruit Tarts, page 178*
>
> Filling *(for a 6½-inch tart; increase amount about ¼ for*
>   *8-inch size):*
> *6 apricots*
> *12 sweet or sour cherries*
> *Blueberries to fill center*

1. Make hazelnut pasta frolla or tart crust following the recipe directions. (If using the recipe for Hazelnut Pasta Frolla, there will be dough left over from a 6½-inch quiche pan for 8 cookie balls or just enough dough for an 8-inch shell.) Preheat the oven when the tart dough is removed from the refrigerator.

2. Bake the shell the length of time needed for a filling that does not require baking. While the crust is baking, make the glaze. Remove from the heat and allow to cool until thickened but not solid.

3. Wash and dry the fruit. Cut the apricots in half and remove the pits. Remove the pits from the cherries but leave them whole. Set the fruit aside on separate plates.

4. When the crust is done, remove it from the oven and place it on a cake rack. With the point of a small knife, loosen the crust from the edge of the pan, cutting away any overlapping sections of crust. This will make it easier, once the crust is filled, to remove the tart from the pan. Allow the crust to cool.

5. When the crust is cool, brush the bottom, sides, and top edge with apple glaze. Brush the cut side of each apricot half with glaze before placing it, cut side down, against the outer edge in a single circle, and then brush the curved tops of the apricots with glaze. Repeat the process with the cherries, forming 2 circles. Mix some of the glaze with the blueberries, fill the center of the shell with a level layer of berries, and cover their top with glaze. Place an "accent" blueberry at the edge of the shell between every two apricot halves. Spoon the remaining glaze over the top of the fruit, smoothing the surface.

6. Place the tart in the refrigerator to set the glaze. Remove shortly before serving since the tart should not be refrigerator cold. Remove the rim of the pan, leaving the tart on the bottom metal disk. Place the tart on a serving dish and allow to come almost to room temperature before serving.

Tartlets

Tartlets are just that—

small tarts or pies, with the same crusts and fillings as the larger tarts and pies, but there are also many special fillings. In a pasticceria there is a varied selection of tartlets for those who want to buy individual servings rather than a large tart or pie; also, as we found, they are very good to take along on a picnic. An assortment of tarts forms a jewel-like serving platter at the end of dinner or to accompany espresso at an evening's entertainment.

Apple Tartlets (Ascoli Piceno)

At the end of the day in the hill town of Ascoli Piceno, we stopped at the local bakery to buy dinner and picnic desserts, waiting while a little girl carefully chose her afternoon treat.

For dinner dessert we bought two apple tartlets that, upon eating, revealed layers of hidden surprises. The top layer of glazed apple slices was arranged in an overlapping pattern; concealed beneath was a thin layer of sweetened chopped apple that covered a powdered cinnamon-topped layer of jam (one tartlet had apricot, the other plum jam) that in turn covered a thin, thin layer of cake. Between the cake and the tartlet's pasta frolla bottom was another layer of jam.

Nine 3¾-inch English muffin rings or tart rings
Notched-wheel cutter
11-x-17-inch baking pan
Serves 9

Tart Crust, page 170
Thin Cake Layer, page 38
12 ounces apricot or plum jam
Juice of 1 lemon
6 to 8 green apples, depending on size
Powdered cinnamon
Sugar to taste
Apple Jelly Glaze, page 177

1. Butter the English muffin rings or tart rings and place them in position on the buttered baking pan.

2. Make the tart dough and chill it in the refrigerator following the recipe directions.

3. While the tart dough is chilling, make and bake a ¼-inch-thick 11-x-11-inch sheet of thin cake layer. When the cake is baked, cool it on a cake rack, then cut it into nine 3½-inch circles. Set aside.

4. Melt the apricot or plum jam in a small saucepan over low heat. Press through a fine-mesh sieve and set aside, discarding the solids.

5. Squeeze the lemon juice into a small bowl. Peel the apples, cut them in quarters, and remove the cores. You will need approximately 14 slices per tartlet. After cutting a sufficient quantity of apple slices, sprinkle them with half of the lemon juice and set aside. Chop the remaining apple into ¼-inch dice, sprinkle with the rest of the lemon juice, and set aside.

6. Remove the tart dough from the refrigerator and roll it out between floured sheets of wax paper to an 18-x-18-inch square. Cut the dough into nine 6-inch circles with a sharp knife or notched-wheel cutter, using a plate or cardboard circle as a pattern. Line the buttered rings with the dough circles, crimping the upper edge of the dough with your fingers.

To Assemble:
1. Preheat the oven to 350°.
2. Brush the sides and bottom of the dough circles with the

sieved jam. Add a thin cake layer on top of each one and spread it with a generous layer of the sieved jam, well sprinkled with powdered cinnamon. Scatter the chopped apples over the jam and add 1 teaspoon of sugar or more to each tart, depending on the sharpness of the apples. Arrange the apple slices over the chopped apples in a flat pattern of 6 overlapping slices across the middle and 2 rows of 2 slices on each side, with the curved edges facing the side.

3. Sprinkle the tops with sugar and bake the tartlets in the oven for 30 to 35 minutes.

4. Make the glaze while the tartlets are baking.

5. When the tartlets are done, remove them from the oven and add the apple glaze, following the recipe directions. Cool the tartlets in their rings because the hot pastry is not self-supporting until cold. Just before serving, remove the tartlets from their rings.

Apple Tartlets (Florence)
"Botticellis"

After a morning spent enjoying the breathtaking collection of paintings and sculptures at the Galleria degli Uffizi, built in the sixteenth century, we reluctantly left the building at the midday closing. We walked out into the pale spring sunshine of modern Florence, with its cars and buses and people all hurrying home for lunch.

We made our way to a favorite restaurant and, as usual, paused at the dessert table facing the door to see just how we would end our meal. In the center of the table, displayed on an oval metal tray, were apple tartlets, pale yellow in color with a center ring of golden-brown pastry. Somehow the pale colors reminded us of the tones of the Botticelli paintings we had just seen, and since we did not know the name of the tartlets, forever after we have called them Botticellis.

Shallow, fluted tartlet pans are lined with pasta frolla. The chopped apple filling is studded with small dice of citron and candied orange peel, and crowned with a small ring of crisp pasta frolla.

10 fluted tart pans, 3 inches x ½ inch
11-x-17-inch baking pan
Serves 5 or 10

> *Tart Crust, page 170*
> *Apple Turnover filling, page 221; double the ingredients*

1. Make the tart dough and place it in the refrigerator to chill for 1 hour.
2. While the dough is chilling, make the apple filling.
3. Preheat the oven to 425°.
4. Butter the tartlet pans. Place the baking pan upside-down on the center shelf of the oven to preheat it.
5. Between 2 sheets of well-floured wax paper, roll out the chilled tart dough into a strip 7 x 17½ inches. Add more flour as the dough is rolled out. Cut the dough into ten 3½-inch squares. Fit each square into a buttered tartlet pan, cutting off the points of dough. Press the dough against the side of each pan so that it is ¼ inch above the edge.
6. Fill the shells with the cooked apple mixture. Add the citron and candied lemon peel dice around the edge of the apple filling. Curl the ¼-inch edge of the dough over the filling so that it leans partially over but does not touch the filling; this will prevent the filling from bubbling over the edge of the pastry shell.
7. Form the dough scraps into thin rolls between the palms of your hands and curve the rolls into circles ¾ to 1 inch in diameter. Place a dough circle in the center of each tart filling and add a dice of candied citron within each circle. Brush the exposed dough around the edge of each tartlet and also the center dough circle with the remainder of the beaten egg from the tart dough. Any extra egg is brushed over the top of the apple filling to give it a gloss.

8. Place the filled tartlet pans on the bottom of the preheated upside-down baking pan. (This exposes the tartlet pans to the full heat of the oven.) Bake in the preheated oven for 15 to 20 minutes. The edges of the tartlet crusts and the dough circles will be golden brown.

9. Remove the tartlet pans from the oven and place them on a baking rack to cool. Loosen the edges of the tarts with a sharp-pointed small knife while the crust is still hot. When the tartlets are almost cool, remove them from the pans and allow them to finish cooling on the rack.

Apple Turnover (Mantua)

One morning we drove south to Mantua through the wide Lombardy plain, through lush green fields outlined with poplars and plane trees. Ocher-colored farmhouse complexes could be seen across the fields, balanced by brick barns with patterned openings at the top. Tree nurseries along the way added color with their ornamental red beeches, yellow shower trees, and pink chestnuts interspersed with low, round, plastic greenhouses for forcing early food crops, such as zucchini, lettuce, and tomatoes.

We parked near the Piazza Erbe and walked to the Palazzo Ducal for our escorted tour of the fascinating collection of rooms. The guide was in a hurry, and the tour was much too fast to absorb all the details before we were ushered out at the noontime closing. Then off to lunch on the square: thin noodle-type pasta with meat sauce, sliced beef and polenta. The highlight was a scalloped-edge apple turnover, golden brown on the surface with an unspiced apple filling, the essence of apple flavor. After lunch we explored the streets on the way to the beautiful garden setting of the Palazzo del Te and its ample, decorated rooms.

10-x-15-inch baking pan
3½-x-6¼-inch fluted cutter

Makes 4 turnovers

> *Tart Crust, page 170*
> *8 ounces green apples*
> *1 tablespoon unsalted butter*
> *3½ or 4 tablespoons sugar*
> *1½ tablespoons diced candied citron*
> *1½ tablespoons diced Candied Lemon Peel, page 50*

1. Make the tart dough, and while it is chilling in the refrigerator, peel, quarter, core, and thinly slice the apples.

2. Put the slices and butter in a small frying pan over low heat. Stir lightly with a fork until the slices are coated with melted butter, cover, and cook for 5 minutes. Remove the cover, add sugar, and stir, breaking up the slices into irregular halves. The slices should be slightly golden and partially translucent but still hold their shape. Remove from the heat and allow to cool.

3. Preheat the oven to 425°.

4. Remove the tart dough from the refrigerator and roll it out between sheets of well-floured wax paper, adding a sifting of flour, top and bottom, as the dough is rolled and the flour is absorbed. Roll out to a 6½-x-14-inch rectangle. Cut 4 pieces with a fluted oval cutter 3½ x 6¼ inches and carefully transfer each piece to the buttered baking pan using 2 wide cake turners. Place the pieces at least 1 inch apart.

5. Heap 1½ to 2 tablespoons of apple filling on half of each oval. Poke about 5 citron and lemon dice into each filling. Brush the edges of the oval with the beaten egg left over from the tart dough. Very carefully, because this is a short and tender crust, bring the other half of the oval over the filling. Press the edges together to seal. If there are any thin spots or cracks, especially along the fold, add small pieces of dough and smooth into place. Brush the tops with beaten egg, reserving some for a second brushing during baking. Prick the center of each top with a table fork.

6. Put the baking pan in the preheated oven for 15 to 20 minutes, taking care not to let the turnover bottoms burn. After 10

minutes, brush the tops of the turnovers with the remaining beaten egg.

7. When done, remove from the oven. If not glossy and deep golden on top, put the turnovers under the broiler for a few minutes, then allow to cool on a baking rack. They can be served at room temperature, or they can be slightly heated in the oven before serving.

Apricot Jam Tartlets (Ferrara)

Part of the charm of the apricot tartlets we ordered at a coffee bar in Ferrara was their rectangular shape. A pasta frolla crust was filled with rum-flavored, chunky apricot jam and topped with four narrow crisscrossed strips of dough. The other part of the charm was relaxing under a sidewalk umbrella with cappuccino coffee and a sweet before us, after a day of walking and photographing while exploring the city.

Tartlet sheet with 12 rectangular openings 2½ x 3¾ x 1¼ inches or
*   10 round fluted tartlet pans 3½ x 1 inch and a baking pan large*
*   enough to hold them*
Notched-wheel cutter
Makes 10 tartlets

> *Tart Crust, page 170; double the recipe*
> *16 to 20 ounces chunky apricot jam, approximately*
> *1 tablespoon dark rum or Amaretto liqueur, or to taste*
> *1 egg, beaten*

1. Butter the tartlet sheet or pans (the recipe is for 10 rectangular or round tartlets).

2. Make the tart dough following the recipe directions and form into two 4-inch disks. Chill for 1 hour.

3. Roll out 1 dough disk between 2 sheets of floured wax

paper to a 13½-x-13½-inch square. With a sharp knife or notched-wheel cutter, cut out 6 pieces 4½ x 5¾ inches. For the round pans, cut six 4½-inch circles. Line 6 of the forms with the cut-out pieces. Gather up the scraps and set aside.

4. Preheat the oven to 375°.

5. Roll out the second dough disk into a 13½-x-13½-inch square. Cut out 4 pieces in the sizes listed in Step 3. Gather together the scraps from both lots, briefly knead, and reroll into a ⅛-inch-thick rectangle. Cut out 40 strips, ¼ inch wide x 3½ inches long, for the rectangular tarts or for the round tartlets. Re-form all leftover pieces of dough, put in plastic wrap, and freeze for another use.

6. Turn over the top edges of the dough lining the pans to thicken them and crimp the edges with your fingers.

7. Put the jam in a bowl and mix in the rum or Amaretto liqueur. Fill the tartlet shells with the mixture, leveling off the top surface.

8. With the dough strips, form two X's on the top of each tartlet. Brush the strips with the beaten egg. Place the tartlet sheet in the oven. Or place the round tartlet pans on a baking pan and then in the oven. Bake for approximately 30 minutes, or until the tops of the X's are well browned.

9. Remove the tartlets from the oven and place on a baking rack to cool. Loosen the edges of the tartlets while they are still hot. Allow to cool in their pans and remove them just before serving.

Lemon Tartlets

Along the Amalfi Drive where lemon and orange trees climb the terraced hills that face the blue-green sea, we stopped one afternoon on our way back from the Greek ruins at Paestum for espresso and the coffee bar/pastry shop's shallow lemon tarts. The filling was the essence of lemon flavor, and the color, the golden yellow of lemon fruit.

2 tart plaques with 9 openings each, 3-x-⁵/₁₆-inch, or small individual
*   tart shells*
3-inch fluted cookie cutter
Makes 16 tarts

> Tart Crust, page 170
> 1 lemon
> 2 tablespoons flour
> 2½ tablespoons cornstarch
> ¾ cup sugar
> ½ teaspoon salt
> 1⅛ cups boiling water
> 2 egg yolks, beaten
> 1 teaspoon butter
> ½ teaspoon lemon extract

1. Butter the openings in the tart plaques or the individual tart shells, and set aside.

2. Make and chill the tart dough following the recipe directions. While the dough is chilling, make the lemon custard.

3. Grate the lemon zest. Squeeze the lemon juice. Set both aside.

4. In the top of a double boiler, mix together the flour, cornstarch, sugar, and salt until all the cornstarch lumps have disappeared.

5. Pour in the boiling water, stirring constantly. Place the pot over simmering water and cook for 15 minutes, stirring to keep the custard from sticking.

6. Blend in the egg yolks and cook the custard 2 minutes more.

7. Blend in the butter, lemon juice, and lemon zest, and remove from the heat.

8. Add the lemon extract, then cool the custard, stirring occasionally, until the custard is cool.

9. Preheat the oven to 375°.

10. Roll out the dough to a 12-x-12-inch square and cut out circles of dough with the cookie cutter. Transfer the circles to the plaque openings and lightly press them into place. Re-form the dough scraps, roll out, cut more circles, and transfer them to the plaque openings. Repeat until all the dough is used up. If you are not using plaques, line individual tart shells with dough as you would a large tart.

11. Brush the circles with the leftover beaten egg and bake for 10 to 12 minutes until only lightly colored.

12. Slide the shells onto baking racks to cool.

13. Place the tart shells on a baking pan. Preheat the broiler to 300°. Fill each shell with about 1 tablespoon of lemon custard, smoothing the tops. Slip the baking pan under the broiler for 1 or 2 minutes, or until the top surface is level and shiny. Remove the pan from the broiler and cool the tarts on a baking rack before serving.

Small Cream Pastries (South Italy)
Pasticcio Crema

After a few days at Sperlonga on the Gulf of Gaeta recovering from jet lag, we drove the rest of the way down the west coast, our destination Reggio di Calabria and the ferry to Sicily. On the way we stopped in a small village to pick up a loaf of bread and local cheese, blood oranges, olives, and several small custard pastries for a noontime picnic on a low hillside where the air was redolent with the herbs of the *macchia*, the coastal thicket of scrubby bushes and small wind-twisted trees.

These pastries are made in small fluted tart pans lined with very thin pasta frolla; they are filled with an almond-flavored egg custard mixed with ricotta cheese and topped with shiny pasta frolla.

11-x-17-inch baking pan
Twelve 2¾-x-1-inch fluted tart pans
3½-inch and 3¼-inch plain or fluted cookie cutters
Notched-wheel cutter
Makes 12 small pies

> *Tart Crust, page 170; double the recipe*
> *Egg Custard, page 237; or Time-Saver Custard, page 240,*
>   *double the recipe and omit the vanilla extract*
> *1 teaspoon almond extract*
> *½ cup ricotta or creamy cottage cheese*
> *1 egg*
> *1 teaspoon cold water*

1. Butter the tart pans.

2. Make the tart dough and put it in the refrigerator to chill, forming the dough into 2 disks, 1 larger than the other.

3. While the dough is chilling, make the custard. When it is cooked, remove the custard from the heat, flavor it with almond extract rather than vanilla extract, and stir in the ricotta or cottage cheese. Pour the mixture into a bowl, cover the top with a round of wax paper to prevent a skin from forming, and set aside.

4. Preheat the oven to 375°.

5. Roll the larger disk of dough into a 12-inch circle between 2 floured sheets of wax paper; the dough should be quite thin. Cut the sheet into 8 circles with the 3½-inch cookie cutter. (If your cutter is only 3 inches in diameter, then press it very lightly against the dough surface, and with a notched-wheel cutter cut out a circle ¼ inch wider all around.)

6. Line 8 tart pans with the dough, leaving a ⅓-inch overhang at the edges. Gather up the dough scraps and reroll, cutting out 4 more circles and lining the remaining tart shells.

7. Roll out the second disk of dough between 2 floured sheets of wax paper, adding any leftover scraps of dough from the previous rolling. Cut the dough into 3¼-inch circles with the cutter, re-form the dough, and reroll and cut out more circles until you have 12 circles. Set aside.

8. Fill the tart shells with the ricotta custard, leveling off the top surface.

9. Cover the filling of each tart with a circle of dough, pressing the two ¼-inch overhangs together. Tuck them under and then flute the edges together with your fingers. Cut a small X with the sharp point of a knife in the center of each tart.

10. Put the tart pans on the baking pan.

11. Beat the egg with the cold water and brush the tops of the tarts with half the egg glaze. Bake for 15 minutes, then brush the tops with the remaining egg glaze. Bake 15 minutes more. If the top crust is not brown enough, put the tarts under a preheated broiler until they are a rich shiny brown but not burned. Remove the baking pan with the tarts to a cake rack to cool. Do not remove the tarts from their pans until they are cold or the sides will collapse.

Small Ricotta Tarts (Matera)

From the coast road along the Gulf of Taranto, we made a detour to Matera to see its old houses that are carved into the rocky hillside. The rows of buildings come down to the narrow road edging a high cliff that overhangs a deep ravine. The buildings, half caves and half stone masonry, have been long abandoned and are falling into ruins; their empty windows stare out into empty streets. The former residents have gradually moved into the "new" town. We did see several buildings that were being fixed up by artists and craftspeople, so perhaps life will return to this fascinating area. As we explored, we realized that some of the narrow streets are actually roofs of houses in the tier below. Across the deep ravine, door openings carved into the opposite cliff lead into the remains of dwellings or burial grounds of an even more ancient people.

We went into the new town for lunch before driving on to Taranto. Our dessert was individual ricotta tarts. Ricotta is a basic ingredient in south Italian cooking, used as part of both main courses and desserts. These small tarts had a filling very similar to the large Ricotta Cheese Pie of Taranto, except that diced candied orange peel was substituted for the raisins in the mixture and the citron and cherries were diced into one-fourth-inch pieces. A one-half-inch-wide cross of pasta frolla topped each tart.

The number of tarts you make depends on the size of the metal forms used. A single recipe of pasta frolla and half a recipe of ricotta filling will be sufficient for four to six tarts.

4 fluted tart pans, 3½ x 1 inch, or a 6-cup muffin pan with each
opening 2½ x 1¼ inches
11-x-17-inch baking pan
Makes 4 to 6 tarts

> *Tart Crust, page 170*
> *Ricotta Cheese Pie filling, page 204; half the recipe. Substi-*
> *tute for the raisins 2⅔ tablespoons diced Candied Or-*
> *ange Peel, page 51*
> *Vanilla-Flavored Confectioners' Sugar, page 40 (optional)*

1. Butter the fluted tart tins or muffin pan.

2. Make and chill the tart crust dough. Reserve the leftover beaten egg for brushing the dough strips on top of the tarts.

3. While the dough is chilling, make the ricotta filling. Follow the recipe directions *but* leave out the raisins, substituting the candied orange peel cut into ¼-inch dice. Cut the citron into less than ¼ inch dice and the candied cherries into ¼-inch pieces. Set the filling aside.

4. Preheat the oven to 375°. Remove the dough from the refrigerator and roll it out into a 12-inch circle between 2 sheets of floured wax paper. Cut out 4 circles of 4¾ inches for the tart tins

or 6 circles of 4 inches for the muffin pan. Line the tart tins or muffin pan openings, flattening the dough edges so they are even with the top edge of the forms. Reroll the scraps to a thin rectangle 7½ x 2 inches if using tart tins or 5½ x 3 inches for the muffin pan. Cut either 4 strips or 6 strips ½ inch wide, lengthwise, then cut each strip in half crosswise.

5. Fill the dough-lined forms with the ricotta or cottage cheese filling, leveling it off just below the top edge of the dough lining. Cross 2 strips of dough on top of each tart, attaching the ends to the edges of the dough lining with a brushing of beaten egg. Brush the tops of the crosspieces with the rest of the beaten egg, finishing up with the top edges of the dough lining.

6. Put the tart tins or the muffin pan on a preheated baking pan on the middle shelf of the oven. Bake for 30 minutes. When done, if the dough strips are not well browned, place the tarts under a preheated broiler until the strips are brown.

7. Remove the tarts from the heat and allow them to cool in the pans before removing. Otherwise the side walls will collapse. The ricotta tarts can be served plain or dusted with vanilla-flavored confectioners' sugar.

Spice Cake Tartlets (Verona)

One of the several varieties of cookies and small cakes we bought at the Pasticceria Castelvecchio in Verona was a small muffin-shaped tartlet of pasta frolla crust filled with a chocolate spice cake. It became part of a picnic lunch high in the mountains at the snow line, with snow coming down to where tiny blue gentians were in bloom in the exposed earth.

2 muffin pans, each with 12 openings 1¾ inches in diameter
3-inch cookie cutter or a 3-inch fluted tart pan
Makes 24 tartlets

*Tart Crust, page 170; double the recipe and add 3 extra
    tablespoons sugar*
½ ounce unsweetened chocolate
3 tablespoons unsalted butter
1 egg
½ cup less 1 tablespoon flour
¾ teaspoon baking powder
⅛ teaspoon powdered cinnamon
1/16 teaspoon freshly grated nutmeg
1/16 teaspoon powdered cloves
Pinch of salt
2 tablespoons raisins
2 tablespoons Almonds, Blanched and Toasted, page 48
1 tablespoons Candied Orange Peel, page 51
¼ cup dark brown sugar
2 or 3 tablespoons milk, as needed
Hard Chocolate Glaze, page 43

1. Make double the amount of tart dough, adding the 3 table-spoons of sugar. Form the dough into 2 flat rounds, wrap them in wax paper, and put them into the refrigerator for 45 minutes. While the dough is chilling, make the chocolate spice cake filling (to be set aside until the muffin tins are lined with the dough).

2. Melt the chocolate in a double boiler over hot water. Remove from the heat and set aside.

3. In a mixing bowl, slice the butter and allow to soften.

4. Beat the egg in a small bowl and set aside.

5. Sift all the dry ingredients (except the brown sugar) into a small bowl and mix until well blended. Set aside.

6. Chop the raisins and mix with ½ teaspoon flour to prevent the pieces from sticking together. Chop the nuts and candied orange peel into ⅛-inch pieces. Set aside.

7. Cream the softened butter, add the brown sugar, and beat until light. Add the beaten egg and mix. Pour in the melted chocolate and blend.

8. Spoon about ⅓ of the dry ingredients into the moist mixture and smooth. Add a little milk if the dough seems stiff. Add another ⅓ of the dry ingredients and beat in. Add the remaining dry ingredients and more milk if needed. Beat the dough for about 3 minutes with a wooden spoon, then fold in the raisins, nuts, and candied orange peel. Set aside.

To Assemble:

1. Preheat the oven to 350°. Butter the 2 muffin pans.

2. Remove 1 chilled round of tart dough from the refrigerator. Roll it out into a 10-x-12-inch oval; the dough will be a little less than ¼ inch thick. Cut out 12 rounds with the cutter or fluted tart form and fit them into the openings of the muffin pan. Place the pan in the refrigerator and remove the other round of dough. Repeat the rolling, cutting, and fitting into the other muffin pan.

3. Gather up the excess dough, if any, wrap it in plastic wrap, and freeze it for future use (see *Note*).

4. Distribute the chocolate spice cake batter evenly among the openings in the 2 muffin pans. The shells will be about ⅔ full.

5. Bake on the middle rack for 20 minutes, checking for doneness with a toothpick or thin metal skewer; if the skewer comes out clean, remove the tartlets from the oven, since you do not want to overcook the chocolate spice cake. If the top edges of the dough are still white, pop the pans under the broiler for a quick browning.

6. Place the pans on a cake rack and allow the tartlets to cool completely in the pans because the edges will crumble if you take them out while still hot.

7. When cool, ice with a thin coat of hard chocolate glaze icing. Serve with coffee.

Note: Leftover tart dough can be used to line small, shallow tart pans to be baked, filled with fresh fruit or jam, and garnished with whipped cream.

Rice Tartlets (Mantua)

Just before we left Mantua to drive back to Desenzano through the wide-stretching fields and the flooded rice paddies, we stopped at a pasticceria and bought the rice tartlets that are a specialty of this area of Lombardy.

Small muffin cups are lined with a very thin pasta frolla and then filled with a mixture of rice, egg, and chopped toasted almonds—all strongly flavored with almond extract.

2 muffin pans, 1¾-inch cup openings
3-inch round fluted or plain cutter
Makes 16 to 18 small pastries

> Tart Crust, page 170
> 4 tablespoons rice
> 1¼ cups water
> 20 to 25 Almonds, Blanched and Toasted, page 48
> 5 tablespoons sugar
> 3 tablespoons beaten egg (reserved egg from tart crust)
> Pinch of salt
> ¾ to 1 teaspoon almond extract
> Powdered cinnamon

1. Make and chill the tart crust dough.
2. Butter the cups in the 2 muffin pans and set aside.
3. Preheat the oven to 200°.
4. While the tart dough is chilling in the refrigerator, put the rice and water into a saucepan and cook until the rice is soft. Pour the rice into a metal sieve, run cold water through the rice, and drain. Place the rice and the sieve into the preheated oven to dry out the excess moisture. When the rice is dry, remove from the oven and cool.
5. While the rice is cooking, prepare the almonds. Chop the toasted almonds into ⅛-inch chunks and set aside.

6. Scrape the cooled rice into a bowl. Mix in the sugar, beaten egg, and pinch of salt, and mix together. Add the chopped almonds and the almond extract. Taste for flavoring and adjust if needed. Set aside.

7. Place wax paper on the pastry board, dust it with flour, and cover with another piece of wax paper.

8. Reset the oven to 400°.

9. Take the tart dough from the refrigerator and place it in the center of the pastry board between floured sheets of wax paper. Roll out to ⅛ inch thick.

10. Stamp out as many rounds as you can with the plain or fluted cutter, pulling away the extra dough from each round as you lift it from the wax paper with a broad spatula. Transfer each round to a muffin cup and fit it in place in the cup, pressing and crimping the edges above the opening. Gather up the scraps of dough, roll out again, and cut more rounds. Repeat until all the dough has been used.

11. Spoon 1 tablespoon of the rice mixture into each lined muffin cup and top it with a dusting of powdered cinnamon. Place the muffin pans in the oven and bake for 20 minutes, then put under a preheated broiler to brown the crust edges. Remove from the broiler and transfer to a cake rack to cool. Remove the rice tartlets from the pans when they have cooled.

Puddings

Puddings are comfortable

and soothing desserts in Italy, made with rich milk and eggs. With each addition of another ingredient, a new pudding name has been invented.

We've had Tiramisu in many guises; its name literally translates as "measured scramble," an apt description though there are other translations. We've also had Mascarpone pudding without any Mascarpone in its mixture and various baked custards with honey whose basic formula goes back to Apicius' cookbook written in Imperial Roman times. And there is, of course, the ever-present zuppa inglese with what seems to be as many changes of ingredients as there are pastry chefs.

Puddings, though, are always lovingly put together, with the best of ingredients, subtly flavored, and elegantly served. We've chosen our favorites—those that have found a place in our regular cooking-at-home desserts.

Egg Custard

This is a perfect "saucepan" egg custard. It is the basis for many puddings and an essential part of many pastry desserts. The Italians serve a thicker custard than the English, whose custard tends to be almost a sauce.

Serves 4

> *2 egg yolks*
> *6 tablespoons sugar*
> *3 teaspoons vanilla extract*
> *3 tablespoons cornstarch*
> *2 cups half-and-half*
> *Pinch of salt*
> *Whipped cream (optional)*
> *Almonds, Blanched and Toasted, page 48, sliced (optional)*

1. Place the egg yolks in a saucepan and, while beating, gradually add the sugar. Continue to beat while mixing in two teaspoons of vanilla extract.

2. Put the cornstarch in a small bowl. Slowly pour in ½ cup of half-and-half, mixing and smoothing the cornstarch with a spoon. When all the lumps are smoothed out, stir in the remaining half-and-half.

3. Slowly add a little of the liquid to the egg-sugar mixture and blend with a wooden spoon or small wire whisk. Gradually add the remaining liquid, smoothing out any lumps. Put the pan over low to moderate heat and stir continuously with an angled-bottom wooden spoon to keep it smooth. Beat the custard vigorously as it starts to thicken. Cook the custard for 8 minutes, scraping the bottom and sides of the pan to keep the custard moving.

4. Take the pan off the heat. Add a pinch of salt and the remaining teaspoon of vanilla extract.

5. If serving as a plain custard dessert, pour into 4 sherbet glasses to cool. Top with whipped cream and/or sliced almonds, if desired.

Chocolate Egg Custard

This rich chocolate custard combines chocolate and coffee flavors in a smooth custard base.

Serves 4

> 2 ounces unsweetened chocolate
> 2 egg yolks
> 6 tablespoons sugar
> 2 teaspoons vanilla extract
> 3 tablespoons cornstarch
> 2 cups half-and-half
> 1 teaspoon instant espresso coffee powder
> Pinch of salt

1. Grate the chocolate in either a food processor or Mouli grater and set aside.

2. Place the egg yolks in a saucepan and, while beating, gradually add the sugar. Continue to beat while mixing in 1 teaspoon of vanilla extract.

3. Put the cornstarch in a small bowl. Slowly pour in ¾ cup of half-and-half, mixing and smoothing the cornstarch with a wooden spoon. Slowly add a little of the liquid to the egg-sugar mixture and blend with the wooden spoon or a small wire whisk. Gradually add the remaining liquid, smoothing out any lumps.

4. Heat the remaining 1¼ cups of half-and-half. Sprinkle the grated chocolate and espresso coffee powder over the surface when the milk begins to warm. Stir until the chocolate has melted, then immediately remove from the heat. Slowly pour this mixture over the egg mixture, whisking rapidly to prevent lumps from forming.

5. Place the pan over low to medium heat. Stir the custard continuously with an angled-bottom wooden spoon to keep it smooth. When the custard starts to thicken, beat it vigorously with

the spoon. Cook for 8 minutes, scraping the bottom and sides of the pan to keep the custard moving.

6. Take the pan off the heat. Add a pinch of salt and the remaining teaspoon of vanilla extract.

Note: The custard can be served plain or with whipped cream, or used in a recipe that calls for chocolate custard.

Time-Saver Custard

Every so often time runs out and shortcuts are in order. We often use vanilla pudding mix with added flavoring instead of an egg custard from scratch. It works well as a cake filling or in a tart as a custard base under fresh fruit.

Makes enough for a 6½-inch cake or tart

>6 tablespoons vanilla pudding powder, or half a box
>1 cup half-and-half
>1 teaspoon vanilla or almond extract

1. In a small saucepan, mix together the pudding powder and a little half-and-half, stirring to form a thick, lumpless mixture. Slowly pour in the remaining half-and-half, stirring and smoothing the mixture.

2. Put the pan over moderate heat and cook the custard according to the manufacturer's instructions.

3. When thickened, remove the custard from the heat. Add the vanilla or almond extract, stir, and pour into a bowl to cool. Cover the top of the custard with a circle of wax paper to prevent a skin from forming and put in the refrigerator until ready to use.

VARIATION
A small amount of whipped cream may be stirred into the

cooled custard to lighten it. Other flavorings that can be used are rum, maraschino liqueur, Marsala, and orange or lemon zest or extract.

Baked Caramel Custard
Crema al Caramello

The ubiquitous caramel custard can be a melt-on-the-tongue joy or a rubbery, watery disaster. Here is a recipe for the ultimate in creamy, quivery texture, topped by golden brown caramel when unmolded. Serve extra caramel syrup in a small pitcher.

4 individual custard ramekins, ⅔-cup size
Serves 4

> ¾ *cup sugar*
> 2 *tablespoons hot water*
> 2 *eggs*
> 4 *tablespoons sugar*
> ⅛ *teaspoon salt*
> 1 *teaspoon vanilla extract*
> 1¾ *cups half-and-half*
> *Grated nutmeg*

1. Place the ¾ cup of sugar in a small saucepan and sprinkle the hot water over the surface. Let the sugar absorb the water, then mix it with a fork until the water is evenly distributed.

2. Place the pan over low heat and let the sugar melt without stirring. When most of the sugar has turned to liquid, you may have to break up some unmelted lumps with a fork. Shake and tip the pan until the liquid is just beyond the golden stage, then quickly remove it from the heat.

3. Drizzle thin ribbons of this caramel syrup on the sides and bottom of each custard ramekin. Do not cover the interior surface

completely because this would be too much caramel; it will only collect and harden on the bottom of the ramekin. Set aside.

4. To make the extra syrup, add a small amount of boiling water to the caramel left in the pan and return the pan to the heat to blend the 2 liquids. Stir the syrup and remove from the heat when the caramel has melted completely. You will have to be the judge of the amount of water to add since it depends on how much caramel syrup is left in the pan.

5. Let the syrup cool in the pan. If it is too thick or too thin when cooled, either add a little hot water to thin or put it back on the heat to boil down to thicken. Cool again and pour into a small pitcher for serving.

6. Preheat the oven to 300°. In the center of the middle rack, place a shallow pan large enough to hold the custard cups without touching and half-fill it with hot water.

7. Beat the eggs in a bowl with a wire whisk. Add the 4 tablespoons of sugar and salt, and beat until the sugar has dissolved. Add the vanilla extract.

8. Pour the half-and-half into a saucepan and scald it over moderate heat. Remove the pan from the heat and slowly pour the half-and-half into the egg-sugar mixture, beating all the time with a wire whisk.

9. Ladle the mixture into the caramel-lined ramekins and grate nutmeg over the tops.

10. Place the ramekins in the pan containing the hot water and bake for about 1 hour. Test by inserting the blade of a table knife into the center of a custard. If it comes out clean, remove the custards from the oven; if some custard clings to the knife blade, then cook the custards until the blade comes out clean.

11. When cooked, place the ramekins on a baking rack to cool. Do not refrigerate because custards should be served at room temperature, and chilling hardens the caramel.

12. To serve, run a broad, thin-bladed knife around the edge of each ramekin to loosen the custard and break the vacuum. Place an individual serving bowl over the top of each ramekin, turn it

over, and the custard will slide into the serving bowl. Scrape out any remaining caramel onto the top of the custard. Serve with the additional caramel syrup.

Black-and-White Pudding (Modena)

This seductive pudding was served to us from a large glass bowl. It was a cross between Mascarpone Pudding I of Ravenna, Mascarpone Pudding II of Faenza, Tiramisu of Venice, and a local variation of zuppa inglese. With that wild introduction let us describe the pudding we ate at a restaurant down a side street off the large market square in back of the Modena cathedral.

Vanilla and chocolate custard were wavily and irregularly layered in the bowl, producing an effect somewhat like marble cake. As the custards were added, three-quarter-inch squares of sponge cake, soaked in maraschino liqueur, were dropped into the bowl. Over the top surface was "floated" a one-quarter-inch-thick layer of transparent caramel jelly. It was delicious.

7-x-3½-inch loaf pan
Glass serving bowl, 10 inches in diameter
Serves 8

> *Sponge Cake, page 32, half the recipe; or leftover plain cake*
> *Egg Custard, page 237; or Time-Saver Custard, page 240,*
> *   double the recipe*
> *Chocolate Egg Custard, page 239*
> *¼ to ½ cup maraschino liqueur*
> *Caramel Jelly:*
> *½ cup sugar*
> *1 tablespoon cold water*
> *Boiling water*
> *2 teaspoons unflavored gelatin*

1. Make and bake the sponge cake. Turn out the cake, allow it to cool, and then cut it into ½- to ¾-inch cubes.

2. Make both of the custards. Pour into separate bowls and cover each top with a circle of wax paper to prevent a skin from forming. Cool the custards to lukewarm or until they thicken enough so they will stay separate when spooned into the glass serving bowl.

To Assemble:

1. When the custards are cold, pour the maraschino liqueur into a small bowl. Dip the cubes of cake lightly into the liqueur and arrange them on a plate; they should absorb some of the liqueur but not be soggy.

2. Alternately ladle the 2 custards into the glass serving bowl in an irregular pattern, placing the maraschino-soaked sponge cake cubes into the bowl as you add the custards. When all the custard and sponge cubes have been added, smooth the top with the edge of a plastic or rubber spatula. Put the bowl in the refrigerator to chill.

3. To make the caramel jelly: Place the sugar in a small saucepan and stir in 1 tablespoon of cold water until it is completely distributed. Put the pan over low heat until the sugar has melted to a medium caramel color; do not let it get too dark or burn. Take the pan off the heat to stop the browning and cool the caramel slightly. The amount of caramel jelly is enough to cover a 10-inch-diameter surface ¼ inch deep.

4. Add ½ cup of boiling water and stir the mixture with a tablespoon to blend the sugar and water, returning the pan to high heat. When blended, add enough boiling water (if needed) to make 1 cup of syrup. Remove from the heat.

5. Soften the gelatin with 3 teaspoons of cold water. When soft, bring the syrup to just below boiling, stir in the softened gelatin, remove the pan from the heat, and continue to stir until the gelatin has melted.

6. Place the pan in the refrigerator until the caramel jelly is a thick syrup. Do not let it stiffen completely because it must be

spooned over the top of the chilled custard into a smooth glassy covering, but it cannot be so soft that it will sink into the custard.

7. When chilled, carefully spoon the caramel jelly over the top of the pudding and return the bowl to the refrigerator to finish setting the jelly. Serve the pudding at table from the glass bowl.

Custard Ladyfinger Pudding (Taormina)

Before a leisurely exploration of Sicily—Syracuse, Piazza Armerina, Agrigento, Palermo, and the countryside in between—we settled into Taormina for a few days to enjoy the town, its shops and restaurants. One night, in the top-floor restaurant of our hotel with its view of brooding Mount Etna, our dinner ended with an elegant custard and ladyfinger dessert. This very soothing, rich dessert of cooked egg custard, ladyfingers, nut brittle, and whipped cream was savored spoonful by spoonful until finally the dish was carefully scraped.

4 shallow glass dessert dishes
Serves 4

> *12 Ladyfingers, page 119, or Sponge Cake, page 32*
> *Egg Custard, page 237; or Time-Saver Custard, page 240,*
>   *double the recipe*
> *4 teaspoons Amaretto liqueur*
> *4 teaspoons crushed Almond Brittle, page 52*
> *¼ cup heavy cream, or to taste*
> *Sugar to taste*
> *Vanilla extract to taste*

1. Preheat the oven to 350°. Make the ladyfingers. If you make the full recipe, you can freeze the remaining ladyfingers for

another use or enjoy them with a glass of white wine or espresso coffee.

2. While the ladyfingers are cooling, make the custard. When cooked, remove the pan from the heat and cool the custard to room temperature, with a circle of wax paper on top to prevent a skin from forming.

3. Arrange 3 single ladyfingers, flat side down, across the bottom of each dessert dish. Sprinkle each set of ladyfingers with 1 teaspoon of Amaretto liqueur. If the ladyfingers are thick, you may use more liqueur, but do not soak the cake.

4. Divide the cooled custard among the 4 dishes, spooning it over the ladyfingers so they are completely covered. Place the dishes in the refrigerator for 10 to 15 minutes to chill the custard.

5. Remove the dishes from the refrigerator and sprinkle 1 teaspoon of crushed almond brittle over the top of each chilled custard (the almond brittle will melt on room-temperature custard). Return the dishes to the refrigerator until 45 minutes to 1 hour before serving. The pudding should not be served refrigerator cold.

6. Whip the cream and add sugar and vanilla extract to taste. Serve the pudding with a dollop of whipped cream in the center.

Honey-Nut Custard (Imperial Rome)

We have often read through the collection of recipes in the Apicius book of recipes from Imperial Rome. We have marveled at some of the food combinations enjoyed by those early Romans and have been impressed by the originality of others. One day, realizing how popular caramel custard (latte imperiale) is in Italy, we decided to work our way through Apicius' honey-nut custard recipe, adapting it to our modern methods. Surprisingly enough, this was not difficult to do, and so this ancient patina versatilis vice dulcis, or nut-custard turnover, was added to our favorite desserts.

4 ramekins, ⅔-cup size
Serves 4

> *24 Toasted Hazelnuts, page 49*
> *10 tablespoons honey; dark honey or wildflower honey is*
> *preferred*
> *2 eggs*
> *⅛ teaspoon salt*
> *1¾ cups half-and-half*
> *Cardamom powder*

1. Prepare the hazelnuts following the directions in the recipe. Place them in a food processor fitted with a steel blade and spin 3 times with a count of 5 each time. Pour into a small bowl and cut up any large pieces with a knife; the chunks will be approximately ⅛ inch.

2. Divide the nuts among the 4 ramekins, Add 1½ tablespoons of honey to each ramekin. Mix the hazelnuts and honey together in each ramekin. Set aside.

3. Preheat the oven to 300°. Place a shallow pan, large enough to hold the 4 ramekins without touching, on the center rack of the oven. Half-fill the pan with hot water.

4. In a bowl, beat the eggs with a wire whisk. Add the salt and the remaining 4 tablespoons of honey, beating all the while.

5. Scald the half-and-half and pour it in a thin stream over the egg-honey mixture, beating all the while.

6. Ladle the mixture into each ramekin. Dust the top of the custard with the cardamom powder. Place the ramekins in the shallow pan of hot water, being careful that they do not touch.

7. Bake the custards for 50 to 60 minutes. Test for doneness by inserting the thin blade of a table knife into the center of the custard. When the blade comes out clean, the custard is done. Remove the ramekins from the oven and place on a baking rack to cool. Do not refrigerate. To serve: Run a knife around the edge of each ramekin. Place a shallow glass dessert dish or a sherbet glass

over the top of the ramekin, turn it over, and the custard will slide in. Scrape out any remaining honey-nut mixture.

Latte Imperiale (Ravenna)

At the Pasticceria Giogioni in Ravenna, we bought half-round slices that were cut from a long loaf of baked custard and cake drenched in honey-flavored caramel syrup.

We were puzzled by the name Latte Imperiale (Imperial Milk), and so when we returned home we looked through Apicius' book on cooking and dining in Imperial Rome. We found recipes for baked custard incorporating honey instead of caramel sauce and realized that down through the centuries the designation Imperiale had become attached to all honey-sauced baked custards.

Since a half-round loaf pan is not standard kitchen equipment, we bake ours in an oven-proof glass bowl with a round bottom, then turn the custard out on a round platter and serve it cut into wedges.

5-inch round cake pan
Oven-proof glass bowl, 5-inches in diameter and 2½ to 3 inches deep,
    with a round bottom
Serves 4

> *Thin Cake Layer, page 38; half the recipe*
> *¾ cup sugar*
> *2 tablespoons cold water*
> *Boiling water*
> *1 tablespoon dark honey*
> *2 eggs*
> *4 tablespoons sugar*
> *Pinch of salt, or to taste*
> *1 teaspoon vanilla extract*
> *1¾ cups half-and-half*

1. Preheat the oven to 475°. Bake the thin cake layer, using the 5-inch cake pan, and then cool, following the recipe directions.

2. Reset the oven to 300°. To make the caramel syrup, measure the ¾ cup of sugar into a small, flat-bottomed saucepan. Stir in the cold water and place the pan over medium heat. With a fork, break up the lumps as the sugar melts. Tip the pan to mix the syrup until it is just beyond the golden stage, but do not let it get too dark or it will become bitter.

3. Pour ¼ to ½ of the caramelized sugar syrup in a thin stream into the glass bowl, turning the bowl so the bottom and sides are covered with a thin coat. Set aside.

4. Add 2 tablespoons of boiling water to the remaining caramel syrup in the saucepan and bring to a boil, stirring with a spoon. Add more boiling water as needed to make a thick syrup. Turn off the heat and stir the honey into the syrup. Set aside.

5. In a mixing bowl, beat the eggs with a wire whisk. Add the 4 tablespoons of sugar and beat well. Add the salt and vanilla.

6. Place the half-and-half in a saucepan and put over medium heat to scald. Stir in 2 tablespoons of the caramel syrup. Pour in a thin stream over the beaten egg mixture, beating constantly.

7. Ladle the custard into the prepared oven-proof glass bowl. Place the bowl in a 1½-inch-deep cake pan containing 1 inch of boiling water. Bake in the preheated oven for 1 hour and 10 minutes, or until a thin-bladed table knife inserted in the center comes out clean. Remove the bowl from the oven and cool the custard on a cake rack.

8. To the leftover thick syrup add 3 to 5 tablespoons of boiling water and bring to a boil, stirring constantly while scraping the bottom and sides of the saucepan. The syrup should not be watery; you'll have to use your own judgment as to the amount of water to add to the leftover syrup. You will need enough syrup to pour over the thin layer cake and to serve on the side with the pudding. You may have to make more caramel sugar for the extra syrup.

9. Trim the thin layer to fit the top of the custard, if necessary. Place the cake on a plate. Pour part of the caramel syrup over the cake, allowing the syrup to soak in but not make the cake mushy.

10. Loosen the edge of the custard with a thin knife. Transfer the caramel-soaked thin layer to the top of the custard. Center a round serving platter with a wall edge over the bowl and turn the platter and bowl over. Remove the bowl and scrape out any syrup in the bottom of the bowl. Cut the pudding into wedges to serve and pass extra syrup in a pitcher.

Mascarpone Pudding I (Ravenna)

There are several types of a creamy custard pudding called Mascarpone, with or without swirls of chocolate. We are including two recipes: One has the rich dessert cheese Mascarpone as an ingredient, as we were served in Ravenna; the other, found in Faenza, has a cooked custard and whipped cream base.

Mascarpone cheese is similar in texture to very thick Devonshire cream and is pale gold in color. It can sometimes be found here in 100-gram (4-ounce) plastic containers in the refrigerated section of specialty stores or sold by weight in fine cheese shops.

4 glass sherbet dishes
Serves 4

> *1 ounce semisweet chocolate*
> *2 eggs*
> *Pinch of cream of tartar*
> *½ cup superfine sugar*
> *2 tablespoons dark rum*
> *100 grams (4 ounces) Mascarpone*
> *Pinch of salt*

1. Break up the chocolate into ½-inch chunks and melt in a double boiler over hot water. Stir, then remove from the heat to cool to lukewarm.

2. Separate the eggs, putting 1 white in a bowl and the other

in a small ramekin to be frozen for another use. If the eggs are small, use both yolks; otherwise, beat 1 yolk and use only half of it (1½ teaspoons) with the other yolk. Put the 1½ or 2 yolks in a small mixing bowl and set aside.

3. Beat the egg white with the cream of tartar. When it peaks, add 2 tablespoons of the superfine sugar. Beat the whites until they are stiff. Set aside.

4. Beat the egg yolks and gradually beat in the remaining sugar with a wire whisk and continue beating until lemon-colored. Add the rum and beat until all ingredients are well blended. Spoon in the Mascarpone and beat until the mixture is light and smooth. Add a pinch of salt to taste if needed.

5. Freshen the beaten egg white with 3 or 4 turns of the beater. Fold the white into the Mascarpone mixture.

6. Spoon ¼ of the custard mixture into a small bowl and lightly fold in the cooled melted chocolate.

7. Alternately spoon the custard mix and the chocolate mix into 4 sherbet glasses, swirling the chocolate with a fork but not blending the 2 mixtures. The pudding should be predominantly golden custard with streaks of chocolate. Cover each glass with a sheet of clear plastic wrap and put the glasses into the refrigerator until it is time to serve. Basic Butter Cookies (page 146) are an excellent accompaniment.

Mascarpone Pudding II (Faenza)

One Sunday in Faenza we spent the morning at the ceramic museum; then we were faced with closed restaurants. Only a few coffee bars were open, and their tired, made-earlier-in-the-day sandwiches were not particularly appetizing. At one of the bars we were given directions to the Pizzeria al Salvatore. After driving through several narrow streets, we turned under an archway into an alley—and there was the Pizzeria. It turned out to be a warm and friendly place with a long bar in the front and a wood fire burning in the open forno where the pizzas were cooked. The inner dining room was plain but comfortable, and the menu listed both dinner dishes and a long list of pizzas. We decided on pizza, and our choice was a revelation: a thin crisp crust, mushrooms, prosciutto, very little tomato sauce, rosemary, and other goodies.

For dessert we had a smooth Mascarpone pudding of creamy goodness served in sherbet glasses. The glass bottoms were heavily sprinkled with ground almond brittle, vanilla-flavored pudding was heaped on top, and a coarse grating of unsweetened chocolate topped it all.

Sherbet glasses
Serves 5 or 6

> *Egg Custard, page 237; or Time-Saver Custard, page 240,*
>   *double the recipe*
> *½ cup heavy cream*
> *5 or 6 tablespoons Almond Brittle, page 52*
> *Unsweetened chocolate*

1. Make the custard following the recipe directions. Spoon the custard into a bowl and cover the top surface with a circle of wax paper or plastic wrap to prevent a skin from forming while it cools.

2. When the custard is completely cool, whip the cream and fold it into the custard. Place the bowl in the refrigerator to chill.

3. Make the almond brittle if you do not have a hoard in a jar in the refrigerator.

To Assemble:

1. Put the dessert together about 1 hour before serving, so that the brittle and grated chocolate are crisp in contrast to the custard pudding. Put ½ tablespoon of almond brittle in the bottom of each sherbet glass. Mound 1 or 2 teaspoons of the custard on top of the brittle, then sprinkle the rest of the brittle between the custard and the sides of the glasses. Add the rest of the custard.

2. Grate the chocolate on the coarse half-moon side of the grater and sprinkle the shavings over the top of the custard. The amount of chocolate depends on the top area of the custard and your own taste, but it should not be so thick that the custard does not show through.

Note: You can also use this formula as the base for Mascarpone Pudding I (page 250).

Tiramisu (Venice)

This version of the pudding tiramisu is a Venetian specialty, but the pudding takes as many forms as zuppa inglese, depending on the Italian city it is served in and the pastry chef who makes it.

In Venice we were served an oblong cut from a large rectangular cake; the Génoise cake had been split into two layers put together with a filling of apricot jam. The top was lavishly covered with an even sieving of unsweetened cocoa powder.

We tried other tiramisus: Some were cake layers filled with a vanilla-flavored custard pudding; others were pure vanilla custard with rum-soaked chunks of cake or ladyfingers mixed in and interlayered with cocoa or chocolate sauce, all spooned from a large bowl into individual dishes. The constant for tiramisu is the thick top covering of cocoa powder or, in the case of the custard, grated unsweetened chocolate.

7-x-7-inch square pan
Serves 4

> *Génoise, page 29*
> *7 tablespoons apricot jam or apricot butter*
> *7 tablespoons Marsala*
> *3 tablespoons plus 1 teaspoon unsweetened cocoa powder*

1. Prepare the Génoise following the recipe directions. When done, remove the cake from the oven and place it under the broiler to crisp the top. Turn the cake out onto a cake rack, remove the wax paper, and turn the cake right side up to cool.

2. When the cake is cool, check the top to see if it is still crisp; if not, place it again under the broiler for a short time but watch it carefully so that the top browns but does not burn. Cool the cake again. Turn the cake over so that the bottom becomes the top. Cut the cake into 4 pieces. Cut each piece in half horizontally and place the halves side by side on a cake rack, cut sides up.

3. Melt the apricot jam or butter. Do not sieve the jam but do break up any large pieces of fruit. Allow to cool slightly before using.

4. Brush the Marsala heavily over the cut sides of the cake squares. Spread the warm apricot jam over the Marsala on the bottom halves of the squares and cover with the top squares.

5. Position the cake rack over a sheet of wax paper. Place the cocoa powder into a fine sieve and sprinkle the top of each square to form an even ⅛-inch-thick covering. Carefully slide each cake onto an individual cake plate.

VARIATION

You can keep the filled and cocoa-dusted cake intact and cut it into squares or into 8 "fingers" at the table.

Zuppa Inglese (Lucca)

We do not know what the original pudding was like except that it probably followed a recipe for the traditional English Trifle, so dear to the hearts of those homesick Victorians who had fled from cold, foggy England to Italy for warmth and romantic scenery. Nowadays, zuppa inglese (English Soup) is almost any mixture of diced fruit, jam, cake, custard sauce, Marsala (to replace sherry), dark rum (to replace brandy), and anything else that the individual

dessert chef adds. It turns up on all the restaurant menus, and it is also the first dessert offered by a waiter if he suspects you are English or American—as happened to us many times.

We did order it in the walled city of Lucca, which seemed to be the epicenter of the Victorian expatriate invasion along the Arno River from Pisa to Florence. Here is a special version of a memory of the past.

2 round cake pans 6 inches in diameter
Oven-proof glass bowl 6 inches in diameter and 4¼ inches deep
Serves 6 to 8

> *Sponge Cake, page 32*
> *Egg Custard, page 237; or Time-Saver Custard, page 240,*
> *   double the recipe. Add additional ½ cup half-and-half*
> *   to either recipe.*
> *6 ounces (8 tablespoons) raspberry jam*
> *Dark rum to taste*

Maraschino liqueur to taste
2 egg whites
Pinch of salt
¼ teaspoon cream of tartar
3 tablespoons sugar
1 teaspoon vanilla extract

Sauce
8 ounces raspberry jam
1 tablespoon maraschino liqueur

1. Cover the bottom of the 2 round pans with buttered wax paper; do not butter the sides of the pans.

2. Preheat the oven to 325°. Make and bake the sponge cake in the 2 cake pans following the recipe directions. When baked, slip the pans under a preheated broiler to dry out the tops; otherwise, they will stick to the cake rack. Remove the pans from the broiler and turn the 2 layers out onto the cake rack. Carefully pull off the wax paper and turn the layers upright on the rack to cool.

3. Make the custard with the additional ½ cup of half-and-half (for a thinner custard) and pour into a small mixing bowl to cool. Cover the top with a circle of wax paper to prevent a skin from forming.

4. Melt the 8 tablespoons of raspberry jam with a tablespoon of water; set aside to cool a little. You may have to add more hot water to make a thinner spread.

To Assemble:

1. Heavily sprinkle the 2 sponge cake layers with the rum and maraschino liqueur—1 side of each layer with rum and the other side of each layer with maraschino liqueur.

2. Spoon ½ of the custard into the oven-proof glass bowl. Measure the width of the top of the custard with a length of thread or string and trim 1 sponge layer to size. Spread the maraschino side with just under ½ of the raspberry jam. Put the layer in place on top of the custard, jam side down.

3. Spoon the rest of the custard over the cake layer. Measure the width of the top of the custard with a length of thread or string, and trim the second layer if necessary. Spread the maraschino side with the rest of the raspberry jam, and put the layer in place on top of the custard, jam side down.

4. Beat the room-temperature egg whites with the salt and cream of tartar until they hold soft peaks. Gradually add the sugar, beating after each addition. Fold in the vanilla extract.

5. Lightly cover the top layer of the sponge cake with the meringue, forming it into irregular peaks and smoothing it against the sides of the bowl so it will not shrink. Place under a preheated broiler to brown the top lightly. If there is not enough space under your broiler, then place the dish in a preheated 300° oven until the top of the meringue has lightly browned. Remove the dish and let it cool to room temperature, then place it in the refrigerator until 30 minutes before serving.

6. For the sauce, melt the 8 ounces of raspberry jam with 1 tablespoon of maraschino liqueur and 3 tablespoons of water or more if the sauce is still too thick to pour. You can sieve the jam to remove the pulp or leave the pulp in the sauce. Transfer to a small pitcher and allow to cool to room temperature. If the sauce becomes too thick on cooling, add sufficient hot water to thin it, then let the sauce cool again.

7. To serve, spoon the pudding into dessert dishes or onto plates and pass the sauce.

VARIATION
Substitute cherry jam for the raspberry jam.

Ice Creams
and Sherbets

While there are

a number of commercial manufacturers of ice cream in Italy, the best of the gelaterias (ice-cream bars) proudly display a sign that their ice cream is made on the premises (nostra produzione). When the worst of winter is over, these gelato bars are in full swing with seemingly endless lists of variously flavored semi-freddo (made with whipped cream) ice creams. Just a few among them are Marsala-raisin, kiwi, avocado, nutella (chestnut puree and liquid chocolate), plus all the nuts and fruits, and combinations thereof, and the standards—chocolate, vanilla, and coffee. Added to these are the fruit sherbets and the "sundae" creations of each individual bar. No wonder that the list posted behind the counter grows longer and longer.

We often bought ice cream at the bars to take home, rather than buy from the freezer at the supermarket. We would specify *a casa,* and tops would be closed over the round "portion" containers. But even more than purchasing ice cream, we like to make our own, taking advantage of seasonal fruits. We prefer the more assertive flavors of Italian ice creams and sherbets as well as the goodness that comes from using fresh ingredients.

One of the difficulties in making home-freezer ice cream and sherbet is eliminating the ice crystals that form in freezer ice cream that is kept for more than a day. The old-fashioned churning added air that created a smooth mixture; however, because there was no "holdover" freezer, the ice cream was eaten the day it was made. But too often the formulas for churned ice cream have just been copied for in-freezer ice cream, with the disastrous result of solid blocks of "ice" with no creaminess. The same applies to fruit sherbets frozen in metal containers to be beaten just before serving to break up the ice crystals—a chore that delays the serving and often results in a wet slush.

We have tested and retested both ice-cream and sherbet formulas and found that by adding a small amount of gelatin to the ice-cream formula we had a smooth and un-iced ice cream—even after it had been packed away in the freezer in containers for up to two weeks. For sherbets we also add corn syrup to the sugar and water, which eliminates the tricky making of a boiled sugar syrup that has to have a perfect balance between the sugar and water quantities and has to be heated to a critical temperature on a candy thermometer (not standard equipment in the average kitchen).

We are now satisfied with our own formulas even though they may go against the accepted "this is the way it has always been" recipes. The main test is that we can serve and enjoy smooth and flavorsome ice cream and sherbet. So try, and enjoy.

Frozen Whipped Cream

This basic recipe is part of the Strawberry Sherbet Cake (page 104) and is an excellent outside "shell" for ice-cream bombes.

Makes approximately 1¼ cups

> *Water*
> *1 packet gelatin*
> *¾ cup heavy cream*
> *2 tablespoons sugar*
> *½ teaspoon vanilla extract*

1. Put 3 tablespoons of water in a small bowl and sprinkle the gelatin over it to soften. Put water in a saucepan and bring it to a boil. Turn off the heat and immediately set the bowl of softened gelatin in the water (which should reach halfway up the bowl).

When the mixture is clear and the gelatin is dissolved, remove the bowl from the hot water and allow to reach room temperature. Do not let the gelatin set.

2. Beat the cream. Add the sugar and vanilla extract, and continue beating until the cream is stiff. Mix 1 tablespoon of the whipped cream with the gelatin mixture, then stir it into the whipped cream. Whip the cream with 2 or 3 turns of the beater to combine and smooth the mixture.

3. Spoon the whipped cream into a plastic container, snap on the cover, and place it in the freezer. After 1 hour, stir the whipped cream to break up the ice crystals.

Note: Double the recipe for serving with fruit or other sauces.

Banana Ice Cream (Asolo)

North and east of Vicenza, beyond Bassano del Grappa, is Asolo, the hill town of Caterina Cornaro, Robert Browning, and Eleonora Duse. The town centers around its sloping market square with the ruins of the castle on one side. All roads lead into the irregularly shaped shop-lined piazza where a sprawling street market is held once a week. One shop has outdoor tables and chairs straggling down a stone-paved slope. It serves the best banana ice cream ever eaten, lushly creamy down to the last scrape of the dish. This is our own re-creation.

Makes approximately 5 cups

> 1½ packets plain gelatin
> ½ cup cold water
> 2 cups heavy cream
> 1 cup half-and-half
> ¾ cup sugar
> 2 large, very ripe bananas (black-spotted skin)

Juice of ½ lemon
⅛ teaspoon salt
2 tablespoons dark rum
3 teaspoons banana extract

1. In a small bowl, sprinkle the gelatin over the surface of the cold water.

2. Heat ½ cup of heavy cream and the half-and-half in the top of a double boiler over simmering water. When the liquid is hot but not boiling, add the sugar and stir until it has melted. Add the softened gelatin and cook for 1 minute.

3. Take the pan off the heat, pour out the hot water, and refill the pan with cold water. Replace the top of the double boiler in the cold water to cool the custard.

4. While the custard is cooling, peel and slice the bananas. Pour the lemon juice over the banana slices, mixing it in with a fork. Scrape them into the container of a food processor fitted with a steel blade and spin until well pureed; no lumps should remain. Measure out the banana puree; at least 1 cup is needed, but a little more is all to the good. Stir in the salt, rum, and banana extract. Set aside.

5. Beat the remaining 1½ cups of heavy cream until stiff but still soft. Add several tablespoons of whipped cream to the custard to thicken it and then mix in the balance.

6. Fold in the pureed banana.

7. Freeze the mixture according to the manufacturer's directions for your ice-cream freezer. When frozen, pack into covered plastic containers for storage in the freezer compartment of the refrigerator.

Coffee Ice Cream (Otranto)

Otranto, on the water near where the Adriatic spills into the Mediterranean, is well south and east of Lecce. With its white buildings, it feels more Arabian than the more northern towns in the heel. Its cathedral was once a mosque, but its mosaic floor, which dates from around 1165, is a mixture of biblical scenes and legendary figures, including one labeled Rex Arturus. We spent most of the morning in the cool cathedral studying the floor, photographing it, and absorbing the medieval world. Outside, the weather was summer, and the ice cream was a welcome finish to lunch and a sweet reminder of the coffee grown in Arabia and shipped across from the Red Sea port of Mocha.

Ours is a smooth and richly flavored ice cream due to the use of instant espresso coffee powder.

Makes 5 or 6 cups

> 1½ *packets plain gelatin*
> ½ *cup cold water*
> 2 *cups heavy cream*
> 2¼ *cups half-and-half*
> 3 *tablespoons instant espresso coffee powder*
> ¾ *cup sugar*
> 1½ *teaspoons vanilla extract*
> ⅛ *teaspoon salt*
> 1 *tablespoon dark rum*

1. In a small bowl, sprinkle the gelatin over the surface of the cold water.

2. Place ½ cup of heavy cream and the half-and-half into the top of a large double boiler and place over simmering water. When the cream is hot, sprinkle the instant coffee powder over the surface. Let it melt, then stir to mix well. Add the sugar, stirring with a wooden spoon until it has melted. Scrape in the softened gelatin and stir for 1 minute.

3. Take the double boiler off the heat. Pour out the hot water from the lower pot and refill it, almost to the top, with cold water. Carefully float the top of the double boiler in the cold water to cool

the custard mixture. Stir in the vanilla extract, salt, and dark rum. Allow the custard to cool, changing water when necessary.

4. Whip the remaining 1½ cups of heavy cream until thick but not stiff. Make sure the custard is cool, then mix in ¼ of the whipped cream. Fold in the remaining cream.

5. Freeze according to the manufacturer's directions for your ice-cream freezer.

6. Store the ice cream in covered plastic containers (2-cup size) in the freezer compartment of your refrigerator. Homemade ice cream sometimes freezes harder than commercial ice cream, so you may have to remove the container or containers from the freezer to the refrigerator compartment or serving table before dinner is served to soften the ice cream.

Rich Chocolate Ice Cream
Cioccolato Gelato Semi-Freddo

When the weather turns warm, Italy goes ice-cream mad. Ice-cream men on bicycles, their stock in a metal box in front of the handlebars, pedal through the streets. White deep-freeze containers plastered with garishly colored drawings of the commercial frozen confections that are inside appear outside small tobacco and grocery stores.

Ice-cream bars specializing exclusively in rich ice creams, sherbets, and ices are packed with customers, and the overflow customers crowd together at tables outside or escape happily to neighboring streets with cones or containers to enjoy while walking.

Here is a recipe for Rome's rich chocolate ice cream (with whipped cream), a delight just as is but whose richness is compounded when made into Tartufo (page 268).

Makes 5 or 6 cups

½ cup cold water
1½ packets plain gelatin
4 ounces unsweetened chocolate
1¾ cups half-and-half
2 cups heavy cream
2 teaspoons instant espresso coffee powder
¾ cup sugar
1½ teaspoons vanilla extract
⅛ teaspoon salt

1. Set the freezer at the coldest temperature.

2. Put the cold water in a small bowl and sprinkle the gelatin over the surface.

3. Break up the chocolate into small chunks and melt them in the top of a small double boiler over simmering water.

4. Pour the half-and-half and ½ cup of heavy cream into the top of a large double boiler with simmering water in the lower half. When hot, sprinkle instant coffee powder over the surface and let it melt. Add the sugar, stirring with a wooden spoon until it has melted. Scrape in the softened gelatin and stir for 1 minute.

5. Remove the pan of melted chocolate from the heat and using a wire whisk quickly beat in approximately 1½ cups of the hot cream mixture. It will thicken quickly. Whisk the mixture back into the large double boiler pot, scraping the chocolate pot with a plastic or rubber spatula. If thick chocolate remains in the bottom of the pot, thin with some of the hot liquid, then pour it back into the rest of the liquid mixture.

6. Remove the double boiler from the heat. Pour the hot water out of the lower pot and fill it almost to the top with cold water. Put the top of the double boiler into the cold water to cool the chocolate mixture. Stir in the vanilla extract and salt and allow the custard to cool, changing water when necessary.

7. When the custard has cooled completely, whip the remaining 1½ cups of heavy cream until thick but not stiff. Mix about ¼ of the whipped cream into the cold chocolate custard to lighten it, then fold in the rest of the whipped cream.

8. Freeze according to the manufacturer's directions for your ice-cream freezer.

9. Store the ice cream in 2-cup covered plastic containers in the freezer compartment of the refrigerator. Remove the containers before dinner is served and allow to stand at room temperature to soften the ice cream.

Chocolate Ice Cream Balls, Sprill-Covered
Tartufo

This is a chocolate ice-cream confection found at the great Roman ice-cream bars. Chocolate on top of chocolate—a chocoholic's dream. The quantities listed are for *one* tartufo made from Rich Chocolate Ice Cream. Increase the ingredients as needed. General directions, though, are for making several tartufi, as you will want to make more than one.

Work very quickly because this chocolate ice cream melts quickly. Also, allow time for freezing between each step.

Ice cube tray

> *½ cup Rich Chocolate Ice Cream, page 266, slightly softened*
> *1 tablespoon chocolate mini-morsels or chips*
> *1 glacéed cherry*
> *1½ tablespoons chocolate sprills, Choc-o-Trims, or similar*
> *   product*
> *Whipped cream to taste*
> *Sugar to taste*
> *Vanilla extract to taste*

1. Put the ice cream into a stainless steel bowl and mix in 1 tablespoon of chocolate mini-morsels per serving. Return the ice cream to the freezer to stiffen.

2. Line 1 or more metal ice cube trays (emptied of compart-

ments) with aluminum foil that should extend 2 inches above the top edge of a tray. Put the trays into the freezer to chill. Also chill a small plate.

3. When the ice cream is stiff enough, form ½ of the bowl's contents into half-balls with a 2½-inch ice-cream scoop, leveling the top. Turn each half out on the chilled plate, then flip it over with a tablespoon into the chilled, aluminum-foil-lined ice cube tray, *flat side up*. Push a glacéed cherry halfway into the middle of each ice-cream half. Return the tray and the bowl with the remaining ice cream to the freezer.

4. When the ice cream has stiffened, form an equal number of half-balls, placing each one on top of a "cherried" lower half. Smooth the joining crack with the flat blade of a table knife. Return the balls to the freezer until solid.

5. Remove only 1 ice cream ball at a time from the freezer. On a chilled plate roll the ball in the chocolate sprills. Work quickly and return the covered ball to the tray in the freezer compartment before taking out the next ball. Repeat until all ice cream balls are covered with chocolate sprills.

6. Put a sheet of aluminum foil loosely over the balls in the tray. Shortly before serving, move the tartufi to the refrigerator.

7. Serve in wide-mouthed sherbet or champagne glasses. Add a dollop of whipped cream that has been slightly sweetened and flavored with vanilla extract. Serve extra whipped cream in a bowl.

VARIATION

The balls of ice cream can be rolled in toasted chopped almonds or crushed nut brittle.

Lemon Ice
Granita

One year we stayed for a week in Sorrento. Our hotel room was several floors up, overlooking the flower-edged lawn. Northward was Vesuvius, and southwest was Capri. Also southward was the coastal road that swooped around the edge of the blue-misted mountains, sometimes above the sea, other times diving to the waterside docks and streets and beaches of small towns. The clouds and sun cast shadow and light over the mountains and sea, changing the colors of land and water. As we drove south the road curved back and forth, and we caught tantalizing glimpses of roofs and houses and terraced fields heavy with orange and lemon trees.

At Amalfi we wandered through the streets to the cathedral with its mix of Arabian, Norman, and baroque architecture. We had lunch in a grottolike restaurant on the waterfront, then strolled down to the docks while enjoying the cool ice flavored with the essence of lemons from those steep hillsides.

Makes 6 cups

> *5 large, thick-skinned lemons, 3 to 4 inches long*
> *¼ cup cold water*
> *1 packet plain gelatin*
> *1¾ cups sugar*
> *¾ cup light corn syrup*
> *2¾ cups water*
> *1 egg white*
> *1 tablespoon sugar*

1. Set the freezer at the coldest temperature.

2. Grate the zest from 3 lemons into a small bowl. Cover the bowl tightly with plastic wrap and set it aside. Squeeze the juice from all 5 lemons and set aside in a small bowl.

3. Pour ¼ cup of water into a small bowl and sprinkle the gelatin over its surface.

4. Put 1¾ cups of sugar, corn syrup, and 2¾ cups of water in a stainless steel saucepan and bring to a boil, stirring continuously until the sugar has melted. Boil for 2 minutes.

5. Turn down the heat to simmer. Add 3 or 4 tablespoons of the hot liquid to the softened gelatin and pour the gelatin into the

rest of the liquid in the saucepan, stirring until the gelatin has melted—this should take less than 1 minute.

6. Take the saucepan off the heat and stir in the grated lemon zest. Cover the pan and set it aside for 30 to 45 minutes to steep and cool to lukewarm.

7. Strain the mixture through a fine plastic or stainless steel (not aluminum) sieve into a stainless steel bowl, pressing all the juice from the grated lemon zest. Stir in the lemon juice and taste for sweetness. If too sharp, add more corn syrup; if too sweet, add more lemon juice.

8. Place the bowl, uncovered, in the freezing compartment of the refrigerator until a *heavy* slush forms throughout the mixture. (See *Note*.)

9. Beat the egg white until stiff and then beat in 1 tablespoon of sugar. When ready, remove the lemon ice from the freeezer and beat vigorously with a spoon until the mixture is of uniform consistency. Fold in the egg white and return the bowl to the freezer.

10. When the ice is almost entirely hard, remove from the freezer and beat with a spoon until well blended and smooth. Spoon into 2-cup covered plastic containers and return to the freezer until firm enough (but not rock-hard) or overnight.

11. To serve, spoon the ice into widemouthed champagne glasses that have been chilled, if you like.

Note: An exact length of time for freezing the ice cannot be given since all freezer compartments are different. It could range from as little as 1 hour to as long as 3 hours. It is only after making the ice once that you can set your own time.

Pistachio Ice Cream (Manfredonia)
Pistacchio Semi-Freddo Gelato

After a long and exciting trip on the Adriatic coast from the "heel of the boot," we came to rest for several days in Manfredonia in a blue-and-white modern hotel with the distinct decor of an ocean liner. Through the window-lined wall of the dining room one looked out on the Adriatic, increasing the sense of a detached leisurely holiday. This summer mood led to ice-cream desserts, and the richly flavored pistachio ice cream reminded us of the link with Eastern cuisine beyond the Adriatic Sea.

Makes 6 cups

> *1½ ounces (⅓ cup) shelled pistachio nuts (3 ounces un-*
> *   shelled, non-red-stained*
> *1 to 1½ teaspoons unsalted butter*
> *¼ cup half-and-half*
> *1½ packets plain gelatin*
> *2 cups heavy cream*
> *1¾ cups half-and-half*
> *¾ cup sugar*
> *⅛ teaspoon salt*
> *1¾ to 2 teaspoons pistachio flavoring or almond extract*
> *4 drops green food coloring, approximately*

1. Set the freezer at the coldest temperature.

2. Put the shelled nuts in boiling water to cover and simmer them for 2 minutes. Remove with a slotted tablespoon; rub off the skins and roughly chop the nuts. Place a small saucepan over low heat, add the nuts, and stir them with a fork to dry them out. When the pan is hot, add the butter and continue stirring the nuts for a few minutes longer. Watch the nuts carefully so they do not get too brown. When done, turn them out on paper towels to blot the excess butter.

3. Pour ¼ cup of half-and-half into a small bowl. Sprinkle the gelatin over the surface and allow to soften, stirring with a fork.

4. Put ½ cup of heavy cream and 1¾ cups of half-and-half in the top of a double boiler over simmering water and scald. Add the sugar and stir with a wooden spoon until the sugar has melted. Add 2 or 3 tablespoons of the hot liquid to the gelatin mixture and stir. Add to the liquid in the double boiler. Cook approximately 1

minute, until the gelatin has melted. Take the pot off the heat and place the top of the double boiler into a saucepan of cold water to cool the mixture.

5. Beat the remaining 1½ cups of heavy cream until it is thick but not too stiff.

6. Add salt, flavoring, and food coloring to the cooled custard. Stir 2 or 3 heaping tablespoons of whipped cream into the custard and mix with a wire whisk. Fold in the remaining whipped cream.

7. Follow the manufacturer's directions for freezing the ice cream and adding the pistachio nuts. When the ice cream is frozen, transfer it to 2-cup covered plastic containers. Place the containers in the freezing compartment until almost ready to serve. Remove the containers just before dinner is served and allow to stand at room temperature to soften the ice cream.

Strawberry Sherbet

The sherbet filling the center of the Strawberry Sherbet Cake in Catanzaro was so good that we kept looking for gelato signs as we drove along the coast road the next day. We stopped at the first one to indulge ourselves again—in strawberry sherbet alone.

This is an intensely flavored sherbet that can be eaten just by itself, served with Pine Nut Cookies (page 157), or as one of the ingredients in Strawberry Sherbet Cake (page 104). Strawberries picked before they ripen are weak in flavor and freezing sherbet or ice cream also lessens the flavor, so the addition of strawberry extract is a must.

Makes 4 cups

> ½ *cup cold water*
> 1 *packet plain gelatin*
> ½ *cup sugar*

4 tablespoons light corn syrup

1 cup water

1 container very ripe strawberries, 4 x 4 x 2¾ inches, ap-
*   proximately 12 ounces (to make 1¼ cups puree)*

2 teaspoons strawberry extract

1 tablespoon dark rum

4 tablespoons white wine

⅛ teaspoon salt, or to taste

1 egg white

1 tablespoon sugar

1. Set the freezer at the coldest temperature.

2. Pour ½ cup of water into a small bowl and sprinkle the gelatin on the surface. Set aside.

3. Mix together ½ cup of sugar, corn syrup, and 1 cup of water in a saucepan. Place over the heat and bring to a boil, stirring until the sugar has melted. Turn down the heat, add the softened gelatin, and stir for 1 minute. Take off the heat and place the saucepan inside a larger pot filled with cold water to cool. Replace the cold water as necessary.

4. Wash and hull the strawberries. Puree in a food processor. Set aside.

5. When the liquid in the saucepan is cool, stir in the strawberry puree, strawberry extract, rum, white wine, and salt. Pour into a deep, flat-bottomed metal container or metal bowl and place in the freezer compartment of the refrigerator. Or follow the manufacturer's directions for an electric ice-cream freezer.

6. Beat the egg white until stiff, then beat in 1 tablespoon of sugar. Remove the semifrozen strawberry mixture from the freezer or ice-cream machine; the unfrozen center will have a slight gelatin-stiffened consistency. Break up the mixture with a large tablespoon, then beat briefly with a wire whisk to smooth any lumps. Fold in the beaten egg white.

7. If you are using an ice-cream machine, freeze the mixture according to the manufacturer's directions. If you are not using a machine, return the strawberry sherbet in the metal container to

the freezer compartment of the refrigerator for 1 hour. Remove from the freezer, break up the lumps again, and beat with the wire whisk for 10 minutes. Spoon into two 2-cup plastic containers, cover, and return to the freezer compartment for 2 or 3 hours, until the sherbet is firm.

8. Serve in stemmed widemouthed champagne or sherbet glasses that have been chilled in the refrigerator.

Zabaglione Ice Cream (Sorrento)
Zabaióne Semi-Freddo Gelato

The outdoor cafes crowd the upper level of the square in Sorrento, and we were lucky one festival night to find a table to share with friends. From there we watched the town's fireworks display which was no more than small bags of colored fire strung on rickety screens of sapling poles. These were set off in a cheerful but haphazard succession at the lower end of the sloping square in the midst of buses trying to navigate the turn onto the main road to Naples. We observed the whole mad, exuberant spectacle as we drank our espresso and spooned the smooth zabaglione ice cream.

This smooth, rich ice cream can be served loosely piled in glass dishes or as the center of a melon-shaped mold lined with an inch-thick layer of Frozen Whipped Cream (page 262). As the center of a mold, mix in candied cherries and chopped toasted almonds, or thickly sprinkle the surface of the frozen whipped cream with Almond Brittle (page 52) before adding the zabaglione.

Makes 3½ cups

>   1 slightly rounded teaspoon plain gelatin
>   2 tablespoons cold water
>   3 egg yolks
>   5 tablespoons sugar
>   Grated zest of ¼ lemon

½ cup dry Marsala
1 cup heavy cream

1. Set the freezer at the coldest temperature.

2. Sprinkle the gelatin over the cold water in a small bowl. When the gelatin has softened, put the bowl in a pan of hot water (heat turned off) to melt the gelatin.

3. Beat the egg yolks with the sugar in the round-bottomed stainless steel top of a double boiler until light-colored and foamy. Beat in the grated lemon zest. Carefully beat in the Marsala, a little at a time.

4. Put the top of the double boiler over the bottom pan containing simmering water; do not let the water touch the bottom of the pan. Beat the mixture with a hand beater for 4 minutes. Add the melted gelatin and beat the mixture 1 minute more. Take the pan off the heat and cool the custard by placing the top pan inside a larger pot filled with cold water.

5. While the custard is cooling, beat the heavy cream until just slightly thicker than the custard. Fold the whipped cream thoroughly into the cooled custard—the mixture should lose any streaks of color. Spoon the zabaglione into a chilled flat-bottomed metal form such as a 4- or 5-cup loaf pan. Cover the pan with aluminum foil and put it in the freezer compartment of the refrigerator for 5 hours.

Fruit Desserts

Italy is both

a fruit-growing and a fruit-eating country; fruit is served and eaten as part of a restaurant meal far more often than in this country. An assortment of fresh fruit is served as a separate course, as is cheese, in addition to and not in place of a sweet. If one eats only fruit or cheese at the end of a meal, it is a personal choice.

Early in the spring everyone serves the sweet, intensely flavored, vine-ripened strawberries doused with maraschino liqueur or white wine. Later on peaches and apricots are bathed in white wine, with sometimes an added teaspoon or two of Amàretto liqueur.

Fruits are also an important part of sweet desserts such as tarts and are poached in sugar syrups to be served alone or combined with custards or cake, or both. A combination of dried fruits served in liqueur-flavored poaching syrup is a traditional favorite.

Ice creams and sherbets are also made with fruits, and for an American the surprise is to find the avocado treated as a fruit. It is served raw with lemon juice and sugar, or as the basis for a pale green ice cream.

Avocado Dice

A surprise dessert "fruit" in Italy is the avocado pear. It can be pureed to make a rich, pale green ice cream or diced and mixed with lemon juice and sugar as an exotic fresh fruit dessert—very good indeed. Since avocado trees are now grown near the Mediterranean, the fruit has become more and more popular in salads and in sweets.

Serves 4

>   *2 large well-ripened avocados*
>   *Juice of 2 lemons*
>   *4 to 6 tablespoons superfine sugar, or to taste*

1. Peel the avocados with a sharp knife. Cut in half and remove the pit. Cut into ½- to ¾-inch dice and place in a shallow bowl.

2. Carefully mix in the lemon juice with the diced fruit, coating all the pieces.

3. Sprinkle the fruit with superfine sugar to taste. Cover the bowl with clear plastic wrap if not ready to serve immediately. Serve in widemouthed champagne glasses.

Banana Slices (Rome)

In a small restaurant, reached from the base of the Spanish Steps, we were served a "tropical" dessert with an Italian flair that turned the fruit into a smoothly luscious confection. The recipe is for a single serving, but you can increase the ingredients according to the number of persons to be served.

Serves 1

>   *¾ tablespoon dark rum*
>   *¾ tablespoon maraschino liqueur*
>   *1 very ripe banana*
>   *Superfine sugar to taste*
>   *¼ cup heavy cream*
>   *Vanilla extract*

1. Mix the rum and maraschino liqueur together in a small bowl.

2. One hour before serving, peel and slice the banana into a flat-bottomed bowl such as a small ramekin. Cover the bottom of the bowl with a single layer of banana slices. Sprinkle the slices with some of the liqueur and dust with superfine sugar. Continue layering until the banana is completely used. Pour any leftover liqueur over the top and finish with a topping of sugar. Cover the bowl with a plate or clear plastic wrap. Do not refrigerate.

3. Whip the cream. When it has thickened into soft peaks, add sugar to taste and 3 or 4 drops of vanilla extract. Continue whipping the cream until stiff but still smooth. Place in the refrigerator until ready to serve.

4. To serve, spoon the banana slices into a widemouthed champagne glass or other shallow glass dessert dish. Pour the juice over the banana slices and top with a generous dollop of whipped cream placed in the center of the banana slices.

Fantastic Pear (Sabboneta)
Pera Fantastico

After a morning spent at the Palazzo Ducale of the Gonzagas, photographing the frescoed ceilings and portrait heads, we went out across Garibaldi Square where the market fair was closing. The self-contained meat, cheese, and clothing trucks (Automarket Alimentari) were still open. Their counters let down from one long side of the truck, the awning over the counter is formed by the rest of the side lifted upward, and inside, the shelves are lined with weighing scales and produce. We stopped to buy some cheese to take home with us, then went on to a lunch that ended with a dessert worthy of a Renaissance court jeweler, though the pastry chef told us it was a new experiment. It begins with leftover cake and pears, and ends as a jewel encased in clear, tawny-colored caramel "enamel."

Either slightly dry Panettone or Plum Cake is a good base for this dessert. Each cake slice is browned lightly in butter, covered with apricot jam, and topped with a poached pear half that is then glazed with caramelized sugar—a fantastic combination of flavors and textures.

Serves 4

> *2 pears, poached (see recipe for Pear Tart, page 198)*
> *1½ tablespoons apricot jam or apricot butter*
> *4 slices dry Panettone, page 95; Plum Cake, page 102;*
>   *Génoise, page 29; or pound cake—all ½ inch thick*
> *1 or 2 tablespoons unsalted butter*
> *½ cup sugar*
> *1¼ tablespoons water*

1. Peel, cut the pears in half, and core. Poach the pears following the recipe directions. Spoon about 1 tablespoon of the syrup over the pears and set them aside in the refrigerator to chill. Poaching can be done early on the day of serving or the day before.

2. About 2 hours before serving, melt the apricot jam or apricot butter in a small pan along with up to 1 tablespoon of poaching syrup. Sieve the jam and set it aside.

3. Cut 4 slices of cake, each one just large enough to hold a pear half. Melt 1 tablespoon of butter in a frying pan large enough to hold the cake slices in a single layer. Swirl the butter around the pan. Put the slices of cake in the pan and brown them lightly on one side. Turn the slices over, add another tablespoon of butter if necessary, and brown the other side. Place each slice of cake in the center of a dessert plate.

4. Brush the melted apricot jam or apricot butter over the top of each slice of cake.

5. To make the caramel, put the sugar in a small saucepan and add the water. Allow the sugar to soak up the liquid, then stir with a fork to mix thoroughly. When mixed, smooth the sugar over the bottom of the saucepan.

6. Put the saucepan over low to moderate heat until the sugar melts. Do not stir. When the sugar has dissolved, turn the pan from side to side to allow the syrup to flow and mix as it slowly turns color; you may have to stir the syrup with a fork. When the syrup is just beyond the light golden stage, remove the pan from the heat.

7. While the sugar is melting, place a chilled pear on top of each slice of cake, rounded side up.

8. Quickly spoon the syrup over the top of each pear half until each is covered. If the syrup hardens in the saucepan before you are finished, put the saucepan back over moderate heat just long enough to melt the rest of the syrup.

9. Set the dessert aside until ready to serve. The caramelized sugar will form a hard transparent glaze over the pear.

Oranges Milanese (Milan)

As we passed the dessert table just inside the dining room door of a restaurant in Milan, we took more than a passing glance at a platter of golden skinless oranges, shiny with syrup. Strips of candied orange peel were piled helter-skelter on top of each one, and a thin pool of orange syrup covered the platter. That vision stayed in our minds all through dinner, so of course we ordered the oranges for dessert. They were served in individual shallow dishes with some of the syrup.

This recipe is for two servings, one orange for each; however, the amount of syrup and the amount of candied peel from two oranges are enough for a serving of four oranges! Our advice is to go right ahead and use all the peel and make all the syrup. Store the extra peel, well dredged with sugar, in a glass jar in the refrigerator; the extra syrup is excellent as a sauce for ice cream or poured in the bottom of the ramekins when making an orange-flavored baked custard.

Serves 2

> 2 *large, thick-skinned seedless oranges*
> 1 *cup sugar*
> *Water*

1. With a swivel peeler, cut 1-inch-wide strips of zest (the orange rind without the white part) from the top to the bottom of the two oranges. With a sharp knife, cut the zest into ⅛-inch-wide strips approximately 2 inches in length.

2. Put the strips into a small saucepan large enough to hold the two oranges side by side. Add 1 cup of water, bring to a boil, and boil gently for 10 minutes.

3. Meanwhile, thoroughly remove *all* the rest of the skin and the membrane from the outside surface of the oranges, slightly cutting away at the flesh of the oranges with a very sharp knife. Set the oranges aside on a plate.

4. With a slotted spoon, remove the cooked peel to a small bowl. Pour the liquid into a measuring cup and add enough water (if needed) to fill the cup to the ¾-cup mark. Pour the liquid back into the saucepan and add the sugar. Boil for 7 to 10 minutes, or until the syrup begins to thicken. Add the orange peel to the syrup and boil 5 minutes more. Test the peel for softness and sweetness, and boil 2 or 3 minutes more—the peel should be slightly translucent. Scoop out the peel with a slotted spoon into a fine-mesh sieve, drain, and spread out on a sheet of wax paper, separating the pieces with a fork and your fingers.

5. Bring the syrup to a boil again and put the peeled oranges into the syrup with a slotted spoon. Keep turning them in the boiling syrup for *no more than 2 minutes*. They should glisten with syrup on the outside but remain uncooked within. With the slotted spoon, remove the oranges from the syrup and drain them as much as possible. Place each orange in the center of an individual shallow glass or china dessert dish.

6. Boil down the syrup for 2 or 3 minutes. Take the pan off the heat, let the foam diminish, and cool. Then spoon the syrup slowly over the oranges; if too thick, add enough hot water to thin. You be the judge of how much syrup you want in each dish. Pile 12 to 14 orange peel strips on top of each orange and add another spoonful of syrup on top of the strips. Cool to room temperature.

Peaches and Cream (Ferrara)

In the wide, flat landscape between Ferrara and the Adriatic coast stretch orchards of espaliered fruit trees: peaches, apricots, pears, apples, and cherries. Grapevines looking like ballet dancers are twisted and woven around vertical and horizontal supports.

Poach fresh peaches in a syrup of sugar, wine, and orange flavoring, then serve them cold with a dollop of whipped cream mixed with ground almond brittle. Two very large peaches will serve four people; increase the ingredient amounts depending on the size of the peaches and the number of servings.

Serves 4

> 2½ to 3 tablespoons Almond Brittle, page 52, crushed
> Strip of orange zest
> 2 very large ripe freestone peaches
> ½ cup sugar
> ½ cup white wine
> 2 tablespoons dark rum
> ¼ teaspoon orange extract
> ¼ cup heavy cream

1. Make and crush the almond brittle.
2. Cut a ½-inch-wide strip of orange zest from around the center of a soft-skinned orange. With a sharp-pointed knife, cut the strip into pieces ⅟₁₆ inch wide by 1½ inches long. (If you have strips of Candied Orange Peel [page 51] stored in the refrigerator, use them instead.)
3. Dip the peaches into boiling water, peel them, and cut in half. Remove the peach pit and a little of the center flesh in order to deepen the center cavity.
4. Put the sugar, wine, and orange zest into a stainless steel saucepan large enough to hold the peaches in a single layer. Bring the ingredients to a boil. Add the peach halves, cut side down, and continue to boil the liquid for 3 or 4 minutes, turning the peaches 3 times during the cooking. Do not overcook; the peaches should remain somewhat uncooked within.
5. Remove the peach halves to a bowl with a slotted spoon. Bring the syrup back to a boil and boil down until thickened drops fall off the side of a spoon. (The syrup should be quite thick because the juice remaining in the peaches will thin the syrup.) Remove the

syrup from the heat. Drain the peaches, adding the juice in the bowl to the syrup. Add the rum and orange extract. Return the peach halves to the bowl and pour the syrup over them. Let the peaches cool to room temperature, then place in the refrigerator if not ready to serve.

6. Shortly before serving, remove the peaches from the refrigerator so they will not be ice cold. Place each peach, cavity side up, in the middle of a shallow glass dessert dish or widemouthed champagne glass. Remove the orange strips from the syrup, placing them on a small plate. Spoon the syrup around the bottom of each peach. Whip the cream and fold in the crushed almond brittle. Heap the whipped cream on the center of each peach and scatter the strips of orange peel on top of the whipped cream. Serve with a spoon and fork.

Pear Pastry (Milan)

In northern Italy there are many variations of individual fruit and cake pastries. One that we ordered in a restaurant in Milan was a light sponge cake topped with a pear half, glazed with sharp currant jelly, and the whole decorated with a piped-on border of whipped cream. The sheet of sponge cake and the poached pears can be made early in the day or the day before serving, but the dessert is put together an hour or so before dinner is served.

7-x-11-x-1-inch baking pan
Serves 6

Sponge Cake, page 32
3 pears
1 cup sugar
¼ cup white wine
¾ cup water
¼ teaspoon vanilla extract

8 tablespoons currant jelly
¾ cup heavy cream
1 tablespoon sugar, or to taste
¼ teaspoon almond extract, or to taste

1. Make and bake the sponge cake. Cool the cake according to the recipe directions and set aside.

2. Peel the pears, cut in half, and core. Scoop out a little extra pear in the center with a melon scoop or small spoon to make a deeper hollow. Set the 6 halves aside.

3. Into a pan large enough to hold the pear halves in a single layer, put 1 cup of sugar, the white wine, water, and vanilla extract. Bring to a boil and boil for 2 or 3 minutes. Add the pears, flat side down, and cook in the bubbling syrup for 5 minutes, basting with the syrup. Take the pan off the heat, lift out the pears with a slotted spoon, and drain them in a fine sieve. Place the pears on a plate to finish draining. (Pour off any juice that gathers in the plate, mix it with any leftover syrup, and save for use in other desserts.) When the pears are cool, place them in the refrigerator until ready to put the pastries together.

4. About 1 hour before serving the pastries, melt the currant jelly over a low flame, then cool until it begins to thicken.

5. Beat the cream and when it begins to thicken, add 1 table-spoon of sugar (or more or less to taste) and the almond extract. Continue beating until the cream is stiff.

To Assemble:

1. Slice off any center hump and cut the sponge cake sheet into six 3½-x-3⅝-inch portions. Place each portion, bottom side up, on a small baking pan.

2. Remove the pears from the refrigerator and dry off the surfaces with paper towels. Fill each hollow with whipped cream, reserving the rest of the whipped cream for decoration. Place each pear half on a portion of cake, filled side down.

3. Spoon the jelly over the curved top of each pear. Return

the pears and cake to the refrigerator to harden the jelly. Put the whipped cream into the refrigerator.

4. When the jelly has hardened, remove the pan from the refrigerator. Spoon the whipped cream into a pastry bag fitted with a number 6 star tube. Pipe the whipped cream all around the edge of the cake surrounding the pear. Add a rosette in the middle of each pear. Return to the refrigerator. Just before serving, transfer the pastries to individual dessert plates.

Strawberries and Clear Maraschino Liqueur

Toward the end of May, red-ripe strawberries both cultivated and wild arrive in the markets and are on the menu of most restaurants. Ripened in the sun, they are incredibly sweet. Unsugared, they are piled in widemouthed champagne glasses, to which the waiter adds a splash of clear maraschino liqueur or white wine. (In Sorrento, the waiter had a heavy hand and the maraschino was a bit raw, drowning out the delicate strawberry flavor!)

Maraschino liqueur is an eau de vie, a clear liquid with an intense flavor. It is not to be confused with the red liquid in which maraschino cherries are packed. The Stock brand is available in the United States, but if you cannot find it, add cherry extract or the maraschino cherry liquid to vodka to approximate the flavor and alcoholic content. The slightly red color blends into the strawberry juice.

About one and a half hours before serving, wash and hull very ripe strawberries. Place them in a bowl and, given our market strawberries, add superfine sugar to sweeten, then cover. Do not place them in the refrigerator. At room temperature the flavor is more intense.

Just before serving, spoon the berries into serving dishes, adding the juice in the bowl. Pour about one tablespoon of maraschino liqueur over each portion, and serve.

Index

About the Authors

Virginie and George Elbert are enthusiastic travelers of Europe, particularly Italy, where they greatly appreciate the immense variety and wonder of dessert. They live in New York City where they can be found recreating their scrumptious discoveries.